# The Poem of my
# CID

*(Poema de Mio Cid)*

Translated with an Introduction & Commentary by

# PETER SUCH & JOHN HODGKINSON

ARIS & PHILLIPS – WARMINSTER

*To Trini and Jesús*

The Spanish text edited by C. C. Smith is reproduced with the kind permission of the editor and Oxford University Press.

The publishers gratefully acknowledge the financial assistance of the Dirección General del Libro y Bibliotecas of the Ministerio de Cultura de España for this translation.

 British Library Cataloguing in Publication Data

[El Cid *(Poem). English*], The poem of my
   Cid : (Poema de Mio Cid – 1207) –
   (Hispanic classics).
   I. Such, Peter   II. Hodgkinson, John
   III. Series
   861'.1            PQ6367.E3

ISBN 0–85668–321–3 (cloth)
ISBN 0–85668–322–1 (limp)

Printed and published by Aris & Phillips Ltd, Teddington House, Warminster, Wiltshire, England.

# CONTENTS

Acknowledgements      iv

Select Bibliography      v

Maps

     Spain at the time of the Cid      viii

     The Cid's route into exile      ix

     The campaigns in the Levante      x

     The route to and from Corpes      xi

Introduction

     I.      Manuscript, date and authorship      1

     II.      The historical background to the events and composition of the *Poema de Mio Cid*      3

     III.      The Spanish epic      5

     IV.      History and fiction in the *Poema de Mio Cid*      7

     V.      Themes      9

     VI.      Characterization      19

     VII.      The poet's craft      24

     VIII.      The Cid in literature and music      34

     IX.      The translation      35

Notes to the Introduction      36

THE POEM AND COMMENTARY

CANTAR I      39

CANTAR II      108

CANTAR III      177

Index of proper names      260

ILLUSTRATIONS

     *Poema de Mio Cid*, fol. 565 (lines 2760−2787)      xii

     The castle of Zorita      39

     The *Puerta del Sol* in Toledo      107

# ACKNOWLEDGEMENTS

We owe an enormous debt of gratitude to Professor Colin Smith, who has been tireless and most generous in giving advice and help during the preparation of this volume. The consequent translation and critical material may not be entirely what he would approve of or agree with, but his support has been greatly valued.

A number of colleagues and students at Sherborne have helped with comments and advice, and some have given us a considerable amount of their time. We are particularly grateful to Rod Beavon, Ronald Murison, Michael Zimmerman, and David Key, and to Michael Weston for his great kindness in helping us to prepare the book for print.

PTS
JH

# SELECT BIBLIOGRAPHY

Details of some books and articles not mentioned here are given in the notes to the Introduction and Text. We have attempted to suggest a very brief selection of works which the student of the *Poema* will find particularly helpful and most (though not all) of which are available in English.

## 1. Editions

R.Menéndez Pidal, *Cantar de Mio Cid*, 3 vols (Madrid, 1911 and later editions); contains a grammatical study, extensive glossary and both palaeographic and critical texts. Not available in translation.

I.Michael, *The Poem of the Cid* (Manchester, 1975 and Harmondsworth, 1984); a critical edition with introduction and notes, accompanied by a prose translation by R.Hamilton and J.Perry. This text is also available in a Spanish edition (Madrid, 1976).

C.C.Smith, *Poema de mio Cid* (Oxford, 1972); a critical edition with introduction and notes. This is also available in an extensively revised Spanish edition (Madrid, 1985), and it is this text which is printed in the present volume.

## 2. Origin and sources

D.Hook, 'The *Poema de Mio Cid* and the Old French Epic: Some Reflections', in *The Medieval Alexander Legend and Romance Epic: Essays in Honour of David J.A.Ross*, edited by Peter Noble, Lucie Polak and Claire Isaz (New York, 1982), pp.107-118.

D.W.Lomax, 'The Date of the *Poema de Mio Cid*', in *Mio Cid Studies*, edited by A.D.Deyermond (London, 1977), pp.73-81. This volume contains several important studies on aspects of the *Poema*.

C.C.Smith, *The Making of the 'Poema de mio Cid'* (Cambridge, 1983); this major study includes and develops material from a number of Smith's earlier articles. We have given details of some of these in the notes.

## 3. Interpretation

A.D.Deyermond, 'The Close of the *Cantar de Mio Cid*', in *The Medieval Alexander Legend and Romance Epic: Essays ... David J.A.Ross* (New York, 1982), pp.11-18.

P.N.Dunn, 'Theme and Myth in the *Poema de Mio Cid*', *Romania*, LXXXIII (1962), 348-369.

P.N.Dunn, 'Levels of Meaning in the *Poema de Mio Cid*', *Modern Language Notes*, LXXXV (1970), 109-119.

R.M.Walker, 'The Role of the King and the Poet's Intentions in the *Poema de Mio Cid*', *Medieval Hispanic Studies presented to Rita Hamilton*, edited by A.D.Deyermond (London, 1976), pp.257-266.

## 4. Legal aspects

D.Hook, 'On Certain Correspondences between the *Poema de Mio Cid* and Contemporary Legal Instruments', *Iberoromania*, 11 (1980), pp.31-53.

M.E.Lacarra, *El 'Poema de Mio Cid': realidad histórica e ideología* (Madrid, 1980); an important study of the legal and historical background, not available in translation.

M.N.Pavlović and R.M.Walker, 'Money, Marriage and the Law in the *Poema de Mio Cid*', *Medium Aevum*, LI (1982), 197-212.

M.N.Pavlović and R.M.Walker, 'Roman Forensic Procedure in the *Cort* Scene in the *Poema de Mio Cid*', *Bulletin of Hispanic Studies*, LX (1983), 95-107.

P.E.Russell, 'Some Problems of Diplomatic in the *Cantar de Mio Cid* and their Implications', *Modern Language Review*, 47 (1952), 340-349.

## 5. Language, style, and structure

E. de Chasca, *El arte juglaresco en el 'Cantar de Mio Cid'*, second edition (Madrid, 1972). See also his general study, *The Poem of the Cid* (Boston, 1976).

A.D.Deyermond, 'Structural and Stylistic Patterns in the *Cantar de Mio Cid*', in *Medieval Studies in Honor of Robert White Linker* (Madrid, 1973), pp.55-71.

A.D.Deyermond and D.Hook, 'Doors and Cloaks: Two Image-patterns in the *Cantar de Mio Cid*', *Modern Language Notes*, 94 (1979), 366-377; this article examines in further detail some of the patterns identified by Deyermond in the earlier study.

T.R.Hart, 'The Rhetoric of (Epic) Fiction: Narrative Technique in the *Cantar de Mio Cid*', *Philological Quarterly*, LI (1972), 23-35.

C.C.Smith, 'Tone of Voice in the *Poema de mio Cid*', *Journal of Hispanic Philology*, IX (1984), 3-19. A large part of *The Making of the 'Poema de mio Cid'* (see above) deals with linguistic and stylistic questions.

## 6. The geography of the 'Poema'

The following two studies by I.Michael are particularly helpful:

'Geographical Problems in the *Poema de Mio Cid*. I: The Exile Route', in *Medieval Hispanic Studies presented to Rita Hamilton* (London, 1976), pp.117-128.

'Geographical Problems in the *Poema de Mio Cid*. II: The Corpes Route', in *Mio Cid Studies*, edited by A.D.Deyermond (London, 1977), pp.83-89.

## 7. The historical background

D.W.Lomax, *The Reconquest of Spain* (London and New York, 1978).

R.Menéndez Pidal, *La España del Cid*, two volumes (Madrid, 1929 and later editions); a shorter form of this work was translated by H.Sutherland as *The Cid and his Spain* (London, 1934).

## 8. The literary background

For a general introduction to the literature of medieval Spain, see A.D.Deyermond, *A Literary History of Spain: The Middle Ages* (London and New York, 1971).

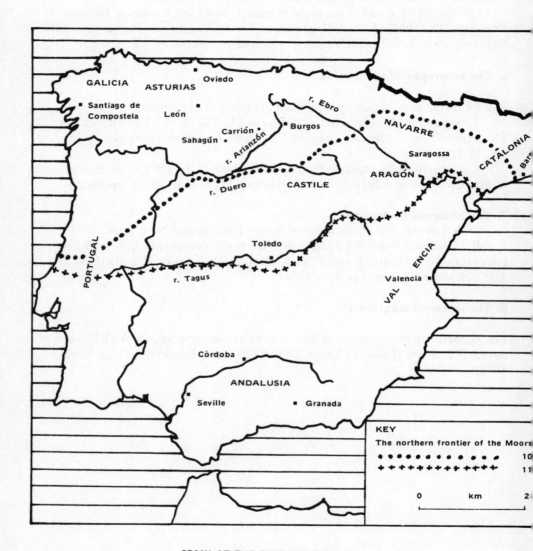

**KEY**

The northern frontier of the Moors

•••••••• 10

+++++++++ 11

0      km    2

SPAIN AT THE TIME OF THE CID

THE CID'S ROUTE INTO EXILE

ix

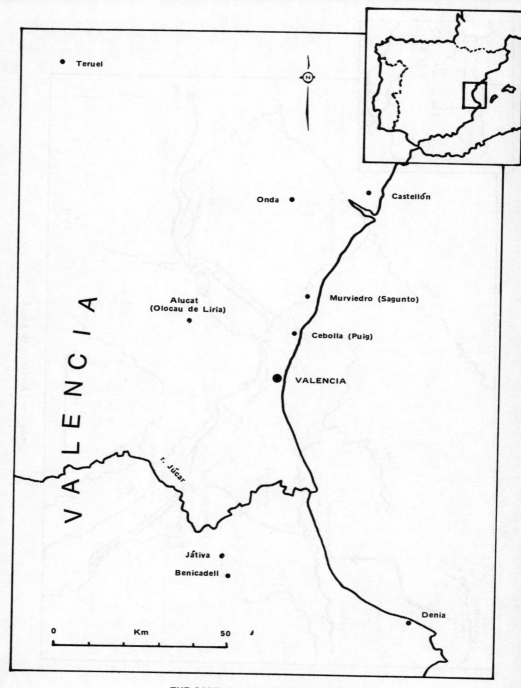

THE CAMPAIGNS IN THE LEVANTE

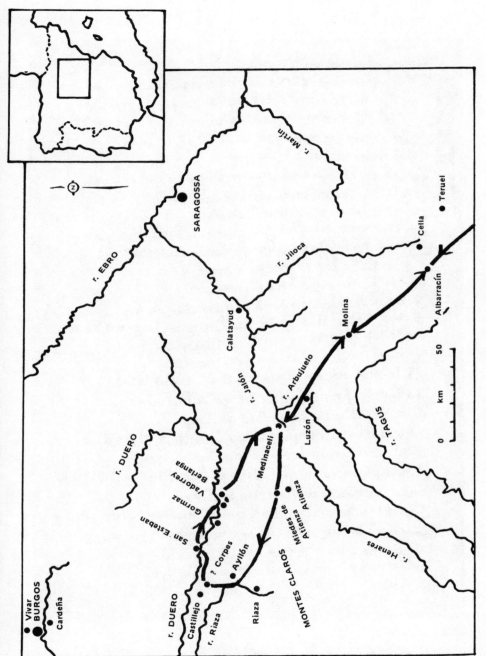

THE ROUTE TO AND FROM CORPES

Poema de Mio Cid, *fol. 56r (lines 2760-2787) of the unique manuscript in the* Biblioteca Nacional, *Madrid.*

# INTRODUCTION

## I MANUSCRIPT, DATE, AND AUTHORSHIP

The *Poema de Mio Cid*, an account of the deeds of the eleventh-century hero Rodrigo Dıaz de Vivar, *El* (or *Mio*) *Cid*, has survived in a single manuscript, dating from the fourteenth century. It is incomplete, lacking the first one or possibly more folios (about fifty lines each), and probably two further folios at later points in the text; but an indication of what the missing sections contained is provided by chronicle accounts which drew on the *Poema*.[1] There is no title page, and, indeed, no universally agreed title: the work is sometimes known as the *Cantar de Mio Cid*, for the poet states at the end of the second of its three sections that the verses of his song (*cantar*) are coming to an end; but generally scholars have accepted the term *Poema*, even though the use of this word is not documented until well after the time of composition.

The dating of the poem, together with the questions of origin and authorship, is the subject of widely differing judgements. Recent years have seen important research into the way in which the *Poema* came to be composed, but there continues to be disagreement on fundamental points which have significant consequences for our understanding of the aims of the poet and the nature of his work. The final lines of the *Poema* are problematic:

> May God grant his paradise to the man who wrote this book! Amen.
> Per Abbat wrote it down, in the month of May,
> in the year 1207.
> (3731-33).

The date which appears in the Spanish text is 'era de mill e .cc xlv. (i.e. MCCXLV) años'. The word *era* relates to the Spanish manner, in the late-Roman and medieval periods, of counting dates from the year 38 B.C. (see note to l.3733 of the text), and the date given is thus A.D. 1207. The distinguished and influential editor of the *Poema*, Ramón Menéndez Pidal, argued that in the gap between *cc* and *xlv* there had originally existed another *c*, and that the year given, 1307, was that in which the copy of the poem was made. Per Abbat (or Pedro Abad) was seen as the fourteenth-century copyist of a poem written down much earlier, according to Pidal (and numerous others) in

1

about 1140, just over forty years after the Cid's death. Other scholars have called this argument into question. There are good reasons to consider the late twelfth or early thirteenth century as the most likely time of composition. Some, for example, are in connection with the poet's sources, but probably the most convincing relate to the social and political background reflected in the *Poema*.[2] The date of 1207 can thus be regarded as a plausible one, and, though few scholars have felt that it is safe to attribute the *Poema* with confidence to a particular named individual, Colin Smith not only has argued that Per Abbat is indeed its author but also has drawn attention to a particular individual bearing this quite common name. This man was a Castilian lawyer, who can be shown to have had an interest in the Cid and who could well have had the knowledge and opportunity to compose the *Poema* at the beginning of the thirteenth century.[3]

For Menéndez Pidal, who stressed what he considered to be the popular and anonymous origins of the *Poema*, the work as we possess it represents the culmination of a long process of development, starting during or shortly after the Cid's lifetime, and in which oral transmission played a very important part. The key figure in this was the *juglar* or minstrel, passing on the poem in a constantly reworked and modified form, in such a way that a narrative originally faithful to historical fact gradually became less 'truthful'; according to such a theory, there could have existed successive written versions of the poem, constituting a record of the development of the legend: Menéndez Pidal postulated the existence of a short epic of 1105 which came to form part of the surviving version of the *Poema*, set down in writing some thirty-five years later. There are certainly features of the *Poema* which appear to be closely linked with oral tradition. Particular attention has been paid to the use made by the poet of the kind of formulae associated with oral improvisation (see Section VII (b), below).[4] However, the presence of these elements does not mean that we must see the *Poema de Mio Cid* as a record of an oral performance, or that it should not be regarded as the work of an individual who consciously incorporates traditional elements of the *juglar*'s art into a complex and original creation.

Whether it is possible to identify a particular individual who wrote the *Poema* or not, there is an increasing amount of evidence to suggest that it is the work of a man of some learning, with access to legal documents and to chronicles and with a good knowledge of legal procedures[5] He also seems to have known French epic poetry and it has been argued that he drew extensively on it. His poem is a carefully elaborated work of art, based on historical fact, but very far from being in essence an accurate record of its hero's life.

## II THE HISTORICAL BACKGROUND TO THE EVENTS AND THE COMPOSITION OF THE POEMA

Rodrigo Díaz de Vivar, El Cid, lived from about 1043 to 1099, and the *Poema de Mio Cid* seems to have been composed about a hundred years after his death. Two factors need to be appreciated if the reader is to understand the lifetime of the Cid and the period of the poem's composition. These are, firstly, the struggle against the forces of Islam, and, secondly, the conflicts and rivalries within and among the Christian kingdoms themselves.

The original conquest of the Spanish Peninsula by Islamic armies from North Africa had begun in the year 711 and the Christian Visigothic state had rapidly been overwhelmed. Resistance only continued in the mountainous areas of the North. The following centuries saw a very gradual southward advance of Christian rule, centred initially on Asturias and, from the beginning of the tenth century, on León. This was no confident and unbroken advance, and the savage raids of al-Mansur in the second half of the tenth century saw the Christian states reduced to a position of powerlessness and humiliation. Nevertheless, the collapse of the caliphate of Córdoba in the early years of the eleventh century saw Moslem Spain divided into numerous independent kingdoms, which became easy targets for exploitation through the imposition of tribute and, in some cases, for conquest.

The county of Castile, which had won independence from León in the mid-tenth century, rose under Fernando I to a position of considerable importance. Fernando ruled both León and Castile from 1035 to 1065 (and his brothers García and Ramiro were kings of Navarre and Aragón respectively), but when he died in battle his lands were divided up, as he had commanded, among his three sons: Alfonso became king of León, Sancho of Castile, and García of Galicia and Portugal. The consequence of this division was to be conflict between the brothers: at first Sancho, his troops commanded by Rodrigo Díaz, was victorious; but after the Castilian monarch's murder in 1072 it was Alfonso of León who was to rule Castile, León and Galicia until his death in 1109. Alfonso VI is one of the principal characters of the *Poema de Mio Cid*.

Alfonso's rule saw increasing Christian domination of the Moslem kingdoms, and commanders such as Rodrigo Díaz and Álvar Fáñez played an important part in the exacting of vast amounts of tribute. Alfonso's most conspicuous achievement was the capture in 1085 of the great city of Toledo, a success which represented a massive strategic blow to the Moslem kingdoms of the South. It provoked an appeal by the king of Seville to the powerful North African empire of the Almoravids, and in 1086 Yusuf ibn Tashufin, at the head of a vast army of African troops and supported by the forces of the Andalusian kingdoms, marched northwards, meeting and defeating the Christian army at

Sagrajas and narrowly failing to capture Alfonso himself. Yusuf asserted his superiority over the Moslem kingdoms of the South, and there followed a series of reverses for the Christian forces, including a heavy defeat in 1108 at Uclés, where Alfonso's son, Sancho, was killed.

It was against this background that there developed the remarkable career of Rodrigo Díaz, also known as *El* (or *Mio*) *Cid*, a name half-Castilian and half-Arabic, derived from the title *Al-Sayyid* and expressing the respect which he won from Christians and Moors alike.[6] The son of a minor Castilian nobleman, Rodrigo Díaz rose to the position of commander-in-chief of the armies of Sancho II of Castile and so played a prominent part in the conflict which followed the death of Fernando I. According to legend, it was Rodrigo who administered an oath to Alfonso, without which the Castilian nobles would not have accepted the Leonese monarch as their king, and clearly he must have appeared to his lord to be a figure not only powerful but also potentially threatening. In 1081, following an unauthorized raid into the kingdom of Toledo, Rodrigo was exiled by Alfonso and his estates were confiscated. Accusations concerning his expedition to collect tribute from Seville may also have been responsible for his banishment (see also note to the text, ll.1-2). He spent some years fighting in the service of the Moorish king of Saragossa, and, although it was a common enough occurrence for a Christian to ally himself with Moslems and fight as a mercenary in this way, it is nevertheless hardly surprising that this stage in the Cid's career does not figure in the *Poema*. In 1087 Alfonso pardoned Rodrigo, but two years later, after the latter had failed at Aledo (through error, it seems) to provide the King with the support he required, banishment was reimposed. The Cid had already set about asserting himself in the East (the Levante), and, by shrewd exploitation of the political situation and outstanding military expertise he took possession of the city of Valencia in June 1094, after a harsh siege. In December of that year he won a major battle over the Almoravid army at Cuarte, and the following years brought him further military successes. He ruled Valencia securely, though not without the need at times to take firm repressive measures, and in 1096 he converted the city's great mosque into a cathedral. His ability to hold the city against the Almoravids was of great strategic importance, being largely responsible for the Moslems' failure to advance rapidly through eastern Spain; no other Christian general in his lifetime defeated the Almoravids in pitched battle. In 1101, two years after the Cid's death, the city of Valencia was abandoned, following the relief by Alfonso of another Almoravid siege; it was not recovered by the Christians until 1236.

Through the illustrious marriages of his daughters (related briefly at the end of the *Poema*), it was in due course to become true, as the poet proclaims (3724), that kings of Spain (in fact of Navarre and of Castile-León, and also,

4

indeed, of Portugal and France) were descended from the Cid.

The twelfth century was to be a period of faltering progress in the reconquest of the Peninsula, the most notable advances being made by the Aragonese, who took Saragossa in 1118. When the Almoravids' grip weakened, they were superseded by the Almohads, a sect originating in the Atlas Mountains. Divisions among the Christian kingdoms prevented effective concerted action. Alfonso VII of Castile and León died in 1157, bequeathing León to one of his sons and Castile to the other, and a long period of instability ensued, plagued by conflicts among the nobility, such as the long-standing feud between the Laras and the Castros.[7] Ascending to the Castilian throne in 1170, at the age of fourteen, Alfonso VIII faced the twin problems of war with León and the struggle against the infidel. He was crushingly defeated by the Almohads at Alarcos in 1195, but, seventeen years later, in alliance with Navarre and Aragón, and having received the sustained support of Pope Innocent III, he won the major and decisive battle of Las Navas de Tolosa, which opened the way for the conquest of southern Spain. By the middle of the thirteenth century all of the Peninsula (with the exception of the kingdom of Granada, which was not conquered till 1492) was in Christian hands.

If the reign of Alfonso VIII, and in particular the early years of the thirteenth century, is to be taken as the period in which the *Poema de Mio Cid* was composed, then some of the characteristics of the age may be significant. Clearly, in a time of preparation for a major campaign against the forces of Islam, the confident achievements of the Cid could provide an inspiring example. Moreover, this was an age which would have had much to learn from the model of a harmonious and united society, ruled by a strong, just, and respected monarch and in which the most illustrious of noblemen scrupulously and, when necessary, obediently observed his obligations towards his vassals, his peers, and his king.


## III THE SPANISH EPIC

The continuing state of conflict and uncertainty which prevailed in twelfth-century Spain went hand-in-hand with an intellectual backwardness and an absence of the kind of aristocratic and royal patronage that did much to stimulate the rich literary creation of France during that period. Thus, for example, the courtly romance flourished in the French courts in the twelfth century but it was not really until the fourteenth century that works reflecting a similar preoccupation with themes of love, idealism, and adventure were to achieve widespread popularity in Spain.

Even so, the contrast is extraordinary between on the one hand the paucity of Spanish epic texts, and on the other the wealth of French epic material, with so many works dating from the twelfth century, before the period of the composition of the *Poema*. By 'epic' the reader should understand a long narrative poem celebrating the exploits and achievements of heroes and warriors; usually such poems would combine history and legend and in most cases would have a national significance. The *Poema de Mio Cid* is the earliest extant epic poem in Spanish and only two others have survived: the *Mocedades de Rodrigo*, a late fourteenth-century reworking of an older poem about the youthful exploits (*mocedades*) of the Cid; and a fragment of *Roncesvalles*, a poem composed in the late thirteenth century and drawing on the subject matter of the *Chanson de Roland*. There is evidence that other Spanish poems existed and were subsequently lost: the *Poema de Fernán González*, which tells of the way in which Castile had achieved independence in the tenth century, is a learned poem of monastic origin composed in about 1250 and seemingly based on an epic which no longer survives. The rich Spanish ballad tradition appears to be related to and predated by a substantial body of epic material, and of particular interest to scholars has been the incorporation of such material into medieval chronicles, both Latin and vernacular. In some of these chronicles in Spanish, the borrowing has been done so directly that assonance and other obviously poetic features have been preserved in the prose. Menéndez Pidal was able to reconstruct, from the text of fourteenth-century chronicles, about 550 lines of the *Siete Infantes de Lara* (*The Seven Princes of Lara*), a sombre tale of treachery and vengeance set against the troubled relations between Moors and Christians in the late tenth century. There is also evidence in the chronicles drawn up under Alfonso X in the late thirteenth century, of the existence of a series of vernacular epic poems which dealt with the events following the death of Fernando I and leading up to those narrated in the *Poema de Mio Cid*. There are a number of other poems that we can confidently consider to have existed, and among them figures the story of Bernardo del Carpio, a Leonese nobleman who is presented as the victor over Roland at Roncevaux. However, though the historical events to which this narrative relates were ancient, the poem itself is entirely fictitious and probably dates from the thirteenth century. Indeed, we must in general be wary of attributing to the Spanish epic an antiquity for which there is little firm evidence. It has been argued that the *Poema de Mio Cid* is the oldest of the Spanish epic poems and that it established a form for those which followed.[8] Many scholars will prefer to emphasize the debt owed by the *Poema* itself to an established tradition; but two points should be clear: firstly, that the *Poema* cannot be taken as a representative work typical of the Spanish epic in general or of the literary creation of its age; secondly, that it is a work of exceptional quality, and this may well have ensured its survival, almost alone among the epic poems of medieval Spain.

# IV HISTORY AND FICTION IN THE 'POEMA DE MIO CID'

The *Poema* gives a chronological account of the deeds of the Cid, without any major digression from the narrative line:

**Cantar I**: The Cid, exiled by King Alfonso, leaves Vivar and rides through Burgos (1-77); with Martín Antolínez's help, he tricks the Jewish money-lenders, Raquel and Vidas, into lending him six hundred marks (78-200); he rides to the monastery of San Pedro de Cardeña, where he bids farewell to his wife and daughters (201-390). Encouraged by a vision of the angel Gabriel, he sets off into exile (391-434). He captures Castejón, and his men raid along the Henares valley (435-541). He takes Alcocer (542-624), where he wins a major battle over a Moorish force sent from Valencia (625-809). As he sets off down the Jalón valley, he sends Álvar Fáñez bearing gifts to Alfonso (810-934). Continued raiding provokes an attack from the Count of Barcelona, whom the Cid defeats, captures, and eventually sets free (935-1084).

**Cantar II**: The Cid's campaigns bring him closer to the Moslem city of Valencia, whose people he defeats in battle (1085-1156). With his army steadily growing, he is able to besiege Valencia, which surrenders in the tenth month (1157-1220). He defeats an army led by the King of Seville, establishes his authority over Valencia, and again sends Álvar Fáñez with gifts to Alfonso (1221-1315). Alfonso allows the Cid to be joined by his wife and daughters, who are escorted in honour to Valencia and richly welcomed (1316-1618). The Emir of Morocco attacks Valencia and the Cid wins a major battle and great booty (1619-1802). Alvar Fanez is sent with a gift of two hundred horses to Alfonso, who agrees to pardon the Cid (1803-1878). The Infantes of Carrión ask Alfonso to request for them the hands of the Cid's daughters in marriage, and Álvar Fáñez carries the news of the pardon back to Valencia (1879-1958). At a meeting on the banks of the Tagus the Cid is reconciled with his monarch and grants the request made by Alfonso on behalf of the Infantes (1959-2166). In Valencia the marriages take place (2167-2277).

**Cantar III**: In Valencia the Infantes are humiliated through their fear of an escaped lion (2278-2310). An army arrives from Morocco and the Infantes fail to distingish themselves in battle; the Cid is victorious and gains further wealth (2311-2531). Shamed by their failures, the Infantes plan vengeance; they set off with their wives for Carrión, further disgracing themselves before the Cid's Moorish friend Abengalbón (2532-2688). They beat their wives and leave them for dead in the oak-wood at Corpes (2689-2762), but the girls are rescued and taken back to Valencia (2763-2897). The Cid requests that Alfonso give him justice, and the King commands the nobility of his kingdom to gather in Toledo (2898-2984). The court gathers and the Cid makes his preparations (2895-3100); he demands justice, formal challenges are issued, and the King commands that the duels be fought at Carrión (3101-3485). The Cid departs to Valencia, and three of his vassals, protected by Alfonso, defeat the Infantes and their brother at Carrión (3486-3709). The Cid's daughters are married to the princes of Navarre and Aragón, amidst great rejoicing (3710-33).

Important elements of the Cid's story as it is presented in the *Poema* (banishment, military success, growing prosperity, the conquest and holding of Valencia, reconciliation with his king, and the ultimate prestigious marriages of his daughters) all quite faithfully mirror historical fact, and it is, indeed, striking that very many details of the narrative prove to be grounded in history and that, for example, even minor characters can be shown to have had an historical existence. It is clear, however, that this poem is far from being in essence a record of historical fact. It fails to mention, for instance, the second banishment or the years spent in the service of the Moslem ruler of Saragossa. Much is made of the role of Álvar Fáñez as the Cid's lieutenant, but this individual, though a distinguished general, seems to have had no historical connection with Rodrigo Díaz. The Cid's campaigns are presented in a fashion so simplified and accelerated as to possess a coherence which they could never in fact have had: from the time that Alcocer is seized, attention is drawn to the alarmed reaction of the people of Valencia, and the king of that city at once sends a force to punish the raiders; yet the lands under threat were in fact under the domination of the Moslem ruler of Saragossa and certainly not protected by the coastal kingdom. The conquest of Valencia itself is presented as a planned and coherent military invasion, and there is no sense of the lengthy and complex process by which political control of the area was in fact achieved.[9] It is surprising, moreover, that the narrative of the taking of Alcocer, a relatively minor town, should be longer and more detailed than that of the capture of the great city of Valencia. In general, the accounts of the Cid's battle tactics are simple, depending largely on a single trick or manoeuvre, and do not give a convincing sense of military experience; indeed, sources have been detected for the Castejón and Alcocer episodes in the works of classical Latin historians.[10]

It seems likely that the author of the *Poema* had a valuable source of historical material available to him in the *Historia Roderici*, the Latin account of the Cid's life composed in the first half of the twelfth century. The *Historia* contains a significant number of elements which reappear in the descriptions in the *Poema* of the departure of the Cid into exile and of the taking of Valencia, and in it the poet may well have found the germ of the richly comic episode with the Count of Barcelona.[11]     However, although the Latin work would have offered the Castilian poet quite an accurate historical source, no more than selective and free use has been made of it.

The way in which the author of the *Poema* moves away from historical fact is most clearly illustrated by the introduction of material which can be safely assumed to have no historical foundation at all. One such element is the comic anti-semitic tale of the tricking of Raquel and Vidas. In the case of other passages, moreover, it is possible to point to parallels in twelfth-century French epic poems so close as to suggest that these were direct sources for the Spanish poet: for example, the scene in which the Cid from the highest part of the citadel shows Valencia to his wife and daughters, and also, possibly, the Corpes episode.[12] Of greatest significance, however, is the introduction into the poem of the Infantes of Carrión, who, though they were historical figures, seem in reality to have had no dealings with the Cid.[13] The whole episode of the first marriages of the Cid's daughters, of their ordeal, and of the process by which honour is restored, the series of events forming the core of the second half of the poem, is unrelated to any known events in the Cid's career. The dramatic centre of the *Poema* is thus a fiction, around which the poet has carefully elaborated a narrative which serves to convey a clear message about the values and workings of society.

The poet constantly enriches his narrative with precise detail of dress and armour, of numbers (always plausible, in contrast with the exaggerated figures of many medieval epics), of monetary value, of financial transactions and legal procedure, of the practice of warfare – drawing our attention to the provision of fodder for the horses or the regulations for the sharing out of booty – and of place-names and the features of the land across which the characters travel. All of this, combined with the restrained and essentially plausible nature of the narrative, can give us the sense that what is recounted in the *Poema* is historically true. The poet succeeds in giving a sense of actual experience, but his creation is nonetheless an elaborate artefact.


## V THEMES

### (a) Heroism

At the root of the *Poema* lies the military prowess of the Cid. He is a powerful and terrifying figure in battle, though the Spanish poet does not claim for him the superhuman feats performed by Roland and other French epic heroes. At Castejón, his appearance, in itself, seems sufficient to ensure victory (470-72); in the battle at Alcocer, he acts in memorable fashion to rescue Álvar Fáñez (748-52); and, when outside Valencia he intervenes to save

Don Jerónimo, he promptly decides the outcome of the whole battle (2392-98). The Emir Yusuf flees from him in fear (1725 ff.), and so too does King Búcar, only to be overtaken and brutally killed (2408-24). The battle descriptions do not lack bloody and macabre details, and we are given a strong sense of the importance of sheer physical courage in the face of an enemy whose ferocity is emphasized by the terrifying pounding of their drums (2345-47). The Cid and his vassals must owe first their survival and then their prosperity to their skill in battle, and it is natural that theirs should be a world in which cowardice is sharply ridiculed: the Infantes' fear of the lion (contrasted with the calm bravery shown by the Cid moments later) and their failure to play their part in battle bring upon them a mockery which cannot be suppressed.

The Cid's courage and his ability as a warrior provide a model to inspire the poet's public; but his valour is always coupled with moderation and good sense:[14] thus, he is concerned to take prudent practical measures (559-63), he avoids unnecessary slaughter (619 ff.), and he does not allow his troops to go rashly into battle (662-63). The Cid is presented as a fearsome warrior and as a great leader of his men in battle, but he inspires not only obedience but also affection from his followers; he is pre-eminently a fine lord to his vassals and a good servant of his king, and, prominent as his martial achievements may be, his other qualities come to receive at least equal emphasis: at the climax of the poem, the Cid, having displayed his worth in the court, does not take part in the duels.

The accounts of battles in the *Poema* are, moreover, much less lengthy and gory than their equivalents in many French epics and, likewise, than those to be found in a Castilian poem of the early thirteenth century which is a product of the learned world of the schools.[15] Our poet does not revel in the description of brutal conflicts. It is significant, too, that, though the Cid's honour is restored through duels which set the courage and firmness of purpose of his vassals against the cowardice of those who have wronged him, the poet chooses to emphasize not the violent punishment of the Infantes and their brother (they do not, in fact, die) but rather the dishonour inflicted upon them and the triumph of justice.

### (b) Survival and prosperity

At the start of the *Poema* the Cid is an outcast, forced to camp with his vassals on the river-bank outside Burgos (59), his misfortune being rumoured to result partly from the slanders of his rivals and partly from his own greed (109-112); but as he goes into exile, the growing number of his followers means greater strength but also greater responsibility – more mouths to feed (304). The Cid and his men must fight to survive in a difficult country whose inhabitants are hostile to them (834-35), and realize that a violent reaction is

10

only to be expected (1103-06). As they travel eastwards, the place-names convey to a Castilian public a sense of the exotic and the unknown. The Moorish lands are dotted with forbidding castles (such as Atienza, 2691), and campaigning in these barren lands has many hazards, among them the loss of the supply of water (661). In battle the Almoravids prove a strange and menacing enemy (2345-47).

These threatening circumstances are also, however, rich with the possibility of material gain. The Cid's men accompany him out of loyalty, but partly, too, in the hope of profit (1198). They go into battle to show 'who deserves his pay' (1126), and when the Cid's wife and daughters are frightened by the Moslem forces attacking Valencia, he calms them by pointing out that they must view the enemy army as a source of profit:

> My daughters and my wife will see me fight.
> They will see what life is like in these alien lands.
> With their own eyes they shall see full well how we earn our bread.
>     (1641-43)

Growing military strength is accompanied by increased wealth. The poet punctuates the first part of the narrative with precise figures telling us how the Cid's force steadily swells (see 16, 291, 419, 723, 917, 1265, 1717), and, when in Valencia the Cid takes stock of his army, the contrast with the size of the band which left Vivar is joyfully underlined. So too, the poet after each battle returns enthusiastically to the subject of the booty seized (506 ff., 794 ff., 1733 ff., 1772 ff., 2482 ff.), and particular importance is attached to the precision and fairness of the procedure by which each man is given his due share (as in 510 ff. and 2484 ff.). Repeatedly the poet tells us how after a battle all of the Cid's followers have gained great wealth; but social advancement can follow too (1213). For the Cid and his family, the taking of Valencia is seen as bringing lasting security; it is the inheritance to pass on to future generations (1607).

Great significance is attached in the *Poema* to the display of wealth as an indication of power and standing. The finery of the ladies of the Cid's household (1424 ff.), the display of elegance which Álvar Fáñez desires to give (1507 ff.), and the Cid's preparations for his meeting with the King (1985 ff.) are all to be understood as clear signs of a prosperity and success which merit respect and admiration. So too, an impressive show of liberality is an important way of underlining wealth. The Cid has no illusions about men's motives, and he takes strict measures to prevent his vassals from stealing away with their gains (1249 ff.); but in a different context he repeatedly displays exceptional generosity. The series of gifts made to Alfonso (815 ff., 1270 ff., 1808 ff.) are a sign both of the Cid's wealth and power and also of his submission to his monarch. The offer of Babieca (3513-15) is beyond all expectation. Generosity, such as that shown to the visitors to the wedding in Valencia, increases the reputation of the Cid and his vassals (2266), and when two hundred silver marks are given to each of the ladies of the household, it is in part so that news of the gift will travel to Castile. The fame of the Cid's wealth is to be carried far and wide.

Material success and honour are linked. Thus, Alfonso promises that the marriages to the Infantes will bring 'honour and greater wealth' (1905, 1929), and it is not surprising that the dishonour inflicted on the two brothers should be accompanied by severe and embarrassing financial loss. Victory for the Cid's vassals in the duels leads on to a triumphant conclusion as the Cid's daughters marry into great and powerful families. The contrast with the humiliation and isolation suffered by the hero at the start of the poem could not be more marked.

### (c) Christianity and Islam

The poet leaves us in no doubt about his hero's piety. As the Cid, unprotected and vulnerable, is about to leave Burgos, he makes for the cathedral and prays to Saint Mary; and at times of much greater security and happiness he is to give thanks to the Virgin for the prosperity that she has brought him (as in 1267 and 1637). Likewise, the night before the court is held in Toledo, he chooses to keep a vigil in San Servando, praying that justice be done (3055-57). The Creator's name is often on the Cid's lips: His aid is invoked in time of battle and praise is duly offered when victory has been gained. There is a strong sense that God is watching over the hero in his troubles, for, as if in answer to the Cid's prayer in the cathedral and Jimena's frenzied plea before the altar at Cardeña, the angel Gabriel appears with a reassuring message (405-09). Perhaps, indeed, the poet was encouraged by a precedent in the *Chanson de Roland* to provide his hero with divine support; but it is nevertheless evident that he has been at pains in the opening section of his poem to underline the Cid's Christian devotion and his submission to God's will.

But the Cid's piety does not show itself solely in prayer. The gifts which he makes to the Church are impressive: among them, payment in gold and silver for a thousand masses in the cathedral, five hundred silver marks for the monastery of Cardeña (with the indication in 1445 ff. that further generosity is well merited and will indeed follow), and the establishment for Bishop Jerónimo of the rich see of Valencia.

The Cid is also an upholder of the cause of Christianity against the infidel. His troops call in battle on Saint James, patron of Christian Spain, whilst his enemies invoke Mahomet (731), and his victories at Valencia are won over vast and threatening Islamic hordes. His success in battle is seen as a triumph for Christendom (770) and spreads terror through Moslem Spain and into Africa (2499-501). The capture of Valencia is followed by the installation of a Christian bishop:

> Lord God, how happy were all Christians
> that in the land of Valencia there was a lord bishop!
> (1305-06)

and Jerónimo, before requesting the right to strike the first blows and plunging heroically into battle, sings mass and grants a full absolution:

> If any man dies here face to face with the enemy
> I absolve him of his sins and God will receive his soul.
> (1704-05)

The role played by the warrior bishop Turpin in the *Chanson de Roland* offers a very close parallel here, and it is tempting to see in the portrayal of Jerónimo a direct imitation of the French poem; but there are striking differences, for this priest has other aims too: we are told that he is granted a see 'through which he could become very rich' (1304), and in this respect he is typical of the Christian troops as they are depicted in the *Poema*. There is a vast gulf between the crusading spirit of the *Chanson de Roland* and the attitude which views a Moslem army principally as a source of material gain.

The Moslems are represented as fearsome enemies, and the tone is exhilarating when the Christian troops slaughter many of their number in battle (722 ff.). However, at other times the Cid is distinguished by the moderation he shows towards those that he captures, notably at Alcocer, where he wins great affection from the Moors (851-56); and there is sympathy, too, from the author of the *Poema* for the plight of the Moslem people of Valencia besieged by the Cid:

> It is a harsh fate, my lords, to have not enough to eat,
> and to see women and children dying of hunger.
> (1178-79)

Far from seeking to convert the Moors to Christianity or to slaughter them, the Cid exploits them: thus, we see him imposing tribute on the Moorish towns (as in 904) and, in return for their payment, proving to be a man of his word (941-42). When he is threatened by a force from Valencia, the Christian hero calls upon the towns under his domination to support him in battle

(1107-10); the poet does not shrink from showing us Christian allied to Moor, though the alliance is never in fact depicted in battle.

The role of the Moor Abengalbón is a particularly striking one: not only is he the friend of the Cid, for love of whom he displays great warmth and generosity and also restraint towards those who sought treacherously to kill him; in addition, he is shown to be the moral superior of two Christian noblemen, towards whom he rightly displays only anger and biting scorn (2675 ff.). His encounter with the Infantes illustrates well the poet's real concern, not so much with the war between Christian and Moslem as with a different kind of moral conflict, in which, in a brutal and testing world, men give evidence of their true worth.

### (d) Honour, vengeance, and royal authority

When the Cid is forced to leave Burgos, we are aware of the intense humiliation which is part of the punishment of the exile, a man shunned and cast out of the city; but by the end of the poem the hero has gained greatly not only in wealth and material security but also in prestige: he is admired by all, and rich in honour.

Honour is in part associated with material prosperity, as was seen above, but its implications are subtle and far-reaching. The notion of honour, as it is represented in the *Poema*, does not relate to the intrinsic worth of an individual, but rather to his status among his fellows and the respect which he is granted by others. Honour furnished a theme which was to be of great importance in the Spanish literature of later centuries, but it is clear from the law codes of medieval Castile and León that conflicts of honour were already a very significant feature of the society of Christian Spain.[16] The loss of honour with which the Cid is threatened by the outrage to his daughters and which is indeed inflicted on the Infantes is of the utmost gravity: the law codes make it clear that a man dishonoured was, whether the dishonour was his own fault or not, socially dead.

Brave conduct and victory in battle win honour (1011, 1861, 2428, 2530), and we see how important it is that good reports should circulate of an individual's worth (2445, 2480, 2526) and in the same way how much is made of displays of wealth and generosity, for by these, too, a man is judged – see (b) above. Prestigious alliances bring not only financial gain but also honour, and this point is underlined repeatedly as the arrangements are being made for the marriages of the Cid's daughters to the Infantes (1905, 2077, 2188, 2198). The Infantes are only too well aware of the honour conferred on them by their rank, as they show when they scornfully condemn their alliances as degrading (for example in 3296-99). In making this point, however, they are trying to justify their own conduct, motivated – we know well – by shame. They first conceived the plan to marry the Cid's daughters as a source of honour for themselves (1883), and it is ironical that through their own moral failings their marriages should in the end bring them such great dishonour.

There are many ways in which a man can be dishonoured. The stain on Diego González's clothing (2291), resulting from his cowardly flight from the lion, represents the stain which his behaviour has left on his honour. Cowardice earns mockery, and word spreads fast: the Infantes know well that, whatever the Cid may try to do, news of their humiliation will soon be carried far afield. Dishonour results, too, from a physical affront, perhaps the cruellest form of humiliation being the pulling of a man's beard (see, for example, the Cid's precaution, 3097-98, his proud boast, 2832 and 3285-86, and his taunting of García Ordóñez, 3287-90). Likewise, verbal taunts can be charged with significance, and such is the case with the repeated accusation levelled in the court against the Infantes of being 'worth less', of having lost honour (3268, 3346, 3369). Moreover, a man is highly vulnerable to any insult to his position as husband or father, and the attack on the Cid's daughters, coupled with violent expressions of scorn for their social origins, is calculated to cause him the greatest possible embarrassment and dishonour.

The Infantes describe their treatment of their wives as 'vengeance' for the affront that they suffered in the affair of the lion (2719, 2758). Some of the law codes which provide evidence of legal practice at the time of the poem's composition indicate that their behaviour could be justified on these grounds (see note to l.2762 of the text). However, it was their own weakness which brought them dishonour, and this is made all the clearer by the form of vengeance that they choose. The Cid, in his turn, is bound to seek vengeance, for it offers the only way of removing the threat of lasting dishonour; but the form which it takes is in keeping with the nobility and moderation of his character and with the respect which he shows for the laws of the kingdom and the authority of Alfonso. The girls' plea at the time of the attack is, perhaps, surprising, but it is very significant. They do not threaten the Infantes with bloody vengeance at their father's hands, but tell them that they 'will be accountable for it at an assembly or at a royal court' (2733), and this is, indeed, precisely what the Cid is to seek of his king (2914 and 2949). He does not pursue a course of private vengeance; his first act is to place the matter in the hands of Alfonso and to show his trust in his monarch as the source of authority and justice. Alfonso, accepting his responsibility and well aware that dishonour to himself accompanies that suffered by his vassal (2950), takes every possible step to see that justice is administered. Repeatedly the poet returns to the notion of justice (*derecho*) (2952, 2960, 2966, 2992, 3133, 3138, 3549, 3576, 3600). The King is all-powerful; he is fair in his treatment of all his vassals, and at the same time anxious to uphold the cause of a good and obedient man who has put his trust in him. The emphasis on the importance of royal authority for the administration of justice – as opposed to the violent and disruptive settling of issues among the nobles themselves – is more than an accidental feature of the *Poema*. It reflects the values of the latter part of the twelfth century and the early years of the thirteenth century, an age in which in Castile-León the revival of Roman law was helping to confirm the role of the Crown as the dispenser of justice and thus to strengthen the grip of royal authority. The court scene has been described as 'a head-on clash between two quite distinct procedural systems': the old, individualistic system based on Germanic customary law is challenged by the more unified and centralized approach based on Roman law.[17] It has been convincingly argued that the author of the *Poema* was trained in Roman law:

The new concept of public law emphasizes the authority of the monarchy in the face of the growing power of the higher nobility. It was the kings, together with the lawyers, who were instrumental in extending the influence of Roman law in order to defend their prerogatives from the attacks of the nobility. The author of the *Poema*, in presenting the conflict in these terms, speaks out in defence of the public law, which the king wishes to establish, and attacks the prevailing law of private vengeance ... The profound knowledge of the law shown by the author and the terms in which he presents the conflict between public and private law mark him as a man of the end of the twelfth century. Possibly he was a trained lawyer upholding the new concept of the law, which at that historic moment both the profession to which he belonged and the Crown itself strove with special energy to implant.[18]

The duels do not lead to the death of the men of Carrión, but rather to their intense humiliation (3705 ff.). There is the strongest of contrasts with the bloody concept of vengeance which dominates works such as *The Seven Princes of Lara*.[19] Royal authority has made possible a more moderate and controlled solution to the conflict, and has, moreover, asserted the worth of the Cid, a loyal and dutiful vassal, over that of men who claim right by birth to greater honour.

## (e) The bonds of society

The exclamation of the people of Burgos brings to our attention one of the most important themes of the *Poema*: 'Lord God, what a good vassal! If only he had a good lord!' (20). The Cid is constant throughout the poem in his humble acceptance of his king's will; he is an ideal vassal. Equally significant is the development in the role played by Alfonso, from victim of the lies of the Cid's enemies to impartial dispenser of justice.

The author of the *Poema* lays great stress on the mutual bond between lord and vassal, one involving duties and responsibilities for both parties. The Cid's concern for the welfare of his men results not only from his characteristic warmth and fairness but also from a practical understanding of the need to command the respect and obedience of his followers. He is concerned, when he leaves Burgos, about how to feed and pay his followers (83, 300-03); he promises them a rich reward for their service, which in due course they receive in such abundance that all are deeply grateful to him: 'One who serves a good lord will always live in happiness!', exclaims the poet (850). Emphasis is placed on the just way in which the booty is distributed – see (b) above – and on the great riches falling to all of those who have served the Cid (as in 806-07). Though harsh penalties are imposed on any who disobey the Cid's commands (1252-54), his vassals hold him in such esteem that they are prepared to accept the toughest demands made on them (430-31), and it is stressed that those who serve him do so of their own free will (1192-93). The Cid and his followers are bound by a mutual affection and respect, and thus he is able confidently to entrust the settlement of his dispute with the Infantes to three of his vassals; for 'all three were of one mind, having the same lord' (3551).

Not only is the Cid depicted as an exemplary figure in his treatment of his vassals, but in addition, he is shown to act towards his own lord, King Alfonso, with a nobility and a humility which distinguish him as the finest and most dutiful of vassals. In spite of the cruel treatment which he has received, he still considers the King to be his 'natural lord' (895, 1272); and he will not cut a single hair of his beard 'for love of King Alfonso' (1240). A series of gifts are sent as tokens of the vassal's love and readiness to submit to his lord's will, and of this Álvar Fáñez offers further testimony when he points out to Alfonso how the Cid 'acknowledges you his lord and calls himself your vassal' (1847; see also 1339). Early in his period of exile, the Cid avoids battle with his king: 'I do not want to fight Alfonso, my lord' (538). And the meaning of his act in humbling himself before Alfonso –

> He went down on his hands and knees
> and took the grass of the field in his teeth,
> with tears flowing from his eyes, so great was his joy;
> for this is the way he knew to show his submission before Alfonso his lord.
> (2021-24)

17

– can only be understood if we bear in mind the immense power which he has by now acquired, so great that his forces could rival those of Alfonso himself on the field of battle. The greatest vassal in the land recognizes wthout question the authority of his king.

On the other hand, if the Cid has proved an exemplary vassal, Alfonso has not yet played his due part as monarch. There is a strong suggestion that he acted unjustly in banishing his vassal, made first in the allusions to the 'evil enemies' (9) and the 'evil intriguers' (267) and in the criticism expressed in l.20, corroborated by the account of the annoyance shown by the Cid's enemies when he is returned to favour (as in 1345), and generally reinforced by the weight of feeling which the poet provokes in his hero's favour. It must not be forgotten that Alfonso could be seen as a Leonese king, who had gained the throne of Castile after a conflict in which he had been opposed by the Cid; and he might be expected to show unjust favour to the Infantes of Carrión, members of the (at least partially Leonese) Vani-Gómez family.

Alfonso's Leonese link, however, is only mentioned from the time when he is starting to show impartiality (see 1927, 3536, 3543, 3718), and it is, for example, at the moments when he restores the Cid to his favour (1867), when he speaks out in his praise (3509), and when he promises to see justice carried out (3140) that he swears by Saint Isidore of León (see note to l.1342). The sense is that this identification of Alfonso with the kingdom of León represents a limitation which he gradually overcomes. During Álvar Fáñez's second visit to the King, Alfonso shows by his crushing reply to García Ordóñez (1348-49) that he fully recognizes the value of the Cid's service; and the reconciliation between monarch and vassal is accompanied by warm hospitality and a number of gestures – such as the unusual act of allowing the Cid to choose where the audience is to take place – by which Alfonso seeks to pay honour to a man well deserving of his favour, and also, perhaps, to compensate for wrong done. The King's error in arranging the marriages shows that his judgement can still be clouded by favouritism, but it will also ultimately give him opportunity to show how far he has grown in stature.

The poet makes clear Alfonso's responsibility for the misjudged marriages in terms of legalistic precision. The King promises that the Cid and his family will gain in honour and in wealth by the alliances (as in 2077), and himself fully accepts the responsibility for them (2099). The Cid stresses that on his side there are reservations, but that he will agree to the marriages in submission to his king's desire (2082-89). He tells Alfonso that 'You are marrying my daughters, not I' (2110), and makes the same point to the girls: 'You should realize that he, and not I, offers you in marriage' (2204). Thus, after the outrage, it is to the King that he turns:

He married my daughters to the Infantes, not I.
Since they have abandoned them, in great dishonour,
if in this there is any affront to my honour,
whether small or great, it is entirely the concern of my lord.
        (2908-11)

Muño Gustioz uses similar words when he addresses Alfonso (2939 ff.) and Alfonso accepts his responsibility – 'for I married his daughters to the Infantes of Carrión' (2956). The point has been logically made and heavily underscored. Alfonso's duty is clear, and the remainder of the poem sees him discharge it to the full. He gives remarkable expression to his sense of the Cid's worth: 'Though this may upset some men, you are finer than us' (3116). He presides over both the court and the duel 'to see that justice was done and to prevent any wrong' (3549); he protects the Cid and his men from harm 'as a lord to his good vassal' (3478), and when the Infantes might well have expected to benefit from favouritism they instead find their king threatening them with stern measures (3140-41, 3600-02). We are told of Alfonso that:

He is King of Castile, and is King of León,
and of the Asturias, and of Oviedo too, the capital.
And as far as Santiago, he is lord of all,
and the counts of Galicia consider him their lord.
        (2923-26)

The poet here emphasizes not only the territorial extent of the King's authority but also the unity of his kingdom. Alfonso is, by the end of the *Poema*, a commanding figure in whose person and relationship with his vassals is expressed the harmony of an idealized society. The exploration of the roles and responsibilities of monarch and nobleman and of the contribution which each must make to the well-being of the kingdom is an essential part of our poet's purpose. He has carefully worked his material into a narrative which embodies an important message for the society in which he lives.


# VI  CHARACTERIZATION

When considering the way in which characters are presented in the *Poema de Mio Cid*, it is important to forget modern ideas of realism or literal portraiture. The poet creates his characters from the standpoint of medieval aesthetics, and medieval art had a very different view of characterization from that which developed subsequently. The visual arts provide a helpful approach to understanding the medieval poet's attitude. A stained glass window, for instance, might show St Martin dividing his cloak with the beggar – St Martin a full-scale figure on horseback, the beggar, though fully mature in years, nonetheless very much smaller than the saint. A tapestry showing Hector seated in state has the hero surrounded by a number of much smaller figures of knights and courtiers.[20] The idea is quite clear: the artist is not interested in a realistic presentation of his figures but places them in the pictorial plane according to their importance or symbolic significance. St Martin dominates the beggar, not only because of their difference in social class but because the Saint is the embodiment of charity and Christian love. It is these virtues which are being portrayed in the figure of the Saint, not any realistic human being. Such a presentation of characters spoke to medieval man of hierarchy, order, and values which were the basis of feudal society. Similarly, it did not matter what the real Hector had been like or what kind of personality the artist believed he might possess – Hector, though pagan, was an exemplification of heroism and honour, and that was his character. The artist made no attempt to convey any feeling through the pose or expression of his figures, but merely ensured that they clearly symbolized particular abstractions.

The poet's technique was very similar to that of the visual artist. He was not interested in 'psychological' depth or expression of subjective emotions. In the *Poema de Mio Cid* when Jimena prays for her husband's safety (330 ff.) she is not really revealing subjective concern but rather something which is altogether more abstract – her prayer is significant in an abstract thematic sense, not in terms of a woman desperate that her husband is leaving his family, to face great dangers. This is precisely how a character who is symbolic of loyalty and obedience, a true noble wife, must respond. It is not the literal nature of the action or of what Doña Jimena says that is important, but the symbolic nature of word and deed. D. W. Robertson, writing of the *Chanson de Roland*, comments that 'characterization is subordinate to the thematic structure of the poem as a whole, and is rendered in simple, straightforward terms with no attempt at "rounding" '.[21] Much the same can be said of the *Poema de Mio Cid*. The poet is concerned with themes of honour, vassalage, feudal dues, and royal authority, and his characters are given life as the embodiment of these themes, as 'ideas in action'. Alfonso, though by no means infallible, is an ideal of a Christian king, a father to his people whose role is to bind his subjects together with a mutual bond of love between lord and vassal. In the great court scene, King Alfonso addresses his vassals demanding that 'both sides be at peace today' (3139). It is 'for love of My Cid ... that he may receive justice' (3132-33) that the court has been summoned. The Cid, the ideal of heroism, refers to his beard when addressing his men: 'For love of King Alfonso, who has exiled me', it will not be cut (1240-41). The poet does not intend us to see anything whimsical or eccentric in the Cid's words – they are not an expression of an individual personality, merely an indication of how completely the character is one with the themes of vassalage and feudal dues. The Cid is, indeed, a faithful vassal who illustrates what the relationship should be between king and subject.

Doña Jimena similarly exemplifies such themes of obedience, but she is, also, a good illustration of another aspect of medieval characterization. Characters might have traits and qualities associated with them which marked them out to be *exempla* of certain vices or virtues. Doña Jimena is an *exemplum* of patience, obedience, and duty. There is, of course, virtually no actual description of her (nor in any developed sense is there of the other characters) and it is through her actions and words that she is presented as the abstraction she is. Hence, actions and words are mostly stylized and elevated in tone. It is the same with the Cid's loyal vassals and with the Infantes who reveal a treachery that symbolizes what happens when the bonds of society are broken. At the other end of the scale from the Cid are those figures (some of them non-Christians) who show none of the qualities and virtues which are at their finest in the poem's hero. Raquel and Vidas and the Count of Barcelona are perhaps the most vivid. In contrast, Abengalbón is a Moor who embraces nobility and shows respect for ideas of hospitality and honour (1520-26). Yet the portrait of Abengalbón is designed to make him not an attractive 'rounded' character but rather an important *exemplum* of essential virtues.

A further aspect of medieval characterization that needs to be appreciated is the dominance of what might be termed 'moral' character over 'psychological' character. When Doña Jimena and her daughters come out to greet the Cid at San Pedro (262 ff.) the poet does not intend us to feel any strong sense of personality on the part of Doña Jimena begging a favour or on the part of the Cid when he replies. It is tempting to feel a great warmth of heart and personal affection in the Cid's words:

> Doña Jimena, my noble wife,
> I have loved you as my own soul!
> (278-79)

But the poet then makes it quite clear that it is not really a question of human love and tenderness that he is concerned with but a matter of moral responsibility. It is right that Doña Jimena should ask her lord for advice on how they are to act when he is absent; it is also right that the Cid should demonstrate his concern and duty as protector to his wife and family. His concern is shown in his desire 'that I myself may yet arrange marriages for these my daughters' and that he may be granted time 'that I may serve you, my honoured wife' (282b-84).

21

It must not, however, be thought that the medieval author kept his characters completely devoid of humanity and personality. The characters need vitality and life if they are to emerge from the rich tapestry which the poet is weaving. In the scene considered above, the poet tells us of the Cid that he was weeping and 'sighed heavily'; when Emir Yusuf is besieging Valencia, we are told that Doña Jimena and her daughters are 'terrified'. Such indications of feeling and reaction help to keep the characters from being dull and flat. The poet also allows us to feel the humour, sadness, anger, bitterness, or affection in his characters: the Cid cannot resist a joke even when Jimena is alarmed – 'Your daughters are of an age to be married and they are bringing you a dowry!' (1650), he remarks. At the battle of Alcocer when Pedro Bermúdez impulsively gallops into the enemy lines with the ensign, the Cid cries out in alarm: 'Do not go, for the love of mercy!' (709): a hero should not allow himself to become desperate or uncertain, but it would be completely unconvincing were the Cid not to react with some anxiety. Yet, though there are many such details, often very acutely observed, the poet makes no attempt to integrate them into a fully realistic portrait. Indeed, his preoccupation is with the functional and the economical. Raquel and Vidas behave as a kind of duo, acting together, thinking as one: to the modern reader it seems rather comic – not entirely so, though, to the medieval public. The fact that Raquel and Vidas act as one gives strength to their actions and significance to what they represent. Why should the poet bother to create individual personalities for them, when they are essentially incidental? The poet's great skill is in allowing his characters a life of their own within the individual scene, but ensuring that they always emerge from within the structure and never threaten to overwhelm the structural and thematic pattern. Count Ramón is a wonderful comic villain, but, despite his vitality, he remains secondary; after all, he is introduced in order to demonstrate the superior qualities of the Cid himself. The Count is a cameo, and is treated as such by the poet.

With one exception, apart from the hero all of the characters of the *Poema* are incidental. Their importance lies in the way they throw the hero into relief, acting as foils to him so that we may appreciate his actions for what they are, the deeds of a superlative individual, a paragon. Those around him represent ordinary humanity, fallible and limited in physical strength, imaginative scope, and nobility of thought. King Alfonso, however, plays something of a different role. In epic form there is usually a structured hierarchy based on a downward progression through three stages: in classical "epic", for example, the gods have supreme control by virtue of their being gods; then comes the hero, and, beneath him, the common run of humanity. Alfonso occupies this 'god-like' position in the *Poema de Mio Cid*; and, as he rises to his full stature by the end of the poem, we come to see him as the fountainhead of justice love, honour, and authority, as the ideal 'lord to his good vassal' (3478).

The *Poema de Mio Cid* is, like all other epics, dominated by the character and actions of its hero. The *Poema* begins with the Cid moved to tears as he contemplates his deserted home before setting out into exile, and ends triumphantly with the Cid having not only vindicated himself but having become the source of a line of honour and greatness: 'all gain in honour through the man born in a favoured hour' (3725). Not that there is any doubt but that the Cid will triumph, and the fascination of his character is not in any psychological depth nor in any development of personality, but in his consistent singlemindedness and absolute resolve. As E.M.W.Tillyard comments, 'Heroic poetry often concerns actions in which men know exactly what they are doing and rise through deliberate valour to a great height of resolution.[22] We do not, of course, remain completely detached from the hero – the poet is skilful in bringing his public into close sympathy with the Cid: the poem begins with the Cid weeping and on many other occasions the poet presents his hero in an emotional state, often with tears in his eyes, and very effectively wins for him our sympathy.

Epic characters are not complex, not ambiguous or contradictory as real humanity is. It is through their essentially 'simple' personalities that they can be epic characters. W.B.Yeats wrote that 'when the imaginary saint or lover or hero moves us most deeply, it is the moment when he awakens within us for an instant our own heroism, our own sanctity, our own desire'. The epic hero is not merely an historical or legendary figure translated into fiction, he is also an archetype. In epic it is important that the hero is not particularized too much – he must remain, in his god-like superiority, above the reader. If, at the end of the *Poema*, the reader feels that he does not really know the Cid, then that is how it should be. Lascelles Abercrombie observed that the epic hero should be a symbol of the 'accepted unconscious metaphysic' of a period of history,[23] and the Cid embodies in his epic character a whole concept of feudal values as well as what Ian Michael calls 'the restless, hardy ethos of Castile in an outward-looking moment when there were lands to conquer and fortunes to be made'.[24]

It is, perhaps, tempting to see the Cid as a rather down-to-earth hero. In comparison with Roland, for example, he certainly is, but it would be wrong to make too much of his unsophisticated nature, talking to his vassals as man to man, or of his much-depicted role as a family man. In whatever milieu he is presented, the Cid remains an embodiment of abstractions, an essentially poetical creation. Several of the characters of the *Poema* have distinctive traits and their words and actions can stamp them in our memory; but we should not attempt to see them in any kind of 'real' world outside the poem. It is irrelevant to consider how much the Cid of the *Poema* is like the Cid of history. Like those around him, he is a poetic character existing only within the world of the poem – and in that world (which he so largely creates) he is real enough.


## VII THE POET'S CRAFT

### (a) Form

It is important to bear in mind the novelty of the task undertaken by the author of the *Poema de Mio Cid*. It seems probable that he had no written Spanish models on which to base his approach to composition, and though by the thirteenth century it was becoming increasingly common for legal documents to be written in the vernacular, at the time of the *Poema*'s composition Castilian was essentially a spoken rather than a written language and would certainly not be seen as the obvious vehicle for literary composition.

A striking feature of the *Poema*'s form is its irregularity. Menéndez Pidal introduced in his critical edition emendations for very short or very long lines, but accepted that the poet composed lines of between ten and twenty syllables. Smith, in the text used in this volume, has to a large extent kept to the manuscript readings, stressing the degree to which the poet's system of versification must be viewed as experimental, and not attempting to impose regularity.[25]

Nearly all the lines of the *Poema* are divided by a clearly indicated caesura, though the two hemistichs are rarely of equal length. In the later Middle Ages octosyllabic couplets were to become the basis of the Spanish ballad form, and a number of lines in the *Poema* fit this pattern. Nevertheless, the proportion is not sufficiently high to make us believe that this is the metre to which the whole poem should conform. Nor is there anything to suggest that the poet had in mind the line of two hemistichs of seven syllables which was to become the Spanish alexandrine. Indeed, it seems that a syllable count does not necessarily help us to understand the rhythms of the *Poema*: it has been plausibly argued that the basis of the poet's technique of versification is really a system of stresses, usually involving two stresses on each hemistich, or two on the first and three on the second, but with considerable flexibility.[26]

The *Poema de Mio Cid* is divided into 152 *tiradas* or *series*, units of sense like the *laisses* of French epic poems. In the manuscript there is no break between these units, but through each there runs assonance in the final syllables of each line (as in the opening lines of the poem: lor*ando*, cat*ando*, cañ*ados*, m*antos*, etc.). Quite often some of the assonances are imperfect, and here again Smith has preferred to see many of those which disrupt the pattern as a natural part of the poet's essentially flexible system, or even as having been deliberately introduced for the sake of variation or emphasis, or, for example, to link two *tiradas*.[27] One significant feature is the 'paragogic *-e*' (or *-ve* following a vowel), added in delivery to a line *ending* in a stressed syllable and serving to complete the assonance, for example in ss*odes*, vos(*e*), Carri*on*(*e*), emperad*ores*, ifanç*ones*, n*os*(*e*), n*o*(*ve*) (3294-3300).

Many of the lines of the poem contain some form of internal assonance, sometimes involvng the final syllables of the first hemistichs of successive lines, for example in 3324-27, t*odos*, m*oro*, t*odos*, fam*oso*, or sometimes within a particular line, for example:

Mas dexan las mar*i*d*as* en briales y en cam*i*s*as* (2750)
(leaving their wives with just their tunics and undergarments)

The poet exploits a range of sound effects, as in the following passage where, in order to maximize the emotive impact of the outrage which the Infantes are committing, he makes very effective use of assonance (c*arnes*, s*angre*), full rhyme for emphasis (çiclat*ones*, coraç*ones*) and alliteration (*camisas*, *carnes*; *salie*, *sangre*, etc.). The repetition of *con* and *sabor* at the beginning and end of successive lines – a device which the grammarians knew as *conplexio* – is likewise used to increase the intensity of the description:

con las çinchas corredizas majan las tan sin sabor,
con las espuelas agudas don ellas an mal sabor
ronpien las camisas e las carnes a ellas amas a dos;
linpia salie la sangre sobre los çiclatones.
Ya lo sienten ellas en los sos coraçones.

(With the saddle-girths they strike them cruelly,
and with their sharp spurs they cut into them to cause them great pain,
tearing through the undergarments of each of them and into their flesh.
Brightly their blood flows out onto the silk.
They feel such pain in their hearts!) (2736-40)

Novel as the poet's enterprise may be, he does not lack the ability to make very skilful use of his medium.

### (b) The language of epic and the written word

We might expect the author of the *Poema* to have been influenced in his approach to composition by the stylistic features of oral poetry, particularly, indeed, since his subject was the life of a hero extensively celebrated in popular tradition. Not surprisingly, then, the *Poema de Mio Cid* contains a substantial body of material which can be categorized as 'oral-formulaic', a formula in this sense being a group of words used repeatedly, though with variations, in such a way as to form a convenient unit for composition. In oral poetry the formula furnishes the performer with an invaluable aid to improvisation; and in the case of the *Poema* such units can provide a ready-made half-line. In a detailed study of this aspect of the poet's art, Edmund de Chasca has shown that a third of the lines of the *Poema* contain at least one formula and that a significant number of lines are entirely formulaic.[28]

Perhaps the most conspicuous type of formulaic expression in this work is the epic epithet, a title or descriptive expression applied approvingly to (nearly always) one of the main characters. The Cid is the subject of the greatest number of these epithets, and is described, for example, as 'My Cid the Battler', 'the man born in a favoured hour', and 'the man from Vivar', all used, with variations, on several occasions. Some of his followers are also seen as worthy of epithets, such as Martín Antolínez, 'worthy man of Burgos'; and so too is King Alfonso, but, significantly, only as he grows in stature in the second half of the poem. Valencia, too, by virtue of its connection with the Cid, is given its own epithet: 'Valencia la mayor' ('the great city of Valencia'). These expressions are an aid to composition, but they are not merely line-fillers. Consistently they are used to lend weight and dignity to an individual; and it is clear that in many cases a particular epithet has a precise function. Thus, for instance, in the second half of the poem the Cid is rarely described as 'the man from Vivar'; 'the man who had won Valencia' now seems to be judged more appropriate to the hero's position of power and authority; but when we do find the former epithet applied to him it is in the mouth of Asur González, who wishes to insult the Cid's origins (3378). Moreover, when Alfonso in the final scenes of the poem is three times designated 'Alfonso of León', it is because the poet wishes to stress the King's impartiality at a time when he could well have been expected to err by unjustly supporting the Leonese family – see V (e) above.

The poem contains numerous other formulae of various kinds. A few in themselves are almost untranslatable; for example *pensar de*, used very extensively with verbs such as *cavalgar* ('he rode off', etc.), but itself adding little to the meaning. On other occasions an expression may be used emphatically and to quite powerful effect, as is the case with the series of variations on *pesol de coraçon* ('he was deeply saddened') which accompany the revelation to successive characters of the outrage against the Cid's daughters (2815, 2821, 2825, 2835-35b, 2954, 2959). A particularly common group of formulae are the various types of 'pair-phrases', binary expressions constituting a half-line unit: sometimes the two terms are synonymous, as is the case with *d'alma e de coraçon* ('in both heart and soul', 1923, 2033, etc.) or *de voluntad e de grado* ('most willingly', for example 149, 1005, 1056); elsewhere they are 'inclusive pairs', as with 'men and women' (16b), 'townsmen and townswomen' (17) or 'Moors and Christians' (1242, 2498, etc.), all three expressions in fact meaning 'everybody'. A further group involve mention of parts of the body in expressions such as *(p)lorando de los ojos* ('weeping from the eyes', for example 18, 370), *diziendo de la boca* ('saying with the mouth', 2289) and similarly *plazme de coraçon* (literally, 'it pleases me in the heart', 1342). The effect of such phrases can be to increase the intensity and emotive force of a passage, though we can imagine too that they would have been associated with an appropriate gesture in performance. Here again, then, formulaic material has played an important part in the process by which the poet sought to influence his public's response to his characters and their actions.

As one might expect in a poem intended for oral performance, direct speech is extensively and effectively used in the *Poema*. It is, moreover, frequently introduced without the appropriate verb of saying or replying - see, for example, the exchange in ll.439 ff. – and we sense that it is in oral delivery that confusion in such passages would have been avoided. Common, too, are comments directly addressed to the public: for example frequent remarks to attract attention, such as *Afevos ...* ('behold ...') and *sabet* ('I tell you'), statements of intention ('I will tell you what he said', 'I want to tell you about ...'), expressions aiming to bring out the immediacy of the scene ('You could see ...'), and a broad range of exclamations of both joy and sorrow, giving the sense of a narrator, present, guiding his public through the events, and deeply involved in the story which he is telling.

The language of the *Poema* is predominantly direct, simple and concrete. The complex similes and figurative devices whose use is recommended by the grammarians of the twelfth and thirteenth centuries as features of an elegant style are entirely absent, and the few similes which are used for instance 'they parted, like the nail from the flesh' (375, see also 2642), are chosen for their directness and immediacy of effect.

The author of the *Poema de Mio Cid* is indebted to the language of epic tradition and his medium has many characteristics of the spoken language. Yet it is difficult to believe that the poem was dictated by an illiterate minstrel, in view, for example, of the growing body of evidence of its author's knowledge of legal matters, of the likely use of Latin sources, and, indeed, of its very carefully worked out structure – see (c) below. There are certainly linguistic features in the *Poema* which point to an author of some learning, such as the use of a constructiuon clearly modelled on the Latin ablative absolute – 'La missa dicha, penssemos de cavalgar' ('When mass is over ...', 320) – and of words evidently borrowed from Latin (for instance, *virtos*, 'numbers', 'forces', 657, 1498 and 1625). A number of expressions used by the poet have direct parallels in Latin and Spanish legal formulae; and inclusive pair-phrases of the kind illustrated above were common in legal documents, though other possible models for their use are present in medieval Latin chronicles, the works of classical historians, and the Bible itself.[29]

Scholars have examined the similarities which exist between the formulaic system so important in the *Poema de Mio Cid* and the formulae characteristic of French epic. The parallels are many and striking, and include most of the kinds of formula described above. Whether or not the author of the *Poema* borrowed directly from particular *chansons de geste*, it seems very likely that he was well acquainted with the techniques and stylistic devices employed by their authors. It is natural that in producing a written poem, owing much to a Spanish oral tradition but distinctive in its style, he should look for guidance both to the learned Latin works known to him and also to the highly developed French epic.[30]

## (c) Structure

The theorists whose ideas dominated the teaching of the art of poetry in the schools of the twelfth and thirteenth centuries saw the narrative line as a thread on which could be hung a series of gems in the form of, for example, elaborate digressions, rich set-piece descriptions, apostrophes or similes, and it is precisely such a form which is envisaged by the Castilian author of the *Libro de Alexandre*, probably composed within about twenty years of the *Poema de Mio Cid*. In contrast, the structure of the *Poema* is essentially that of a simple, chronological narrative, divided into three main sections or *cantares* (probably each forming a unit of length suitable for performance), and from which there are no major digressions. Indeed, at points in the narrative which seem positively to invite descriptive digression – the sights of the kingdom of Valencia, or trophies taken in battle, such as the tent of the Emir of Morocco (1785-86) – the poet passes rapidly on, in the case of the booty dwelling only on the monetary value. Descriptive elements are usually briefly expressed and are incorporated into the narrative, for example in the passage recounting the arrival of the Infantes and their wives in the oak-wood at Corpes (2697-2700). Moreover, when the poet does introduce descriptive material, its function is not to provide stylistic ornament but rather to achieve a particular effect or to convey a precise idea – as in the Corpes scene, which creates a powerful impression of beauty and purity set against a menacing and hostile background, or in the case of the description of the Cid's preparations for his appearance in court (3084 ff.), which effectively conveys the splendour, power and dignity of the poem's hero.

28

However, though the structure of the *Poema* is simple, the work is shot through with a wealth of recurring details and symbols and of parallels and contrasts.[31] On the one hand these can involve major aspects of the narrative: in the nature and outcome of the series of journeys which are an essential part of the narrative structure there are a number of significant contrasts – for example that between the journey into prosperity and honour which follows the Cid's first parting with his wife and daughters and, following the second parting described in the poem, the girls' journey with their husbands into dishonour. Important, too, are the contrasts between characters – for example the noble Abengalbón and the contemptible Infantes, and the silent but worthy Pedro Bermúdez and the boisterous Asur González – and between the notions of honour and dishonour, valour and cowardice.

Particularly significant is the way in which details recur throughout the narrative in such a way as to comment implicitly on the characters and their actions. Perhaps the poet's technique here, demanding from his public a sharp memory and attention to detail, is similar to that which Eugene Vinaver has discerned in texts of much more complex structure and termed 'the poetry of interlace'.[32] It is revealing, for example, to trace the history in the *Poema* of the two swords, Colada and Tizón. They are both gained in battle and on each occasion the poet stresses the honour won at the same time (1010-11, 2426-28). When they are given to the Infantes as they set out with their wives from Valencia, the Cid points out that he won them 'in manly combat' (2575-76). At Corpes the girls plead with their husbands, rather than inflicting such dishonour on them, to kill them cleanly with the swords, which they name (2726-27). Later, at the royal court, the Cid's first claim on the Infantes is for the return of the swords 'won in manly combat' (3153-54). They are indeed handed over to the King, who draws them, dazzling the whole court (3177), and the Cid promptly promises that they will be the instruments of vengeance (3187). When the time of the decisive combat arrives, the Infantes plead that the use of the swords should not be allowed (3555-56), and the word which they use to describe them (*tajador*, 'keen-edged') is the same as that used by the Cid's daughters at Corpes. The King turns down their request, and in his command that they fight he repeats the phrase 'in manly combat' (3563), twice before used in connection with the swords. So great, indeed, is the effect of seeing Tizón in his opponent's hand that Fernando González, throwing down his own weapon, immediately declares himself to be defeated (3643-44). This series of details, some of which involve precise verbal parallels, form a conspicuous thread running through the poem. The swords, identified with valour and manly performance in battle, are given to the Infantes in order that, properly used, they may bring them honour. In their hands, they come to be identified with the least manly and most dishonourable of conduct, and

29

attention is drawn to the contrast between the claims to valour of the Cid's sons-in-law and their true cowardice. The reappearance of the swords at the end of the poem underlines the irony of the situation: the weapons which the Infantes should have used to bring themselves honour are to be the instruments of their own dishonour; we are reminded of the young men's responsibility for the suffering that they bring on themselves and also of their powerlessness to prevent justice being done.

Clearly the author of the *Poema* intended his public to notice and draw conclusions from such echoes and parallels. It would seem that the medieval public was very alert to details of form, the appreciation of some of which would involve no small effort of concentration and memory. Some of these devices are very obvious, such as the juxtaposition of two passages involving repetition of the formulaic '*so many* ... mules, *so many* palfreys' (etc.) (1967 ff. and 1987 ff.): the first describes the preparations made for the audience by the King, the second those of the Cid. Repetition here is surely not a reflection of limited descriptive resources but a manner of emphasizing the equal footing (as regards power and possessions) on which the Cid now finds himself with Alfonso.

Elsewhere, the poet relies on the recall of particular words to remind us of the context in which they were previously used. There are many points in the second and third *cantares* at which mention of honour anticipates the contrast between the good which the marriages should have brought both the Cid and the Infantes and, on the other hand, the dishonour which comes to each in turn. But other close verbal echoes highlight the wrong done by the Infantes (and the error of the King in arranging the marriages). When the Cid entrusts his daughters to his sons-in-law, he describes the girls as his 'heart-strings' (2578), and when at Toledo he makes his accusation of the Infantes, he again uses the same emotive phrase (3260), underlining the extent to which his love and trust have been betrayed. Similarly, when the Infantes first approach the King about the possibility of marriage to the Cid's daughters (1889), his reaction is identical to that of the Cid when, shortly afterwards, he hears of the proposal: 'for a good hour he thought and reflected' (1932). When each in turn is told of the outrageous behaviour of the Infantes, the same words are again used to describe their response (2828, 2953; there is a small variation in the case of Alfonso). Our attention is directed back to the original, erroneous decision of the King to ask the Cid to allow the marriages, to the doubts which existed at that time, and to Alfonso's responsibility to take action on behalf of his vassal. So too, on each of the two occasions when we see the Cid parting from his daughters, the very powerful and memorable simile ('like the nail from the flesh ...') is used (375 and 2642), highlighting the parallel between the two situations, though ironically, in view of their different outcomes. Often, then, repetition is accompanied by a sense of irony. Alan Deyermond points to the emphasis on sorrow (with the verb *pesar* repeatedly used), firstly in the series of scenes in which news of the outrage spreads, and later, in contrast, when the day of retribution arrives and it is the turn of the Infantes to grieve: verbal repetition stresses the justness of the punishment.[33]

The reader will be able to detect numerous such motifs and verbal parallels – they are so frequent and significant that it is difficult to imagine their use to be other than deliberate. This subtle technique of repetition and variation, emphasizing parallels and contrasts and often illuminating irony of situation or drawing attention to the disparity between appearance and reality or intention and outcome, is a very important aspect of our poet's art.

**(d) The sense of the dramatic**

The narrative of the *Poema de Mio Cid* moves rapidly forward with a strong sense of plot: the work is rich in incident, and we are constantly brought to anticipate subsequent events and changes in the fortunes of the characters. As in many epic poems, the movement of the plot is emphasized by a series of physical journeys, themselves charged with symbolic significance. Within the narrative there are contained several episodes of particular dramatic quality, incidents which are varied but follow swiftly on, and reinforce, one another. They are described in a style which is taut and spare, constantly achieving an effect of sharpness and spontaneity; but the very impression of simplicity which results conceals a highly developed art and is in itself part of the poet's design.

The opening scene of the poem is stark and powerful. It contains few precise descriptive details: the open gates and empty hooks, the crows as the Cid with his followers leaves Vivar and arrives in Burgos, the townspeople at the windows, the text of the King's decree, the closed door and the appearance in the street of the frightened little girl; but these are such as to stamp themselves sharply on our minds. No further description or commentary is necessary, for we are given enough for our imagination to create a clear visual picture of the scene. The effect of the visual elements combines with that of details of great emotive force. Throughout the *Poema* much is made of the sorrow or the joy provoked by events – emotions which the poet intends us to share – and here the bitterness of the moment finds expression in the tears of the Cid and of the townspeople. Particularly striking, too, is the repetition by a terrified child of the chilling words that she has been made to learn by heart; for fear of the Cid's rage, no adult will appear, and the delivery of the message by the child makes only too clear the hero's isolation.

In his battle scenes, the author of the *Poema* resists any temptation to over-use the clichés which are a stock part of the medieval poet's narrative technique: for example, the list of heroes, the stylized description of combats,

31

and the extensive use of devices of repetition, all of which are present but none to excess. The description of the pitched battle at Alcocer is a distinctive and memorable account which illustrates well the poet's sense of what will work dramatically. As we are told at some length of the discussions which precede the battle, of the preparations, and of the disposition of the forces, tension mounts. Pedro Bermúdez is given the ensign and, unable to endure the wait, he suddenly rushes forward to plant it in the enemy line. The Cid's reaction, a sharp cry of command, is an entirely convincing one, and Pedro's terse reply gives us the sense of words hastily spoken, perhaps with a backwards glance, as he gallops on his way. Here, as often in the *Poema*, narrative is interspersed with direct speech to considerable effect. Now the Cid's urgent cry rings out and the wall of horsemen moves into its charge; the controlled build-up of the scene has given way to sudden action and we find ourselves drawn into the events.

The court scene at Toledo forms the climax of the poem, and here, in the account of the Cid's preparations and of his arrival before the King, we can see how the poet uses a limited number of visual details in order to achieve a carefully contrived effect. The Cid declares that he is to be accompanied by a hundred men wearing 'cuirasses shining white like the sun' (3074) and fur and ermine; and the shirt that he dons is described by the same simile (3087). In the list of clothes that he wears, silver and gold are repeatedly mentioned (3088-96). When he enters, his majestic appearance causes every man to gaze on him, except the Infantes who, as he sits amidst his retainers, 'could not look on him for shame' (3126). They are as men who have to avert their eyes from the brilliance of the sun. Shortly afterwards, the whole court is dazzled by the appearance of the golden pommels and cross-guards of Colada and Tizón (3177-79); these are to be the instruments of the Infantes' punishment. The poet does not have to point out his meaning in explicit fashion or to include a more extensive description of the scene: the details included are such as to suggest the most vivid of pictures and to bring out in dramatic fashion the contrast between the moral stature of the Cid and the baseness of the Infantes. Here, as he does repeatedly in the *Poema*, our poet shows that he has a keen sense of atmosphere and of what makes powerful drama, and we see how much he is able to convey by means of a few well- chosen touches.

## (e) Humour

In the comic scenes, too, the ability to suggest a great deal by the use of a few telling details is a very important feature of the poet's artistry.

In the course of the Cid's encounter with the Count of Barcelona we are presented with a series of memorable visual images: of the Cid, for example, towering over the fearful Count, who hastens to gorge himself with food in order to gain his freedom; we can imagine Ramón's shudder of terror when the Cid suggests that the two of them will never part, and the uneasy glance which he casts behind him as he rides off into safety. We sense, too, how much could be made in performance of direct spech in this episode: of the Cid's repeated taunt to the Count that he will never give back what he has won from him in battle; his mocking invitation to him to eat: 'Come, come, Count ...' (1033); or the trembling voice in which the prisoner agrees that he will eat most willingly if it means separation from his captor. There is a strong sense of the absurd; we watch with pleasure a potentially dangerous threat to the Cid being defused, and we rejoice in the mockery of his enemy, who from the moment he appeared had been roundly condemned as a braggart and a blusterer.

The element of caricature is all the more marked in the depiction of Raquel and Vidas. The two Jews never appear apart; they speak with one voice and are sometimes even made the subject of a singular verb. We can picture them withdrawing together in earnest discussion, working out their schemes and calculations. Their words are an accurate expression of their characters: they stress to Martín Antolínez that in all their dealings they must make a profit (123), and that they always 'take first and then give' (140). Here, too, we can imagine that a performer might make much of their manner and gestures. They are comic because of the contrast between on the one hand their calculated approach and their confidence of success and gain, and on the other hand their role as victims of the Cid's superior wit. When they meet Álvar Fáñez during his visit to Castile to collect Jimena and her daughters, they provoke laughter by their desperate plea for the return of the money and their ineffectual threat to go and collect their debt from the Cid in person (1438).

A third comic scene, but one which at the same time has ominous overtones, is the episode in which the Infantes are humiliated through their fear of the escaped lion. The poet stresses the contrast between the undignified panic which overtakes the two noblemen and the calm control of the Cid. For a time the tone is that of farce, with the Infantes 'stricken with fear in the middle of the hall' (2283), Fernando crawling under the couch in his terror and Diego hiding behind the wine press and emerging with his clothes covered in dirt. Our imagination creates a colourful and entertaining picture. When the Cid asks for his sons-in-law – the lion having been returned safely to its cage – we are told simply that 'they were not to be found' (2304). We imagine his honest and innocent enquiry and the mirth which it provokes in those who, like us, know the truth. As the poet describes the joking which spreads through the court, we share in the hilarity at the Infantes' expense.

In all three of these episodes the humour is cruel, and derives from the humiliation of individuals who are outsiders (Raquel and Vidas) or in one way or another the Cid's enemies. Perhaps it is not a type of comedy which the twentieth-century reader finds it easy to appreciate; but its importance in the *Poema* must not be underestimated. The ridiculing of the Infantes in the lion episode is an effective means of lowering their standing and throwing into sharp relief the huge superiority of the man on whom they consider themselves entitled to take vengeance. Humour offers the plot a method of commenting on character, it increases the range of mood and provides a way of temporarily relieving the tension of the narrative, and it makes a substantial contribution to the *Poema*'s considerable power to entertain.

## VIII THE CID IN LITERATURE AND MUSIC

The *Poema de Mio Cid* was not the first text in which its hero's achievements were celebrated. By the middle of the twelfth century, the Cid had already figured prominently in a number of Arab chronicles and been the subject of both the *Carmen Campidoctoris*, a heroic Latin poem, and also of a more comprehensive Latin chronicle of his deeds, the *Historia Roderici*. In the thirteenth century, the promotion of the cult of the Cid by the monks of the monastery of Cardeña (see note to l.209 of the text), where the hero was buried with Jimena and some of his followers, led to the production and diffusion of a considerable body of fictitious material; this included some of the more picturesque legends which have come to be associated with the Cid, among them that of the the the use of his dead body, strapped to Babieca, taking part in a sally from the city of Valencia and striking terror into the Moslem troops. Accounts of the Cid's life and exploits continued to appear in chronicles, both Latin and Spanish, and his deeds are prominent in the vernacular compilations of the thirteenth and fourteenth centuries. The later Middle Ages and the sixteenth century saw an increase in the popularity of the ballad, and numerous of these *romances* treating episodes from the life of the Cid were collected in the *Romancero del Cid*, published in 1605 and frequently reprinted.[34] In the second half of the fourteenth century, there appeared a far-fetched verse account of the deeds performed by the Cid during his youth; this poem, the *Mocedades de Rodrigo*, was adapted from an epic now lost and it is this epic which, through the ballad-cycle derived from it, was to give birth to Guillén de Castro's two-part play *Las Mocedades del Cid*, published in 1618. The first part of this work tells of an insult inflicted by Doña Jimena's father on that of Rodrigo, and of the dilemma of the Cid, torn between love and the need to avenge his father. It provided the model for a much more celebrated work, Corneille's *Le Cid*, first produced in 1637 and enormously influential in the history of French drama and of the European theatre in general. An English version of Corneille's play was performed within a year of the appearance of the original. Henceforth, the writers who treated the story of the Cid were for the most part to concern themselves with the protagonist of the conflict between love and duty rather than with the epic hero. Thus, for example, although the Cid figures in several operas – some fifteen between 1715 and 1887, the most famous of them by Massenet (1885) – these do not deal with the events recounted in the *Poema de Mio Cid*. Manrique de Lara (1863-1929), a Spanish soldier and composer, began an opera based more clearly on the Cid's epic qualities, but it was not completed. It is surprising that the Cid's deeds have not in the last two hundred years been the subject of more distinguished works of literature and music; and it is perhaps sad that, though the *Poema de Mio Cid* and ballads dealing with the later part of the Cid's life have reached a wider public in translation, outside Spain it is more common for the figure of the Cid to be equated with the young lover of Corneille's play or the hero of a Hollywood film than with the imposing warrior and lord so vividly depicted in the medieval epic poem.

## IX THE TRANSLATION

We have sought in our version of the *Poema* to reproduce something of the style and flavour of the original and have tried, therefore, to reflect both its heroic tone and stylized form. We have endeavoured where possible to be consistent in the rendering of the formulae which are so important a feature of the poet's style, and in general it has been our aim to preserve details of form as far as to do so would produce an acceptable English reading. However, we have at times found it necessary to depart rather more than is our principle from the literal rendering, in order that our translation should work as a convincing English version. It would, for example, have been wrong to follow too closely the tenses used in the *Poema*, for they change sharply and often according to no clear pattern. Above all, we felt that it would be pointless to try to reproduce in English the verse-structure, assonance and rhythm of the Spanish text.

Our aims in this volume could find no better expression than the description of the translator's art included by Tobias Smollett in the preface to his translation, published in 1755, of *Don Quixote*:

*He has endeavoured to retain the spirit and ideas, without servilely adhering to the literal expression of the original; from which, however, he has not so far deviated, as to destroy that formality of idiom, so peculiar to the Spaniards, and so essential to the character of the work.*

## NOTES TO THE INTRODUCTION

**Where full details of books and articles are not given below, they are to be found in the Select Bibliography.**

**1.** For discussion of the evidence which survives for the content of the opening section of the *Poema* and the two other major lacunae, see C.C.Smith, 'On editing the *Poema de Mio Cid*', *Iberoromania*, 23 (1986), 3-19 (pp.10-13).

**2.** This conclusion is supported, for example, by D.W.Lomax, 'The Date of the *Poema de Mio Cid*'. For discussion of the poet's knowledge of legal procedure, see the studies by P.E.Russell, D.Hook, M.E.Lacarra, and M.N.Pavlović and R.M.Walker listed in the Bibliography.

**3.** 'Per Abbat and the *Poema de mio Cid*', *Medium Aevum*, XLII (1973), 1-17; Smith's arguments are further developed in *The Making of the 'Poema de mio Cid'*, especially chapter 3.

**4.** E. de Chasca includes in *El arte juglaresco en el 'Cantar de Mio Cid'* a detailed study of the use of formulae (pp.167-218) and a complete register of expressions which he classifies as formulaic (pp.332-82).

**5.** The poet's knowledge of and interest in matters of law is evident not only in the use that he makes of terms and expressions directly related to legal formulae, but also in the way in which, both in details of his narrative and in the overall treatment of legal issues, he shows a very good understanding of correct procedure; these points are dealt with in the notes to the text and in Section V (d) of the Introduction. If the poet was, indeed, a trained administrator, he could well have had access to legal documents from which to draw the names of his characters and some information about them (see note to ll.733-41 of the text).

**6.** For the use of this title, see R.Menéndez Pidal, *La España del Cid*, p.555.

**7.** Lacarra suggests that the emphasis in the *Poema* on the role of the Vani-Gómez family as the Cid's adversaries reflects the part played in the conflicts of the twelfth century by the Castro family, who were related to both the Vani-Gómez clan and to García Ordóñez, and whose enemies, the Laras, could claim descent from the Cid; see *El 'Poema de Mio Cid': realidad histórica e ideología*, pp.141-59.

**8.** Smith, *The Making ...*, chapter 4.

**9.** For an analysis of this campaign, see D.Hook, 'The Conquest of Valencia in the *Cantar de Mio Cid*', *Bulletin of Hispanic Studies*, 50 (1973), 120-26.

**10.** Smith, 'Literary Sources of Two Episodes in the *Poema de mio Cid*',

*Bulletin of Hispanic Studies*, 52 (1975), 109-22; also *The Making* ..., pp.149-52.

**11.** Smith, *The Making* ..., pp.143-46.

**12.** Smith, *The Making* ..., pp.161-64; see also note 30, below.

**13.** For a possible explanation for the depiction of the Infantes as the villains of the *Poema*, see note 7, above; and for an argument based on monastic rivalries, Smith, *The Making* ..., pp.175-76.

**14.** In this respect, he embodies two of the cardinal virtues (Fortitude and Prudence) often mentioned by medieval scholars and depicted in the visual arts. In the *Chanson de Roland* one of these virtues is represented by each of two sharply contrasted characters – Roland (*proz*) and Olivier (*sage*).

**15.** The *Libro de Alexandre*, edited by J.Cañas Murillo (Madrid, 1978), is in many respects a scholarly work and has its origins in the teachings of the literary theorists; but its battle scenes are long and violent.

**16.** Lacarra, pp.77-84.

**17.** Pavlović and Walker, 'Roman Forensic Procedure in the *Cort* Scene in the *Poema de Mio Cid*', p.104. This important analysis of the legal background to the climax of the *Poema* will be referred to on a number of occasions in the notes to the text.

**18.** Lacarra, pp.101-02.

**19.** Deyermond has emphasized the extent to which our understanding of the final section of the *Poema* depends on a knowledge of epic tradition and recognition of the extent to which it has been modified by the poet. He points out how the work's plot follows a pattern traditional in epic poetry – 'the epic pattern of insult, treacherous violence, and vengeance' – but how this is adapted to a subtler sequence of offence and punishment. See 'The Close of the *Cantar de Mio Cid*: Epic Tradition and Individual Variation'.

**20.** Two such works of art can be seen in the Cloisters Museum, New York.

**21.** *A Preface to Chaucer: Studies in Medieval Perspectives* (Princeton, 1962), p.163.

**22.** *The English Epic and its Background* (London, 1954), p.11.

**23.** Lascelles Abercrombie in *The Epic*, quoted by Tillyard, p.13.

**24.** *The Poem of the Cid*. p.4.

**25.** Smith sets out the principles which he has followed in his text in *Poema de mio Cid*, pp.xc-xcviii; for a fuller explanation of the notion of the experimental nature of the poet's enterprise, see *The Making* ..., pp.104 ff. Smith's conservative approach to the editing of the text is shared by Michael (see Bibliography).

**26.** See Smith, *The Making* ..., chapter 4, especially pp.112-32.

**27.** *The Making* ..., pp.108-11.

**28.** See note 4, above. For the fundamental study of the improvisatory technique of epic singers, see A.B.Lord, *The Singer of Tales; the Making of*

*Homeric Verse* (Cambridge, Massachusetts, 1960).

**29.** Smith, though pointing out that 'pair-phrases' relate to a much more general mental habit, shows that they often have close parallels in Latin usage and, specifically, often seem to be used in the *Poema* in imitation of legal expressions; see *The Making* ..., pp.183-84, and, for a more extensive treatment of binary expressions, *Estudios cidianos* (Madrid, 1977), chapter 7. Hook examines further parallels betwen expressions used in the *Poema* and Latin legal formulae in 'On Certain Correspondences between the *Poema de Mio Cid* and Contemporary Legal Instruments'. Some examples will be given in the notes to the text.

**30.** For detailed analysis of the stylistic parallels with French epic, see Smith, *The Making* ..., chapter 6, especially pp.186-202. Smith discusses, for example, the use made in the French poems of the formulae of direct address to the public, of 'physical phrases', and of a number of elements which the accounts of the battles share with the *Poema*. He points not only to general similarities but also to quite precise verbal parallels, and suggests that the Spanish poet, if not borrowing slavishly, certainly seems at times to have particular passages and, indeed, individual lines in mind. Smith also includes a detailed survey of the evidence that the author of the *Poema* imitated details from a number of episodes and scenes in French epic; see chapter 5, pp.155-66. A number of studies have appeared in recent years on possible French influences on the Spanish poet's treatment of major episodes: see, for example, those on possible sources of the Corpes incident referred to in the note to l.2698 of the text. In 'The *Poema de Mio Cid* and the Old French Epic: Some Reflections', Hook, while examining possible sources for the opening scene of the poem, considers how far parallels are evidence of direct borrowing from a given source or the result of the use of a stock motif.

**31.** For a general study of such patterns in the *Poema*, see A.D.Deyermond, 'Structural and Stylistic Patterns in the *Cantar de Mio Cid*' and the more detailed examination of two series of images by Deyermond and Hook in 'Doors and Cloaks: Two Image-patterns in the *Cantar de Mio Cid*'.

**32.** Vinaver's subject here is Arthurian prose romance, but some of the points which he makes about the aims and techniques of the medieval writer and artist are of more general application. See *The Rise of Romance* (Oxford, 1971), chapter 5.

**33.** 'Structural and Stylistic Patterns', pp.63-65.

**34.** Several such poems (with English verse translations) are included by Roger Wright in *Spanish Ballads* (Warminster, 1987), pp.64-99. Of these, however, only three are directly related to scenes from the *Poema*.

# CANTAR I

*The castle of Zorita was handed over to Alfonso VI by King al-Qadir of Toledo in 1080. At the time of the events of the* Poema, *the lands of Zorita were governed by Álvar Fáñez (courtesy Spanish National Tourist Office).*

1 De los sos ojos    tan fuerte mientre lorando
   tornava la cabeça    y estava los catando.
   Vio puertas abiertas    e uços sin cañados,
   alcandaras vazias    sin pielles e sin mantos
   e sin falcones    e sin adtores mudados.          5
   Sospiro mio Çid    ca mucho avie grandes cuidados.
   Ffablo mio Çid    bien e tan mesurado:
   '¡Grado a ti, señor,    padre que estas en alto!
   ¡Esto me an buelto    mios enemigos malos!'

2 Alli pienssan de aguijar,    alli sueltan las riendas.   10
   A la exida de Bivar    ovieron la corneja diestra
   y entrando a Burgos    ovieron la siniestra.
   Meçio mio Çid los ombros    y engrameo la tiesta:

**1-2** The Cid is about to leave his home in Vivar, a village nine kilometres to the north of Burgos, and ride into the city with a group of relatives and vassals, on his way into exile. He weeps as he looks upon the deserted houses.

The opening section of the *Poema* is very effective as it stands, but these are unlikely to have been the initial lines of the work in its full form; certainly one folio is missing from the beginning, and this may have contained up to fifty lines of verse; it is possible that more than one folio has been lost. The history of the events leading up to the Cid's banishment is recounted in a number of chronicles. The Latin *Historia Roderici* was probably composed in the mid-twelfth century; there is evidence that the author of the *Poema* drew on it, and it certainly provided a source for later vernacular chronicles such as the fourteenth-century *Crónica de veinte reyes de Castilla* (*Chronicle of Twenty Kings of Castile*) which incorporates a prosified version of the first *cantar* of the *Poema* (and short sections of the second). According to the account included in these two chronicles, the punishment was brought upon the hero by the envy and slanders of his enemies, among whom would have figured Count García Ordóñez (see note to l.1345): it was the consequence of an expedition by the Cid to Seville and his intervention on behalf of the tribute-paying King of Seville against the ruler of Granada. It is possible that the *Poema* opened with a prose account of this episode and of the punishment imposed by King Alfonso. However, vernacular chronicles have been used by some editors to reconstruct what may have been the first lines of verse: in their accounts of the events immediately preceding those described in the opening section of the *Poema* it is possible to discern the rhythm and assonance of verse, and it can be argued that here they are drawing upon a reworking of the *Poema* in its full form. The following passage, based on the corresponding sections in fourteenth-century chronicles, was reconstructed by Ramón Menéndez Pidal:

*… He sent for his relatives and vassals, and told them how the King was ordering him to leave his kingdom, that he was giving him only nine days to do so, and that he wished to know from them who wanted to go and who wanted to remain:*
*'May those who go with me receive God's favour!*
*With those who remain I shall be well content.'*
*Then Álvar Fáñez, his nephew, spoke:*

With the tears flowing so freely from his eyes
he turned his head and gazed upon them.
He saw gates open and doors with their locks struck off,
hooks empty without furs and without cloaks,
with neither falcons nor moulted hawks.                                      5
My Cid sighed, for he was greatly troubled.
My Cid spoke with dignity and with such wisdom:
"Thanks be to you, our Father on high!
This has been brought upon me by my evil enemies."

Now they ride off at a gallop, now they loosen the reins.          10
On leaving Vivar they saw a crow on their right hand side
and on entering Burgos they saw one to their left.
My Cid shrugged his shoulders and shook his head:

'We shall go with you, Cid, through settlement and country,
for we shall never fail you as long as we have our health.
With you we shall tire out our mules and horses
and use up our possessions and our clothes.
We shall always serve you as loyal vassals.'
Then every man gave his support to all Álvar had said,
and warmly My Cid gave thanks to them.
My Cid left Vivar, on his way to Burgos,
leaving his mansions empty and deserted.

**3** The King's officials have presumably struck the locks from the doors as a sign that these houses are no longer to be a safe refuge.

**4-5** Such property has probably already been confiscated at Alfonso's command. A moulted hawk is one which has completed its change of plumage and is ready for hunting: a bird of considerable value.

**7** The Cid's *mesura* – 'prudence' or 'discretion' – is one of the distinguishing features of his character. It is in obvious contrast, for example, with the bravery carried to dangerous excess which characterizes the behaviour of the hero of the *Chanson de Roland*, the most famous of the French epic poems.

**9** There is a source for this detail in the *Historia Roderici*, whose author tells us that the Cid was banished 'through envy', and through the influence of intriguers at court: these *curiales invidentes* are again alluded to in the *Poema* in l.267. The Cid has been exiled because of the malicious rumour that he has kept back part of the tribute, and the poet wishes us to see that the punishment is unjust and that Alfonso's judgement has not been an impartial one.

**11-13** The two crows are omens, the one on the right indicating good fortune, the one on the left seen on entering Burgos signifying bad fortune, probably anticipating the cold reception which awaits the Cid in that city. The hero shakes his head to cast off the ill omen. There are further allusions to the interpretation of such auguries in l.859 and l.2615.

'¡Albriçia, Albar Ffañez,     ca echados somos de tierra!'

3 Mio Çid Ruy Diaz     por Burgos entrava,                    15
  en su compaña     .lx. pendones levava.

  Exien lo ver     mugieres e varones,                        16b
  burgeses e burgesas     por las finiestras son,
  plorando de los ojos     tanto avien el dolor.
  De las sus bocas     todos dizian una razon:
  '¡Dios, que buen vassalo!     ¡Si oviesse buen señor!'       20

4 Conbidar le ien de grado     mas ninguno non osava;
  el rey don Alfonsso     tanto avie la grand saña,
  antes de la noche     en Burgos del entro su carta
  con grand recabdo     e fuerte mientre sellada,
  que a mio Çid Ruy Diaz     que nadi nol diesse(n) posada, 25
  e aquel que gela diesse     sopiesse — vera palabra —
  que perderie los averes     e mas los ojos de la cara
  e aun demas     los cuerpos e las almas.
  Grande duelo avien     las yentes christianas;
  asconden se de mio Çid     ca nol osan dezir nada.           30
  El Campeador     adeliño a su posada;
  asi commo lego a la puerta     falola bien çerrada
  por miedo del rey Alfonsso     que assi lo avien parado
  que si non la quebrantas por fuerça     que non gela abriese
                                                      nadi.

14 *Albriçia* means literally 'a reward for good news'. The Cid's bitter irony here typifies the attitude of grim but uncomplaining acceptance which he adopts in the face of misfortune. More striking, perhaps, is the gratitude which he expresses to God in l.8, where he offers thanks for the opportunity which he has been given to prove his true worth.

  Álvar Fáñez (or Háñez) is represented in the *Poema* as the Cid's nephew and right-hand man. In fact he was a distinguished warrior in his own right, in the service of Alfonso VI and as Governor of Toledo, which he defended against the Almoravids in 1109. Though he does appear in a document of 1075 as a witness to part of the wedding settlement between the Cid and Jimena, and is described as the former's *sobrinus* or nephew, there is no doubt that his historical connection with the Cid was much less close than that portrayed in the *Poema*, and he could not have been his constant companion during his time in exile. The two warriors were already mentioned together as the heroes of their age by the author of the Latin *Poema de Almería* (composed between 1147 and 1149).

16 This means that sixty knights accompanied the Cid. With each of these there presumably went a number of his own vassals, and the company would thus already have been quite substantial.

16b Such line numbering in the text indicates that the copyist has written two lines as one.

20 The meaning of this line is disputed, some editors preferring to take it as a single sentence: the sense is then that the Cid would have proved the most obedient of vassals if only the King had treated him fairly. Smith's reading seems more consistent with the point, repeatedly made throughout the first half of the poem, that even though the Cid is rejected by Alfonso and therefore has none of the advantages or duties of vassalage, he nevertheless continues to look to Alfonso as his lord and to do all within his power to win back his favour.

22 The allusion here is to the *ira regia*, quite literally 'royal anger', an institution extensively documented in medieval Spanish law codes: a nobleman who had incurred the wrath of his monarch would be given a fixed

"This is good, Álvar Fáñez; we are cast out of our land!"

My Cid Ruy Díaz was entering Burgos,                                    15
with a company of sixty pennants.

Men and women came out to see him;                                      16b
townsmen and townswomen were at the windows,
tears flowing from their eyes, so great was their pain.
The same words were in the mouths of all:
"Lord God, what a good vassal! If only he had a good lord!"             20

They would willingly have invited him in, but none dared do so;
the King, Don Alfonso, was in so great a rage.
The night before, his decree had reached Burgos,
brought with great precaution and carrying a heavy seal,
commanding that nobody give lodging to My Cid Ruy Díaz,                 25
and that anyone who did so should be aware, for certain,
that he would lose his possessions and his eyes as well,
and what is more his body and his soul.
Great was the sorrow among the Christian people;
they hid from My Cid, for they dared say nothing to him.                30
The Battler made straight for his place of lodging;
when he reached the door he found it firmly closed
for fear of King Alfonso — it had been ordered
that it should not be opened unless it were broken down by force.

period of time in which to leave the kingdom. The punishment inflicted on the Cid largely coincides with the description of the penalty in the law codes and charters of medieval Spain, but, significantly, some aspects of the King's decree are exceptionally severe. The Cid is given just nine days to leave Castile (ll.306-10), whilst normally at least thirty would be allowed; his vassals are forbidden to accompany him (as is made clear by the King's subsequent comments, ll.1361-66), though, had the usual laws of Castile been followed, they would have been expected to go with him; and, whereas those laws indicated that the banished nobleman should be allowed to purchase provisions before his departure, Alfonso has taken every step to ensure that the Cid cannot obtain even the most essential supplies. For a fuller discussion of the workings of the *ira regia* and their reflection in the *Poema*, see M.E.Lacarra, *El Poema de Mio Cid': realidad histórica e ideología*, pp.8-37.

**24** The decree carries a large pendant seal. There is no evidence that Alfonso VI used such seals, other than on important charters, and they are not known to have been used on writs before about 1185. This fact has been used to support the argument that the *Poema* could not have been composed before the late twelfth century. The evidence is far from conclusive. See P.E.Russell, 'Some Problems of Diplomatic in the *Cantar de Mio Cid* and their Implications', p.344; and D.W.Lomax, 'The Date of the *Poema de Mio Cid*', pp.77-78.

**26-28** In this warning there are some echoes of the 'malediction clause', a kind of ritual curse often used in royal documents, invoking a series of punishments – confiscation of possessions, blinding, death, and damnation – for any who disobeyed their terms. For a discussion of these and their dating, see Lacarra, pp.234-35; and Russell, pp.344-46.

**31** The epithet *Campeador*, meaning 'winner of battles' was applied to the Cid in his own lifetime, as contemporary documents indicate, and a latinized form of the title is used in the *Carmen Campidoctoris*.

Los de mio Çid    a altas vozes laman,    35
los de dentro    non les querien tornar palabra.
Aguijo mio Çid,    a la puerta se legava,
saco el pie del estribera,    una feridal dava;
non se abre la puerta    ca bien era çerrada.
Una niña de nuef años    a ojo se parava:    40
'¡Ya Campeador    en buen ora çinxiestes espada!
El rey lo ha vedado,    anoch del entro su carta
con grant recabdo    e fuerte mientre sellada.
Non vos osariemos abrir    nin coger por nada;
si non, perderiemos    los averes e las casas    45
e demas    los ojos de las caras.
Çid, en el nuestro mal    vos non ganades nada;
mas ¡el Criador vos vala    con todas sus vertudes santas!'
Esto la niña dixo    e tornos pora su casa.
Ya lo vee el Çid    que del rey non avie graçia.    50
Partios de la puerta,    por Burgos aguijava,
lego a Santa Maria,    luego descavalga,
finco los inojos,    de coraçon rogava.
La oraçion fecha    luego cavalgava;
salio por la puerta    e (en) Arlançon p[a]sava.    55
Cabo essa villa    en la glera posava,
fincava la tienda    e luego descavalgava.
Mio Çid Ruy Diaz    el que en buen ora çinxo espada
poso en la glera    quando nol coge nadi en casa,
derredor del    una buena conpaña.    60
Assi poso mio Çid    commo si fuesse en montaña.
Vedada l'an compra    dentro en Burgos la casa
de todas cosas    quantas son de vianda;
non le osarien vender    al menos dinarada.

5 Martin Antolinez    el burgales complido    65

45 'Our possessions and our homes' (that is, everything) is an example of a 'pair-phrase' with close parallels i
Latin legal documents. For the importance of this stylistic feature, see Introduction, VII (b) and note 29.
48 The word *vertudes* is used in its Latin sense of 'strength' or 'grace'.
52 The Cid goes to pray in the cathedral of Burgos. This would not, however, have been the present magnificen
building, begun under Fernando III in 1221, but the earlier Romanesque cathedral whose construction had bee
undertaken during the reign of Alfonso VI.
54 Literally, '(with) the prayer finished, he rode on'; the poet is imitating the Latin ablative absolut
construction, as he does on a number of other occasions (for example in l.147 and l.366).
59 A.D.Deyermond points out that in the twelfth century a leper-house stood outside the city walls near a bridg
over the river Arlanzón, and that the poet here seems to suggest to his audience that the Cid was 'being treated a
a metaphorical leper thanks to Alfonso's hostility'; see 'Structural and Stlylistic Patterns in the *Cantar de Mi
Cid*', p.59.
62-63 See note to l.22, above. By emphasizing how far the King has gone beyond what is considered normal an
fitting punishment, the poet underlines the inhumane and unreasonable nature of his action and suggests that th

My Cid's men called out in loud voices, 35
but those within would not say a single word in answer.
My Cid spurred on his horse, and approached the door;
he took his foot from the stirrup; he kicked the door,
but it would not open, for it was firmly closed.
A little girl, but nine years old, came out to him: 40
"O Battler, in a favoured hour you girded your sword!
The King has forbidden us to take you in; his decree arrived last
night,
brought with great precaution and carrying a heavy seal.
Nothing could persuade us to open to you or admit you,
for if we did we would lose our possessions and our homes, 45
and our eyes as well.
Cid, by our misfortune you gain nothing;
but may the Creator assist you with all his sacred power!"
Having said this, the girl returned to her house.
Now the Cid could see how he was out of favour with the King. 50
He turned from the door, and rode off through Burgos;
he reached Santa María and then dismounted.
He knelt down and prayed from his heart
When his prayer was finished, he mounted his horse;
he went through the city gate and crossed the Arlanzón. 55
Near the town he camped on the river - bank;
he dismounted and pitched his tent.
My Cid Ruy Díaz, the man who girded his sword in a
favoured hour,
camped on the river - bank since no one would take him into
his house,
with a loyal company of men around him. 60
My Cid camped as if he were in the mountains.
He had been forbidden to purchase, while in the city of Burgos,
anything whatsoever that he might eat.
They did not even dare to sell him a penny worth.

Martín Antolínez, worthy citizen of Burgos, 65

treatment received by the Cid has been fundamentally unjust.
**65** The historical existence of Martín Antolínez is not documented. He is a significant figure in the *Poema* in that
he saves and upholds the honour of the city of Burgos: the 'loyal man of Burgos' provides the Cid, at the time of
his greatest need, with the help so signally lacking elsewhere, and accompanies him in exile, offering him devoted
support. He is, perhaps, an unusual figure in this world of epic qualities, for one of his outstanding characteristics
is his sharpness of wit.

a mio Çid e a los suyos    abastales de pan e de vino;
non lo conpra,    ca el selo avie consigo;
de todo conducho    bien los ovo bastidos.
Pagos mio Çid    el Campeador [conplido]
e todos los otros    que van a so çervicio.       69b
Fablo Martin Antolinez,    odredes lo que a dicho:    70
'¡Ya Canpeador    en buen ora fuestes naçido!
Esta noch y[a]gamos    e vay[a]mos nos al matino,
ca acusado sere    de lo que vos he servido;
en ira del rey Alfonsso    yo sere metido.
Si con vusco    escapo sano o bivo    75
aun çerca o tarde    el rey querer me ha por amigo;
si non, quanto dexo    ¡no lo preçio un figo!'

6 Fablo mio Çid    el que en buen ora çinxo espada:
'¡Martin Antolinez    sodes ardida lança!
Si yo bivo    doblar vos he la soldada.    80
Espeso e el oro    e toda la plata;
bien lo vedes    que yo no trayo [nada],
e huebos me serie    pora toda mi compaña;
fer lo he amidos,    de grado non avrie nada.
Con vuestro consego    bastir quiero dos archas;    85
incamos las d'arena    ca bien seran pesadas,
cubiertas de guadalmeçi    e bien enclaveadas.

7 Los guadameçis vermejos    e los clavos bien dorados.
Por Rachel e Vidas    vayades me privado;
quando en Burgos me vedaron compra    y el rey me a
                                            airado,  90

---

**67** This fact does not affect the degree to which Martín Antolínez would be liable to be punished (as ll.73-74 make clear). The quantities involved are considerable; the destination of the food and wine would probably have been obvious, and he could not have made the purchases without attracting suspicion.

**78** See also l.41. This is one of the commonest epithets applied by the poet to his hero; the reference is to a favourable conjunction of planets, and the repeated use of this expression makes us see the Cid as a warrior favoured from the outset by fortune, set above other men, and destined to achieve success and honour.

**79** Literally, Martín Antolínez is described as 'a brave lance': the representation of the warrior by his weapon is a figurative device defined by the grammarians as *intellectio* (synecdoche); but there is no need to attribute to a learned source such an expression which could well be drawn from everyday speech.

**80** The poet makes a distinction between those vassals (such as Muño Gustioz, l.737) who form part of the Cid's houshold, and those such as Martín Antolínez whose bond with him is essentially an economic one. Our attention is frequently drawn to the financial benefit which the Cid's men gain from serving him, for generosity and concern for his vassals' welfare are clearly essential characteristics in a man who is to be seen as an ideal lord; see Introduction, V (e).

**84** Here and in ll.94-95 the Cid is most insistent that he acts only out of urgent need. Lacarra (pp.190-91) argues that he here refers not to the trick he is to play but to the act of requesting a loan, for this was forbidden by the Church. It does seem, however, that the poet deliberately makes as much as possible of this episode, which is certainly longer than is necessary for the development of the plot. Since the Church condemned usury, in Spain,

supplied My Cid and his men with bread and wine;
he did not buy these, as he had his own supply;
he had given them good provision of all the food they needed.
My Cid, the worthy Battler, was well pleased,
as were all those who served him.
Martín Antolínez spoke; you will hear what he said:     70
"O Battler, you were born in a favoured hour!
Let us rest tonight and set off at dawn,
for I shall be accused of having helped you,
and incur the anger of King Alfonso.
If I escape with you, alive and well,                    75
sooner or later the King will want me as his friend;
if not, I do not give a fig for all I leave behind!"

This was the reply of My Cid, who girded his sword in a
                                favoured hour:
"Martín Antolínez, you are a valiant warrior!
If I live, I shall double what you are paid.             80
I have spent the gold, and all the silver too;
as you can see very well, I bring nothing with me,
and I will need to pay my whole company;
what I propose, I shall do unwillingly; by choice I would
                                take nothing.
With your help I want to prepare two chests;            85
let us fill them with sand, so they will be very heavy,
and cover them with embossed leather, finely studded:

bright red leather with brightly gilded studs.
Go quickly for me to Raquel and Vidas; tell them:
in Burgos I am forbidden to make purchases, and the King has
                                exiled me;                90

---

as in other Christian countries, money-lending in the earlier Middle Ages was largely the prerogative of Jews.
The Jewish communities of Spain were particularly large and prosperous. They did not suffer – until the later
Middle Ages – the brutal persecution inflicted on Jews in some parts of northern Europe, but they were,
nevertheless, the object of suspicion and resentment, and would be an obvious target for wit. The medieval
audience would relish for its own sake this tale of the deception of the grasping and, in their way, rather sinister
pair of money-lenders; and thus, for example, the fact that Martín Antolínez, on top of the six hundred marks,
wins for himself another thirty (willingly given by the Jews as a reward for what he has done for them!) gives the
story an extra humorous twist.

**89** It is to be assumed that both the Jews are men: a woman would not engage in business.

47

non puedo traer el aver    ca mucho es pesado,
enpeñar gelo he    por lo que fuere guisado.
De noche lo lieven    que non lo vean christianos;
vealo el Criador    con todos los sos santos,
yo mas non puedo    e amidos lo fago.'      95

8 Martin Antolinez    non lo detar[da]va,
  por Rachel e Vidas    a priessa demandava.
  Passo por Burgos,    al castiello entrava,
  por Rachel e Vidas    a priessa demandava.

9 Rachel e Vidas    en uno estavan amos      100
  en cuenta de sus averes,    de los que avien ganados.
  Lego Martin Antolinez    a guisa de menbrado:
  '¿O sodes, Rachel e Vidas,    los mios amigos caros?
  En poridad    f(l)ablar querria con amos.'
  Non lo detardan,    todos tres se apartaron:      105
  'Rachel e Vidas:    amos me dat las manos
  que non me descubrades    a moros nin a christianos;
  por siempre vos fare ricos,    que non seades menguados.
  El Campeador    por las parias fue entrado,
  grandes averes priso    e mucho sobejanos;      110
  retovo dellos    quanto que fue algo,
  por en vino a aquesto    por que fue acusado.
  Tiene dos arcas    lennas de oro esmerado.
  Ya lo vedes    que el rey le a airado.
  Dexado ha heredades    e casas e palaçios;      115
  aquelas non las puede levar,    si non, ser ien ventadas;
  el Campeador dexar las ha    en vuestra mano,
  e prestalde de aver    lo que sea guisado.
  Prended las archas    e meted las en vuestro salvo;
  con grand jura    meted i las fes amos      120
  que non las catedes    en todo aqueste año.'
  Rachel e Vidas    seyen se consejando:
  'Nos huebos avemos    en todo de ganar algo.
  Bien lo sabemos    que el algo gaño,
  quando a tierra de moros entro    que grant aver saco;    125

---

**98** The Jews live in the ghetto which is known to have been situated close to or within the walls of the castle.
**107** 'Neither to Moor nor to Christian', meaning simply 'to nobody', is an example of a 'pair-phrase' common in the poem.
**109 ff.** This is the first that we are told of the substance of the accusations against the Cid. Martín Antolínez alludes to the expedition to Seville to collect tribute for Alfonso from its Moslem ruler, which, according to some chronicle accounts (see note to ll.1-2), led to the Cid's banishment. He seems to admit that the Cid was guilty of retaining for himself some of the tribute and that he thus deserves his punishment; but it is more likely that we should see him as simply telling the Jews what is current in popular gossip, in order to convince them of the Cid's wealth and of his value as a client.

I cannot take my valuables with me; they weigh too much,
and so I will pledge them for a suitable sum;
let them be taken by night, that none shall see;
may the Creator, with all his saints, be my witness
that I can do no more, and that I act against my will."          95

Martín Antolínez did not delay;
he asked urgently for Raquel and Vidas.
He made his way through Burgos and entered the castle,
asking urgently for Raquel and Vidas.

Raquel and Vidas were both together,                              100
counting their money and their profits.
Martín Antolínez arrived, a clever man:
"Where are you, Raquel and Vidas, my dear friends?
I would like to speak to both of you in confidence."
Without delay all three went off together:                        105
"Raquel and Vidas: promise me both of you
that you will give me away neither to Moor nor to Christian.
I shall make you rich for life, so that you will never be in need.
The Battler went to collect the tribute;
what he received in payment was very great of value               110
and he kept back from it a considerable amount;
that is how he came to be accused.
He has two chests full of pure gold.
And, as you are aware, the King has exiled him.
He has left his inheritance, both houses and manors;              115
he cannot take the chests lest their existence be discovered.
The Battler will entrust them into your hands;
you are to lend him as much money as would be appropriate.
Take the chests into your safe - keeping;
promise both of you with a sacred oath                            120
that you will not look into them for a year from this day."
Raquel and Vidas considered between themselves:
"In all our business we need to make a profit.
We know full well that he acquired riches;
from the lands of the Moors he brought back great wealth;         125

---

**115** It is not entirely clear whether the Cid's houses and lands have been confiscated or not; l.1271 seems to indicate that he still has property in Castile. Certainly those who accompany him into exile stand to lose all their possessions (see note to l.289).

49

non duerme sin sospecha     qui aver trae monedado.
Estas archas     prendamos las amas,
en logar las metamos     que non sean ventadas.
Mas dezid nos del Çid:     ¿de que sera pagado,
o que gançia nos dara     por todo aqueste año?'     130
Respuso Martin Antolinez     a guisa de menbrado:
'Mio Çid querra     lo que ssea aguisado,
pedir vos a poco     por dexar so aver en salvo;
acogen sele omnes     de todas partes menguados;
a menester     seis çientos marcos.'     135
Dixo Rachel e Vidas:     'Dar gelos [hemos] de grado.'
'Ya vedes que entra la noch,     el Çid es presurado;
huebos avemos     que nos dedes los marchos.'
Dixo Rachel e Vidas:     'Non se faze assi el mercado,
si non primero prendiendo     e despues dando.'     140
Dixo Martin Antolinez:     'Yo desso me pago.

Amos tred     al Campeador contado,
e nos vos ayudaremos     que assi es aguisado
por aduzir las archas     e meter las en vuestro salvo,
que non lo sepan     moros nin christianos.'     145
Dixo Rachel e Vidas:     'Nos desto nos pagamos;
las archas aduchas,     prendet seyes çientos marcos.'
Martin Antolinez     cavalgo privado
con Rachel e Vidas     de voluntad e de grado.
Non viene a la pueent     ca por el agua a passado     150
que gelo non venta(n)ssen     de Burgos omne nado.
Afevos los a la tienda     del Campeador contado:
assi commo entraron     al Çid besaron le las manos,
sonrrisos mio Çid,     estavalos fablando:
'¡Ya don Rachel e Vidas     avedes me olbidado!     155
Ya me exco de tierra     ca del rey so airado;
a lo quem semeja     de lo mio avredes algo,
mientras que vivades     non seredes menguados.'
Don Rachel e Vidas     a mio Çid besaron le las manos.
Martin Antolinez     el pleito a parado     160
que sobre aquelas archas     dar le ien .vi. çientos marcos
e bien gelas guardarien     fasta cabo del año;

---

**135** One mark was equivalent in value to eight ounces of gold or silver, and the sum of money involved is thus considerable. One hundred marks are considered ample payment to the monastery of Cardeña for providing for all the needs of Jimena, her daughters, and their ladies for a year (see ll.253-54).

**136** In the Spanish text, the first verb is in the singular, a device which emphasizes the oneness and lack of individual personality of the two Jews.

**153** There is a good deal of kissing of hands in the *Poema*. In several cases this is a ritual gesture which is actually performed, but elsewhere the expression is used by the poet to signify the asking of formal permission (as in l.1252) or simply the making of a request (for example, l.179). In this case the gesture is particularly appropriate

a man who carries great treasure with him will not sleep easily.
Let us take both these chests
and let us put them where they will not be discovered.
Now then, tell us what sum will satisfy the Cid,
and what interest he will pay us for this whole year."          130
Martín Antolínez, a clever man, replied:
"My Cid will want whatever is appropriate,
and since he leaves his valuables in safe hands will ask little of you;
from all sides men are gathering around him;
he requires six hundred marks."                                 135
Raquel and Vidas said: "We will provide them willingly."
"You can see that night is falling, the Cid must hurry:
we need you to give us the marks."
Raquel and Vidas said: "That's not the way of business:
we take first and then give."                                   140
Martín Antolínez said: "I am satisfied with this.
Both of you come to the celebrated Battler,
and we shall help you, as is proper,
to convey the chests into your safe - keeping,
so that neither Moor nor Christian shall know of them."         145
Rachel and Vidas said: "We are satisfied with this:
when the chests have been brought, you will get six hundred marks."
Martín Antolínez rode speedily,
accompanied most willingly by Raquel and Vidas.
He did not pass over the bridge; instead he forded the river     150
so that no man of Burgos should suspect his presence.
Now here they are at the tent of the celebrated Battler:
as soon as they entered, they kissed the Cid's hands.
My Cid smiled and spoke to them:
"Now, Raquel and Vidas, have you really forgotten me?            155
I am leaving this land, for I have been exiled by the King;
I think that you will gain something of my wealth,
and as long as you live you will never be in need."
Raquel and Vidas kissed My Cid's hands.
Martín Antolínez settled the agreement:                          160
that against the security of the chests they should give the Cid
                              six hundred marks,
and that they should have custody of the chests till the end of
                              the year;

to the unctuous and servile behaviour of the Jews in the face of an apparent source of income.

ca assil dieran la fe    e gelo avien jurado  
que si antes las catassen    que fuessen perjurados,  
non les diesse mio Çid    de la ganançia un dinero malo.  165  
Dixo Martin Antolinez:    'Cargen las archas privado.  
Levaldas, Rachel e Vidas,    poned las en vuestro salvo;  
yo ire con vus[c]o    que adugamos los marcos,  
ca a mover a mio Çid    ante que cante el gallo.'  
Al cargar de las archas    veriedes gozo tanto:    170  
non las podien poner en somo    mager eran esforçados.  
Gradan se Rachel e Vidas    con averes monedados,  
ca mientra que visquiessen    refechos eran amos.

10 Rachel a mio Çid    la manol ba besar:

'¡Ya Campeador    en buen ora çinxiestes espada!    175  
De Castiella vos ides    pora las yentes estrañas;  
assi es vuestra ventura,    grandes son vuestras gananças,  
una piel vermeja    morisca e ondrada  
Çid, beso vuestra mano    en don que la yo aya.'  
'Plazme', dixo el Çid,    'D'aqui sea mandada;    180  
si vos la aduxier d'alla;    si non, contalda sobre las arcas.'  
En medio del palaçio    tendieron un almofalla,  
sobr'ella una savana    de rançal e muy blanca;  
a tod el primer colpe    .iii.ᶜᶜᶜ marcos de plata echa[va]n,  
notolos don Martino,    sin peso los tomava;    185  
los otros .ccc.    en oro gelos pagavan.  
Cinco escuderos tiene don Martino,    a todos los cargava.  
Quando esto ovo fecho    odredes lo que fablava:  
'Ya don Rachel e Vidas    en vuestras manos son las arcas;  
yo, que esto vos gane,    bien mereçia calças.'    190

11 Entre Rachel e Vidas    aparte ixieron amos:  
'Demos le buen don    ca el no' lo ha buscado.  
Martin Antolinez    un burgales contado  
vos lo mereçedes,    darvos queremos buen dado  
de que fagades calças    e rica piel e buen manto;    195

**170** This form of direct address – 'you could see …' – emphasizing the immediacy of the scene, is used several times in the *Poema*, and is most common in accounts of battles (see, for example, ll.697, 1141, 2400, 2404). A direct equivalent (*là veïssiez*) is much used in French epic poetry.  
**181** A biting remark, likely to produce much humour, if we believe that the Cid does not intend to repay the Jews.  
**185** Coins might be irregular in form and their weight was what counted. Clipping their edges would lessen their value. By not insisting that the coins be weighed, Martín Antolínez is making a display of trust in the Jews' honesty, to comic effect in view of our knowledge that they are the ones being tricked.  
**187** The number of coins does not seem sufficient to constitute a heavy load for five squires. The detail is not included in order to give us a realistic picture of the scene but simply to convince us that an enormous amount of money is involved.  
**190** Such an article of clothing would be usual as a reward for the kind of service which Raquel and Vidas think

that they should promise and swear to him
that if they looked into them before then they should be
                              considered perjurers,
and My Cid should not give them a miserable penny of interest. 165
Martín Antolínez said: "Load the chests quickly.
Take them, Raquel and Vidas, into your safe - keeping.
I will go with you, so that we may bring the marks,
for My Cid has to be on the move before the cock crows."
As the chests were being loaded, what joy you could see!        170
They found difficulty in lifting them, in spite of their strength.
Raquel and Vidas were delighted with their treasure;
for as long as they lived they were both to be rich.

Raquel goes and kisses My Cid's hand:

"O Battler, who girded your sword in a favoured hour!        175
You are leaving Castile for the lands of foreign peoples;
such is your good fortune, so great will be your profit,
that a fine red tunic, in Moorish style,
I ask of you, Cid, as a gift."
"I grant it," said the Cid.  "Let it now be settled,        180
if I can bring it back to you; if not, deduct its value from
                              the chests."
In the middle of their residence, they spread out a mat,
and on it a sheet of fine white cloth;
first, in one go, they threw down three hundred silver marks;
Don Martín counted them, but did not weigh them.        185
They paid him the other three hundred in gold.
Don Martín had five squires, all of whom he loaded with the money.
You will hear what he said when he had done this:
"Now, Don Raquel and Vidas, the chests are in your hands;
I, who gained you this business, well deserve a pair of breeches." 190

Raquel and Vidas turned aside to one another:
"Let us make him a worthy gift, for he has brought us this business.
Martín Antolínez, eminent citizen of Burgos,
you deserve it, we want to make you a worthy gift
from which you may buy yourself breeches and in addition a
                              rich tunic and a fine cloak;        195

Martín Antolínez has rendered them. It is ironical that in their gratitude and their desire to make sure of their
gains they should give him more than he has requested.

53

damos vos en don      a vos .xxx. marchos.
Mereçer no' lo hedes,      ca esto es aguisado,
atorgar nos hedes      esto que avemos parado.'
Gradeçiolo don Martino      e reçibio los marchos;
grado exir de la posada      y espidios de amos.                   200
Exido es de Burgos      e Arlançon a passado,
vino pora la tienda      del que en buen ora nasco;
reçibiolo el Çid      abiertos amos los braços:
'¿Venides, Martin Antolinez,      el mio fiel vassalo?
¡Aun vea el dia      que de mi ayades algo!'                   205
'Vengo, Campeador,      con todo buen recabdo;
vos .vi. çientos      e yo .xxx. he ganados.
Mandad coger la tienda      e vayamos privado,
en San Pero de Cardeña      i nos cante el gallo;
veremos vuestra mugier      menbrada fija dalgo;                   210
mesuraremos la posada      e quitaremos el reinado,
mucho es huebos      ca çerca viene el plazo.'

12 Estas palabras dichas,      la tienda es cogida,
Mio Çid e sus conpañas      cavalgan tan aina.
La cara del cavallo      torno a Santa Maria,                   215
alço su mano diestra,      la cara se santigua:
'¡A ti lo gradesco, Dios,      que çielo e tierra guias!
¡Valan me tus vertudes      gloriosa Santa Maria!
D'aqui quito Castiella      pues que el rey he en ira;
non se si entrare i mas      en todos los mios dias.                   220
¡Vuestra vertud me vala      Gloriosa, en mi exida,
e me ayude e(l) me acorra      de noch e de dia!

**209** Three times the poet mentions cock-crow in connection with the timing of events at Cardeña. This detail could well be related to the office of *gallicantum* or *gallicinium* which precedes matins (see Smith, *The Making of the Poema de mio Cid'*, p.185).

   The monastery of Cardeña is situated eight kilometres from Burgos. It plays a prominent role in the *Poema*, providing the Cid with the welcome and the protection for his family which the King has sought to deny him, though it is highly unlikely that the monks' defiance of royal authority as it is here depicted coincides with historical fact. This powerful monastery was much favoured by Alfonso VI, who appointed its abbot to the important bishopric of Santiago de Compostela. In 1142, however, Alfonso VII handed the monastery over to the Cluniac order, in whose hands it remained until it regained its independence four years later through the intervention of the Pope. In the twelfth century Cardeña suffered not only from some insecurity with regard to the preservation of its independence but also from steady economic decline; and at some stage, perhaps in the twelfth century, more probably not until after the diffusion of the *Poema* itself in the early thirteenth century, it began actively to promote a cult of the hero, stressing his relationship with the monastery (for the importance of the *Leyenda de Cardeña*, see also Introduction, VIII). The advantage for Cardeña of association with so illustrious a figure was considerable: his generosity towards the community, which the author of the *Poema* draws to our attention, is to serve as a model for other wealthy patrons, and ll.1442-46 are an appeal to the poet's audience as well as to the Cid. Moreover, Cardeña was situated very near the pilgrim route to Santiago de Compostela, and the presence of so important a tomb enabled the monks to attract numerous visitors, bringing great commercial benefit. The *Poema* does not tell us that the Cid was buried at Cardeña, a fact which suggests

we make you a gift of thirty marks.
You will earn it — it is fitting —
as you will see this business through for us."
Don Martín thanked them and took the marks;
he wished to leave the house and he bade them both farewell.        200
He left Burgos and crossed the Arlanzón,
and came to the tent of the one born in a favoured hour.
The Cid welcomed him with arms outstretched:
"You are come, Martín Antolínez, my faithful vassal!
May I see the day when you are rewarded by me!"                     205
"I am come, Battler, and I have acted prudently;
you have gained six hundred marks and I have thirty for myself.
Order camp to be struck and let us be off quickly,
and by cock - crow let us be at San Pedro de Cardeña;
we shall see your wife, so wise and noble a lady;        _JIMENA_   210
we shall make only a brief stay and we shall leave the kingdom;
it is important that we do so, for the time allowed you is nearly
                              at an end."


As soon as these words had been said, the camp was struck.
My Cid and his companions rode off at a gallop.
With his horse's head turned towards Santa María,                   215
he raised his right hand and on his forehead made the sign of
                              the cross:
"I thank you, Lord God, who rule both heaven and earth!
May your blessings support me, glorious Saint Mary!
Now I am leaving Castile, since I have incurred the anger of the King;
I know not whether I shall enter it again in all my days.           220
May your grace support me, Mother in Glory, in my departure,
and help me and aid me through night and day!

that at the time of the work's composition the tomb cult did not exist. Nevertheless, the emphasis which the poet places on the Cid's connection with Cardeña indicates that the monastery had a particular significance for him, and it has been argued that he may have been a lawyer or notary closely linked with the monastery and thus able to consult material in its library and archives. For a discussion of the possibility that the *Poema* was composed at Cardeña, see Smith, ' Se escribió en Cardeña el *Poema de mio Cid?*', in *Homenaje a Álvaro Galmés de Fuentes: II* (Madrid, 1986), pp.463-473.

**210** Jimena is described as a *fija dalgo*. The term *hidalgo* is applied to those who, through their birth, have noble status. It is a generic term, taking in a number of different ranks of nobility. Though Jimena was a daughter of the Count of Oviedo and granddaughter of Alfonso V of León, her illustrious descent is not mentioned in the *Poema*. She married the Cid in 1074, some seven years before the date of the events with which the poem opens.

**215 ff.** Looking towards the cathedral, dedicated to Saint Mary, the Cid prays to the Virgin. The poet is at pains to emphasize his hero's piety, and more precisely his exemplary (and well-rewarded) generosity towards the Church. We can imagine that the ritual gesture in 1.216 would have been illustrated in performance.

Si vos assi lo fizieredes    e la ventura me fuere complida
mando al vuestro altar    buenas donas e ricas;
esto e yo en debdo    que faga i cantar mill missas.     225

13 Spidios el caboso    de cuer e de veluntad.
Sueltan las riendas    e pienssan de aguijar.
Dixo Martin Antolinez:    'Vere a la mugier a todo mio solaz,
castigar los he    commo abran a far.
Si el rey melo quisiere tomar    ¡a mi non m'inchal!    230
Antes sere con vusco    que el sol quiera rayar.'

14 Tornavas Martin Antolinez a Burgos    e mio Çid aguij[o]
pora San Pero de Cardeña    quanto pudo a espol[on]
con estos cavalleros    quel sirven a so sabor.
A priessa cantan los gallos    e quieren quebrar albores    235
quando lego a San Pero    el buen Campeador.
El abbat don Sancho    christiano del Criador
rezava los matines    abuelta de los albores;
i estava doña Ximena    con çinco dueñas de pro
rogando a San Pero    e al Criador:    240
'¡Tu que a todos guias    val a mio Çid el Campeador!'

15 Lamavan a la puerta,    i sopieron el mandado;
¡Dios, que alegre fue    el abbat don Sancho!
Con lumbres e con candelas    al corral dieron salto,
con tan grant gozo reçiben    al que en buen ora nasco:    245
'¡Gradesco lo a Dios, mio Çid!'    dixo el abbat don Sancho;
'Pues que aqui vos veo    prendet de mi ospedado.'
Dixo el Çid: 'Graçias, don abbat,    e so vuestro pagado.
Yo adobare conducho    pora mi e pora mis vassallos;
mas por que me vo de tierra    dovos .l. marchos,    250
si yo algun dia visquier    servos han doblados.
Non quiero fazer en el monesterio    un dinero de daño;
evades aqui pora doña Ximena    dovos .c. marchos,

237 It is surprising that the poet – particularly if he had access to documents relating to the monastery – should not have given the correct name of the abbot at the time of these events, Sisebuto (1056-1086). He does, however, tend to use the name at the end of a line (see ll.243, 246 and 256), and undoubtedly Sancho would fit more easily into a scheme of assonance than the unwieldy Sisebuto.

245 The welcome which follows the hammering on the gate at Cardeña contrasts sharply with the response which the Cid received in Burgos. A.D.Deyermond and D.Hook analyze in detail the references in the *Poema* to doors and gates, in 'Doors and Cloaks: Two Image-patterns in the *Cantar de Mio Cid*'.

252-60 The fact that the Cid needs to ensure the safety of his family in this way indicates that they, too, face considerable danger through the anger of the King. It was not uncommon for large monastic communities to offer care and protection to a family, as, in times of growing financial problems for the monasteries, such arrangements could provide a valuable source of income. A formal financial agreement would be made. Only a noble family could pay with money (as is the case here); others paid in kind, and, where a family possessed lands and property, payment could take the form of the eventual transference of these to the monastery (see Lacarra, pp.15-16). There are close parallels with the transaction between the Cid and the abbot in details of arrangements recorded

If you do so, and I enjoy good fortune,
I shall offer at your altar fine and rich gifts;
it shall be my duty to have a thousand masses sung."          225

The most noble one, deeply moved, took his leave.
They loosened the reins and rode off.
Martín Antolínez said: "I shall take my pleasure with my wife;
I shall instruct my people how they must act.
If the King wants to confiscate my property, I could not care less!
I will be with you again before the sun shines."

Martín Antolínez went back to Burgos and My Cid spurred on
towards San Pedro de Cardeña with all possible speed,
with these warriors who had chosen to serve him.
They heard the rousing song of the cocks as dawn was about to
                                    break          235
when the good Battler reached San Pedro.
The abbot, Don Sancho. a truly Christian man,
was saying matins as dawn broke;
present was Doña Jimena with five worthy ladies,
praying to Saint Peter and to the Creator:                     240
"You who guide us all, support My Cid the Battler."

They hammered at the gate; news of their arrival spread.
Lord God, how happy was the abbot, Don Sancho!
With torches and candles they hurried out into the yard;
with great joy they welcomed the man born in a favoured hour:  245
"Thanks be to God, My Cid!" said the abbot, Don Sancho,
"Receive my hospitality, now you are come."
The Cid said: "Thank you, lord abbot; I am grateful to you.
I shall get ready provisions both for myself and for my vassals.
But, as I am going into exile, I give you fifty marks;         250
If I live for any length of time, they will be doubled.
I do not wish the monastery to suffer any loss:
to provide for Doña Jimena I give you one hundred marks

in documents from monastic archives (see D. Hook. 'The Legal Basis of the Cid's Agreement with Abbot Sancho'. *Romania*. 101 (1980). 517-26. What is perhaps surprising is that the Cid's wife and daughters are to be lodged in a monastery rather than a nunnery: but this poses no difficulty if we see them as staying at Cardeña. outside the actual monastic precinct.

The Cid's daughters were in fact called Cristina and María. born in about 1077 and 1080 respectively. Possibly they also bore the names by which they are known in the *Poema* (Elvira = Cristina and Sol = María). The historical Cid also had a son. Diego. who was killed in battle in 1097.

a ella e a sus fijas e a sus dueñas     sirvades las est año.

Dues fijas dexo niñas    e prendet las en los braços,     255
aquellas vos acomiendo a vos,    abbat don Sancho;
dellas e de mi mugier    fagades todo recabdo.
Si essa despenssa vos falleçiere    o vos menguare algo,
bien las abastad,    yo assi vos lo mando;
por un marcho que despendades    al monesterio dare yo
                                      quatro'.

16 Otorgado gelo avie    el abbat de grado.     261
Afevos doña Ximena    con sus fijas do va legando,
señas dueñas las traen    e aduzen las adelant.
Ant'el Campeador    doña Ximena finco los inojos amos,
lorava de los ojos,    quisol besar las manos:     265
'¡Merçed, Campeador,    en ora buena fuestes nado!
Por malos mestureros    de tierra sodes echado.

¡Merçed, ya Çid,    barba tan complida!
Fem ante vos    yo e vuestras fijas
—iffantes son    e de dias chicas—     269b
con aquestas mis dueñas    de quien so yo servida.     270
Yo lo veo    que estades vos en ida
e nos de vos    partir nos hemos en vida:
¡Da(n)d nos consejo    por amor de Santa Maria!'
Enclino las manos    [el de] la barba velida,
a las sus fijas    en braço' las prendia,     275
legolas al coraçon    ca mucho las queria.
Lora de los ojos,    tan fuerte mientre sospira:
'¡Ya doña Ximena    la mi mugier tan complida,
commo a la mi alma    yo tanto vos queria!
Ya lo vedes    que partir nos emos en vida,     280
yo ire    e vos fincaredes remanida.
¡Plega a Dios    e a Santa Maria
que aun con mis manos    case estas mis fijas,     282b
o que de ventura    e algunos dias vida
e vos, mugier ondrada,    de mi seades servida!'

17 Grand yantar le fazen    al buen Campeador.     285
Tañen las campanas    en San Pero a clamor.
Por Castiella    oyendo van los pregones

---

**267** See note to l.9.

**268** The Cid's beard is often mentioned in the *Poema*. It is an obvious symbol of virility and manly strength, but for a man's beard to be pulled is the harshest of insults (see note to l.2832). The Cid's beard is also, by virtue of his vow not to cut it until accepted back by the King, to be identified with his devotion to his lord.

**282b** The poet is here anticipating what is to be an important element in the second half of the poem: the Cid's desire to see his daughters suitably and honourably married. It is possible that his words here are intended to foreshadow the fact that the girls' first marriages will be arranged not by the Cid but by King Alfonso.

that you may serve her, her daughters and ladies for this year.
I leave two young daughters; take them into your protection;    255
I commend them to you, abbot, Don Sancho;
take every care of them and of my wife.
If this sum should prove insufficient, or if you should need more,
I order you to provide for them well;
for each mark that you spend, I shall give four to the monastery."
The abbot had granted it willingly.
Here is Doña Jimena, arriving with her daughters,
each attended and brought forward by a lady.
Doña Jimena sank to her knees before the Battler,
tears flowing from her eyes, as she made to kiss his hands:    265
"I pray you, O Battler, born in a favoured hour,
you who have been cast into exile because of evil intriguers;

I pray you, O Cid, noble of beard!
Here I am before you, your daughters too,
who are but children, young in days,                            269b
and here are these ladies, who wait on me.                      270
I can see that you are leaving
and that we must be separated from you during our lifetime;
give us your counsel, for the love of Saint Mary!"
The man with the fine beard, stretching out his hands
to his daughters, gathered them in his arms                     275
and took them to his breast, for he loved them greatly.
Tears flowed from his eyes and he sighed heavily:
"Doña Jimena, my noble wife,
I have loved you as my own soul!
You can see that we shall be separated in our lifetime;         280
for I shall go and you are to stay behind.
May God and Saint Mary grant
that I myself may yet arrange marriages for these my daughters; 282b
may I be granted good fortune and time on earth,
that I may serve you, my honoured wife."

A great feast is prepared for the good Battler.                 285
The bells ring out in San Pedro.
Throughout Castile the proclamation is carried

commo se va de tierra    mio Çid el Campeador;
unos dexan casas    e otros onores,
en aques dia    a la puent de Arlançon      290
çiento quinze cavalleros    todos juntados son;
todos demandan    por mio Çid el Campeador.
Martin Antolinez    con ellos cojo;
vansse pora San Pero    do esta el que en buen punto naçio.

18 Quando lo sopo    mio Çid el de Bivar      295
quel creçe compaña    por que mas valdra,
a priessa cavalga,    reçebir los sal(i)e,
tornos a sonrisar,    legan le todos, la manol ban besar.
Fablo mio Çid    de toda voluntad:
'Yo ruego a Dios    e al Padre spirital,      300
vos, que por mi dexades    casas y heredades,
enantes que yo muera    algun bien vos pueda far,
lo que perdedes    doblado vos lo cobrar.'
Plogo a mio Çid    por que creçio en la yantar,
plogo a los otros omnes todos    quantos con el estan.    305
Los .vi. dias de plazo    passados los an,
tres an por troçir    sepades que non mas.
Mando el rey    a mio Çid (a) aguardar,
que si despues del plazo    en su tierral pudies tomar
por oro nin por plata    non podrie escapar.    310
El dia es exido,    la noch querie entrar,
a sus cavalleros    mandolos todos juntar:
'¡Oid, varones,    non vos caya en pesar!
Poco aver trayo,    dar vos quiero vuestra part.
Sed membrados    commo lo devedes far;    315
a la mañana    quando los gallos cantaran
non vos tardedes,    mandedes ensellar;
en San Pero a matines    tandra el buen abbat,
la missa nos dira,    esta sera de Santa Trinidad;
la missa dicha,    penssemos de cavalgar,    320
ca el plazo viene açerca,    mucho avemos de andar.'
Cuemo lo mando mio Çid    assi lo an todos ha far.
Passando va la noch,    viniendo la man;
a los mediados gallos    pienssan de [ensellar].
Tañen a matines    a una priessa tan grand;    325

**289** These are to be confiscated, as is made clear by the King's comments when, later in the poem, he pardons the Cid's followers and mentions the action originally taken (ll.1362-63; see also ll.886-87).
**319** Compare l.2370, where the Mass of the Holy Trinity is said by Jerónimo before the battle with Búcar's forces. This mass was popular with soldiers, and would be substituted for the mass of the day.
**324** *a los mediados gallos*: midway between the office of night and that of *gallicantum* (see note to l.209).

of how My Cid the Battler is going into exile;
some men leave houses and others their estates.
On this day, at the bridge over the Arlanzón,                    290
a hundred and fifteen knights come together,
all asking for My Cid the Battler.
Martín Antolínez joins up with them;
they set off for San Pedro where waits the man born in a fortunate
                                    hour.

When My Cid, the man from Vivar,                                 295
knew that his company was growing and with it his prestige,
he rode out quickly to greet them;
he smiled again, and they all came to him and kissed his hand.
With deep feeling, My Cid spoke:
"I pray to God, our Heavenly Father,                             300
that you, who on my behalf leave houses and estates,
may receive reward from me before I die,
and may win back twice what you lose."
My Cid was pleased that he had more men to feed,
and all those in his company were equally glad.                 305
Of the time he had been given, six days had passed
and but three remained, no more, I tell you.
The King ordered that My Cid should be watched,
so that if, when the time had expired, he should catch him in his
                                    lands,
neither gold nor silver would save him.
The day was closing in and darkness was descending;
he ordered all of his knights to come together:
"Listen, my men, do not be downcast!
I have little money with me, but I want to share it with you.
Be prudent as you must;                                         315
in the morning, at cock - crow,
have your horses saddled without delay;
at San Pedro the good abbot will ring the bell for matins
and will say the Mass of the Holy Trinity for us.
When mass is over, let us set off,                              320
for our time is running out and we have far to go."
They all did as My Cid commanded.

Night passed and day approached;
some time before dawn, horses were saddled.
Bells were ringing out the summons to matins.                   325

61

mio Çid e su mugier    a la eglesia van.
Echos doña Ximena    en los grados delant'el altar
rogando al Criador    quanto ella mejor sabe
que a mio Çid el Campeador    que Dios le curias de mal:
'¡Ya Señor glorioso,    Padre que en çielo estas!    330
Fezist çielo e tierra,    el terçero el mar,
fezist estrelas e luna    y el sol pora escalentar;
prisist encarnaçion    en Santa Maria madre,
en Belleem apareçist    commo fue tu veluntad;
pastores te glorifficaron,    ovieron [t]e a laudare,    335
tres reyes de Arabia    te vinieron adorar
—Melchior    e Gaspar e Baltasar—
oro e tus e mirra    te offreçieron commo fue tu veluntad;
[salvest] a Jonas    quando cayo en la mar,
salvest a Daniel    con los leones en la mala carçel,    340
salvest dentro en Roma    al señor San Sabastian,
salvest a Santa Susanna    del falso criminal;
por tierra andidiste .xxxii. años,    Señor spirital,
mostrando los miraclos    por en avemos que fablar:
del agua fezist vino    e de la piedra pan,    345
resuçitest a Lazaro    ca fue tu voluntad;
a los judios te dexeste prender;    do dizen monte Calvarie
pusieron te en cruz    por nombre en Golgota,
dos ladrones contigo,    estos de señas partes,
el uno es en paraiso    ca el otro non entro ala;    350
estando en la cruz    vertud fezist muy grant:
Longinos era çiego    que nunquas vio alguandre,
diot con la lança en el costado    dont ixio la sangre,
corrio la sangre por el astil ayuso,    las manos se ovo de
untar,
alçolas arriba,    legolas a la faz,    355
abrio sos ojos,    cato a todas partes,
en ti crovo al ora    por end es salvo de mal;
en el monumento    resuçitest,
fust a los infiernos    commo fue tu voluntad,
quebranteste las puertas    e saqueste los santos padres.    360
Tu eres rey de los reyes    e de tod el mundo padre,
a ti adoro e creo    de toda voluntad,

---

**327** Though Doña Jimena's invoking of God's help follows a pattern which is to be found in several French texts.
it is unusual in that in medieval epic such prayers are usually spoken on the battlefield where combat is about to
take place, and also in the very fact that a woman speaks so freely in a church, where she would normally be
expected to remain silent. For a detailed analysis of the prayer, see P.E.Russell, *Temas de 'La Celestina' y otros
estudios (del 'Cid' al 'Quijote')* (Barcelona, 1978), pp.113-58.
**339-42** This passage imitates the repetition of *salvasti* which is found in several Latin prayers.
**341** Russell points out (*Temas*, p.124) that there existed a special veneration for Saint Sebastian in Spain.
**352-57** The story of Longinus is derived from John, 19.34: according to later legend, Longinus was a blind soldier

My Cid and his wife went to the church.
Doña Jimena threw herself on the steps before the altar,
beseeching the Creator, with all her heart,
that he might keep My Cid the Battler from all harm:
"O glorious Lord, Father in Heaven!                                    330
You made heaven and earth and then the sea;
you made stars and moon and the sun to give warmth.
You became flesh by Mary the Holy Mother;
you were born in Bethlehem according to your will.
Shepherds worshipped and praised you;                                  335
three kings came from Arabia to honour you —
Melchior and Caspar and Balthazar —
gold and frankincense and myrrh they offered you according to
                                    your will.
You saved Jonah when he fell into the sea;
you saved Daniel among the lions in the evil den;                      340
you saved Saint Sebastian in Rome;
you saved Saint Susannah from the false accuser.
You walked on earth for thirty two years, heavenly Lord,
performing miracles which we talk of now;
from water you made wine and from the stone bread;                     345
you raised Lazarus, as was your will.
You allowed yourself to be taken by the Jews and on Mount Calvary
they put you on a cross in the place called Golgotha.
Two thieves were with you on either side;
one is in Paradise, but the other did not enter there.                 350
When on the cross, you performed a very great miracle:
Longinus was blind and had never had sight;
he thrust his lance into your side from where the blood flowed
down the shaft and covered his hands,
which he raised up to his face;                                        355
he opened his eyes, looked all around;
he believed in you from then and so was saved.
In the tomb you rose again;
you went down into Hell, according to your will,
broke down the gates and released the holy prophets.                   360
You are King of Kings and Father of the whole world.
I worship you and believe in you with all my heart.

who, after wounding Christ in the side with his lance, wiped his eyes with his blood-stained hand and miraculously
recovered his sight; he underwent conversion as a result and gained salvation. Longinus came to be identified
with the figure of the knight, and his lance was linked with Arthurian tradition.

63

e ruego a San Peydro    que me ayude a rogar
por mio Çid el Campeador    que Dios le curie de mal,
¡quando oy nos partimos    en vida nos faz juntar!'    365
La oraçion fecha,    la missa acabada la an,
salieron de la eglesia,    ya quieren cavalgar.
El Çid a doña Ximena    iva la abraçar,
doña Ximena al Çid    la manol va besar,
lorando de los oios    que non sabe que se far.    370
Y el a las niñas    torno las a catar:
'A Dios vos acomiendo, fijas,    e a la mugier e al Padre spirital;
agora nos partimos,    Dios sabe el ajuntar.'
Lorando de los ojos    que non viestes atal,
asis parten unos d'otros    commo la uña de la carne.    375
Mio Çid con los sos vassallos    pensso de cavalgar;
a todos esperando    la cabeça tornando va.
A tan grand sabor    fablo Minaya Albar Fañez:
'Çid ¿do son vuestros esfuerços?    ¡En buen ora nasquiestes
de madre!
Pensemos de ir nuestra via,    esto sea de vagar.    380
Aun todos estos duelos    en gozo se tornaran;
Dios que nos dio las almas    consejo nos dara.
Al abbat don Sancho    tornan de castigar
commo sirva a doña Ximena    e a la[s] fijas que ha,
e a todas sus dueñas    que con ellas estan;    385
bien sepa el abbat    que buen galardon dello prendra.
Tornado es don Sancho    e fablo Albar Fañez:
'Si vieredes yentes venir    por connusco ir, abbat,
dezildes que prendan el rastro    e pienssen de andar,
ca en yermo o en poblado    poder nos [han] alcançar.'    390
Soltaron las riendas,    pienssan de andar;
çerca viene el plazo    por el reino quitar.
Vino mio Çid yazer    a Spinaz de Can;
grandes yentes sele acogen    essa noch de todas partes.    395
Otro dia mañana    pienssa de cavalgar.    394
Ixiendos va de tierra    el Campeador leal;

---

**372** Smith's text includes the phrase 'a la mugier' – '(to) the woman' – but most editors emend this line which seems to make little sense as it stands.

**378** The author of the *Poema* frequently applies the title *Minaya* to Álvar Fáñez, possibly in error, as it is not documented elsewhere. Menéndez Pidal suggests a link between this term and the Ibero-Basque *anai* ('brother'): see *Cantar de Mio Cid*, p.1211.

**394-95** Smith has followed Menéndez Pidal in inverting the order of these lines, thus making it clear that it was at Spinaz de Can that the Cid was joined by the new arrivals. This place has not been precisely identified; for an explanation of this and other details of the geography of the *Poema*, up to the fall of Valencia, see I.Michael. 'Geographical Problems in the *Poema de Mio Cid*: I The Exile Route'.

I pray to Saint Peter that he may intercede
for My Cid the Battler, that God may keep him from evil.
Since we are separated today, bring us together again in our lifetime."
The prayer said, the mass was finished;
they left the church, and were ready to ride.
The Cid went to embrace Doña Jimena,
and Doña Jimena kissed the Cid's hand;
tears flowed from her eyes, she knew not what to do.                 370
He looked again at the girls:
"My daughters, I commend you to God, our heavenly Father;
now we are parting; God knows when we shall meet again."
With tears flowing from their eyes, more than you have ever seen,
they parted, like the nail from the flesh.                               375
My Cid with his vassals made ready to leave;
he turned to look on all those waiting:
Minaya Álvar Fáñez spoke becomingly:
"Cid, where is your strength!  Your mother bore you in a favoured
                                hour!
Let us be on our way, leave this till later.                         380
All this sorrow will yet turn to joy.
God who gave us our souls will give us aid."
Again, the abbot, Don Sancho, is instructed
how he should serve Doña Jimena and her daughters
and all the ladies who accompany them;                               385
the abbot should understand that he will be well rewarded.
As Don Sancho turned away, Álvar Fáñez spoke:
"Should you see men coming to join us, abbot,
tell them to set out on our trail,
for, whether we be in open country or in town, they will be able
                                to join us."                          390
They loosened the reins, they rode on their way;
the hour approached when they must leave the kingdom.
My Cid halted at Spinaz de Can;
many men from all around joined him that night.                      395
Next morning he rode on his way again.                               394
The loyal Battler was going into exile;

de siniestro Sant Estevan    —una buena,çipdad—
de diestro Alilon las torres    que moros las han,
passo por Alcobiella    que de Castiella fin es ya,
la Calçada de Quinea    iva la traspassar,       400
sobre Navas de Palos    el Duero va pasar,
a la Figeruela    mio Çid iva posar.
Vanssele acogiendo    yentes de todas partes.

19 I se echava mio Çid    despues que fue çenado.

Un sueñol priso dulçe,    tan bien se adurmio.     405
El angel Gabriel    a el vino en [vision]:
'Cavalgad, Çid,    el buen Campeador,
ca nunqua en tan buen punto    cavalgo varon:
mientra que visquieredes    bien se fara lo to.'
Quando desperto el Çid    la cara se santigo;     410
sinava la cara,    a Dios se acomendo.

20 Mucho era pagado    del sueño que a soñado.

Otro dia mañana    pienssan de cavalgar;
es dia a de plazo,    sepades que non mas.
A la sierra de Miedes    ellos ivan posar.     415

21 Aun era de dia,    non era puesto el sol,
mando ver sus yentes    mio Çid el Campeador;
sin las peonadas    e omnes valientes que son
noto trezientas lanças    que todos tienen pendones.

22 '¡Temprano dat çebada,    si el Criador vos salve!    420
El que quisiere comer;    e qui no, cavalge.
Passaremos la sierra    que fiera es e grand;
la tierra del rey Alfonsso    esta noch la podemos quitar.
Despues qui nos buscare    fallar nos podra.'

**397** San Esteban de Gormaz is situated on the north bank of the Duero, along which the Cid passes. Ayllón was some fifteen kilometres to the south-west, and it is unlikely that a poet who knew the region well would have suggested that the Cid was within sight of the town's towers (see Michael, 'Geographical Problems: I', pp.119-20). Ayllón could not, moreover, have been in territory dominated by Moors, and the mention of this detail serves mainly to emphasize the hostility of the territory through which the Cid travels.

San Esteban, here introduced as 'a fine town', is later to receive further attention and praise, its inhabitants being shown to behave with exemplary warmth and nobility towards the Cid and his daughters. The apparent affection shown by the poet towards this town has led some scholars to conclude that he was closely connected with it. Lacarra, however (pp.182-87) offers a different explanation for the prominence of this community in the *Poema*, pointing to the events of 1163, when the people of San Esteban aided the Lara family to prevent the Castilian child king, Alfonso VIII, from falling into Leonese hands.

**399** Alcubilla, though described as being 'on the frontiers of Castile', is well within the limits of the Christian territory. The mountains of Miedes, some thirty kilometres to the south, are still in lands dominated by Alfonso (see ll.422-23 and note to l.415).

**400** This Road of Quinea shares its name with other Roman roads of the Peninsula, the most famous of which linked Mérida and Astorga.

**405 ff.** This episode provides the only supernatural element in the *Poema*, and it serves to emphasize the

to the left, San Esteban, a fine town,
to the right, the towers of Ayllón, in the hands of the Moors.
He passed through Alcubilla, on the frontiers of Castile.
He cut across the Road of Quinea;                                    400
My Cid crossed the Duero at Navas de Palos
and halted at Figueruela.
Men joined him from all around.

There, after eating, My Cid lay down to sleep.

In a deep sleep, he dreamed a pleasant dream;                       405
in a vision the angel Gabriel came to him:
"Ride forth, O Cid, good Battler!
For never has man ridden at so fortunate a time;
while you live all will go well for you."
When the Cid awoke, he made the sign of the cross                   410
on his face and commended himself to God.

He was greatly heartened by the dream he had dreamed.

Next morning they rode on;
I tell you but one day remained.
They halted at the mountains of Miedes.                             415

It was still day, the sun had not yet set.
My Cid the Battler commanded a review of his men.
Not counting the foot soldiers, valiant as they were,
he reckoned three hundred lances, each with his pennant.

"Feed the horses early, so may the Creator protect you!            420
Any man who wants to eat may do so, the others ride on.
We shall cross the mountains, wide and inhospitable;
we shall be able to leave the land of King Alfonso this night.
After that anyone who seeks us may find us."

uncommon importance and stature of the Cid, but also his fundamental goodness and his piety. Possibly the poet is here imitating the scene in the *Chanson de Roland* in which Gabriel appears to the Emperor Charlemagne.
**415** Probably the Sierra de Pela, north-west of the village of Miedes de Atienza (see Michael, 'Geographical Problems: I', p.121).
**420** The poet's attention to the detail of the provision of fodder for the horses is not necessarily to be seen as reflecting a first-hand knowledge of the realities of life during a campaign; it has, for example, parallels in legal documents and charters (see D.Hook, 'On Certain Correspondences between the *Poema de Mio Cid* and Contemporary Legal Instruments', p.45).

De noch passan la sierra,     vinida es la man,                    425
e por la loma ayuso     pienssan de andar;
en medio d'una montaña     maravillosa e grand
fizo mio Çid posar     e çevada dar.
Dixoles a todos     commo querie trasnochar;
vassallos tan buenos     por coraçon lo an,                        430
mandado de so señor     todo lo han a far.
Ante que anochesca     pienssan de cavalgar,
por tal lo faze mio Çid     que no lo ventasse nadi.
Andidieron de noch     que vagar non se dan.
O dizen Castejon     el que es sobre Fenares                       435
mio Çid se echo en çelada     con aquelos que el trae.

23 Toda la noche yaze en çelada     el que en buen ora nasco
commo los consejava     ˏMinaya Albar Fañez.

'¡Ya Çid     en buen ora çinxiestes espada!
Vos con .c.     de aquesta nuestra conpaña                         440
pues que a Castejon     sacaremos a çelada...'
'Vos con los .cc.     id vos en algara;
ala vaya Albar A[l]barez     e Albar Salvadorez sin falla,
e Galin Garçia     —una fardida lança—                             443b
cavalleros buenos     que aconpañen a Minaya.
Aosadas corred     que por miedo non dexedes nada.                 445
Fita ayuso     e por Guadalfajara
fata Alcala     legen las alg[aras],                               446b
e bien acojan     todas las gananças,
que por miedo de los moros     non dexen nada.
E yo con lo[s] .c.     aqui fincare en la çaga;
terne yo Castejon     don abremos grand enpara.                    450
Si cueta vos fuere     alguna al algara
fazed me mandado     muy privado a la çaga;
¡d'aqueste acorro     fablara toda España!'
Nonbrados son     los que iran en el algara,
e los que con mio Çid     ficaran en la çaga                       455
Ya quiebran los albores     e vinie la mañana,
ixie el sol,     ¡Dios, que fermoso apuntava!

---

427 The term *montaña* could apply to forest or woodland rather than to mountains as its present-day meaning would suggest. The forest inspires wonder and a sense, perhaps, of the supernatural.

435 This is the town today known as Castejón de Henares. Smith argues, from a number of precise parallels, that the author of the *Poema* here draws on the account of the taking of the city of Capsa in Sallust's *Bellum Jugurthinum* (see 'Literary Sources of Two Episodes in the *Poema de mio Cid*', *Bulletin of Hispanic Studies*, 52 (1975), pp.109-22, and *The Making ...*, pp.149-52).

441 After this line there is a lacuna in the text. Menéndez Pidal freely reconstructs four lines, on which we have drawn to complete the sense.

443-443b The three knights mentioned here are all historical figures. Álvar Álvarez and Álvar Salvadórez are both mentioned as witnesses in documents of the wedding settlement of the Cid and Jimena, the former being described as the Cid's nephew. Álvar Savadórez was the younger brother of Gonzalo, Count of Lara. Galindo

By night they crossed the mountains; the morning came,                    425
and they began to head downwards;
in the middle of a forest, immense and threatening,
My Cid called a halt and ordered the horses to be fed.
He told them all how he wanted to travel by night.
Such good vassals accepted willingly;                                     430
what their lord willed, all were to do.
Before nightfall they rode on their way,
My Cid acting thus to avoid discovery.
They travelled through the night; they gave themselves no respite.
At the place known as Castejón, beside the river Henares,                 435
My Cid prepared an ambush with his followers.

Through the night the man born in a favoured hour lay in wait,
according to the advice of Minaya Álvar Fáñez:

"O Cid, you girded on your sword in a favoured hour!
With a hundred of our men,                                                440
since we are laying a trap for the people of Castejón,
[you should stay back to protect our rear."
My Cid replied:] "You, with two hundred men, make a raid.
Álvar Álvarez should go, and the matchless Álvar Salvadórez
and Galindo García, a brave warrior;                                      443b
let the good knights accompany Minaya.
Attack courageously, and lose nothing through fear.                       445
Down past Hita and Guadalajara,
as far as Alcalá let the raids extend;                                    446b
they should make sure they take all the booty
and leave nothing for fear of the Moors.
And I shall stay here in the rear with my hundred men.
I shall take Castejón, where we shall be well protected.                  450
If you should encounter any danger in the advance,
send me word immediately to the rear.
All Spain shall talk of this deed."
Those who were to go with the raiding party were named,
and those who were to remain at the rear with My Cid.                     455
Now dawn was breaking and morning coming;
the sun rose, Lord God how beautifully it shone!

García was lord of Estada and Ligüerre in Aragón.
**456** On a number of occasions the author of the *Poema* mentions daybreak and sunrise. They are powerful and
emotive images of hope and optimism, and full use is made of their suggestive power – ironically in this case, for
the day is to bring disaster to the inhabitants of Castejón.

En Castejon      todos se levantavan,
abren las puertas,      de fuera salto davan
por ver sus lavores      e todas sus heredades.                    460
Todos son exidos,      las puertas abiertas han dexadas
con pocas de gentes      que en Castejon fincar[a]n;
las yentes de fuera      todas son deramadas.
El Campeador      salio de la çelada,
corrie      a Castejon sin falla.                                  464b
Moros e moras      avien los de ganançia,                          465
e essos gañados      quantos en derredor andan.
Mio Çid don Rodrigo      a la puerta adeliñava;
los que la tienen      quando vieron la rebata
ovieron miedo      e fue desemparada.
Mio Çid Ruy Diaz      por las puertas entrava,                     470
en mano trae      desnuda el espada,
quinze moros matava      de los que alcançava.
Gaño a Castejon      y el oro e la plata.
Sos cavalleros      legan con la ganançia,
dexan la a mio Çid,      todo esto non preçia nada.                475
Afevos los .cciii.      en el algara,
e sin dubda corren;      fasta Alcala lego la seña de Minaya,
e desi arriba      tornan se con la ganançia
Fenares arriba      e por Guadalfajara.
Tanto traen      las grandes ganançias                            480
muchos gañados      de ovejas e de vacas
e de ropas      e de otras riquizas largas.                       481b
Derecha viene      la seña de Minaya;
non osa ninguno      dar salto a la çaga.
Con aqueste aver      tornan se essa conpaña,
fellos en Castejon      o el Campeador estava.                    485
El castielo dexo en so poder;      el Campeador cavalga,
saliolos reçebir      con esta su mesnada.
Los braços abiertos      reçibe a Minaya:
'¿Venides, Albar Fañez,      una fardida lança?
¡Do yo vos enbias      bien abria tal esperança!                  490
Esso con esto      sea ajuntado;
dovos la quinta      si la quisieredes, Minaya.'

---

**473** The taking of Castejón is the only episode mentioned in the *Poema* which brings the Cid into near conflict with King Alfonso. He has entered the Moorish kingdom of Toledo, bound to Alfonso by a written agreement, and it is likely that the King will now take swift action. Alfonso was renowned for the vigour with which he defended the Moors paying him tribute and thus under his protection. It is, moreover, possible that this passage recalls the unauthorized raid into the kingdom of Toledo which in history was a principal cause of Rodrigo's banishment.

**492** Those taking part in a raid were entitled to share among them one fifth of the wealth they seized (see Lacarra, p.33). The Cid is thus showing exceptional generosity to Álvar Fáñez in offering him a fifth of *all* the booty. This

The inhabitants of Castejón rose from their beds,
opened the gates and went out
to go about their labours and work their land.                    460
They had all left, leaving gates open,
with few people remaining in Castejón.
The people had all scattered outside the town.
The Battler left his hiding place
and fell at once upon Castejón.                                   464b
They captured Moorish men and women                              465
and took all the cattle near the town.
My Cid Don Rodrigo made straight for the gate;
those who guarded it, when they saw the attack,
took fright; it was left unprotected;
My Cid entered through the gate,                                  470
his sword unsheathed in his hand;
he killed fifteen Moors that he found in his path.
He took Castejón, and the gold and silver.
His knights arrived with the booty;
They left it with My Cid; they valued it as nothing.             475
Now behold the two hundred and three men of the raiding party
riding on fearlessly; Minaya's ensign reached Alcalá,
and from that point they returned with their booty
up the Henares valley past Guadalajara.
They brought such great wealth;                                   480
many cattle and flocks of sheep,
clothing and other riches.                                       481b
Minaya's ensign moved ahead;
none dared to attack the rear.
The force returned with this booty,
and now they came to Castejón, where the Battler had remained. 485
The Battler left the citadel well—guarded and rode out,
going out with his troops to meet them.
With arms outspread he welcomed Minaya:
"It is you, Álvar Fáñez, noble warrior!
Wherever I sent you, such success was to be expected!            490
Let all the booty be put together;
I will give you a fifth of it all, if you accept it, Minaya."

passage contains the only mention in the poem of the seizure of cattle and sheep; usually the booty mentioned
consists largely of gold, silver, arms and horses.

24 'Mucho vos lo gradesco,     Campeador contado;
     d'aquesta quinta     que me avedes mand[ad]o
     pagar se ia della     Alfonsso el Castellano.                    495
     Yo vos la suelt[o]     e avello quitado.
     A Dios lo prometo,     a aquel que esta en alto:
     fata que yo me page     sobre mio buen cavallo
     lidiando     con moros en el campo,
     que enpleye la lança     e al espada meta mano          500
     e por el cobdo ayuso     la sangre destelando
     ante Ruy Diaz     el lidiador contado,
     non prendre de vos     quanto vale un dinero malo.
     Pues que por mi ganaredes     ques quier que sea d'algo
     todo lo otro     afelo en vuestra mano.'                       505

25 Estas ganançias     alli eran juntadas.
     Comidios mio Çid     el que en buen ora fue nado
     al rey Alfonsso     que legarien sus compañas,
     quel buscarie mal     con todas sus mesnadas.
     Mando partir     tod aqueste aver [sin falla]                 510
     sos quiñoneros     que gelos diessen por carta.
     Sos cavalleros     i an arribança,
     a cada uno dellos     caen .c. marchos de plata
     e a los peones     la meatad sin falla:
     toda la quinta     a mio Çid fincava.                          515
     Aqui non lo pueden vender     nin dar en presentaja,
     nin cativos nin cativas     non quiso traer en su compaña;
     fablo con los de Castejon     y envio a Fita e a Guadalfagara,
     esta quinta     por quanto serie conprada;
     aun de lo que diessen     oviessen grand ganançia.       520
     Asmaron los moros     .iii. mill marcos de plata;
     plogo a mio Çid     d'aquesta presentaja.
     A terçer dia     dados fueron sin falla.
     Asmo mio Çid     con toda su conpaña
     que en el castiello     non i avrie morada,                    525
     e que serie retenedor     mas non i avrie agua.
     'Moros en paz,     ca escripta es la carta,
     buscar nos ie el rey Alfonsso     con toda su mesnada.
     Quitar quiero Castejon:     ¡oid, escuellas e Min(y)aya!

**510 ff.** The author of the *Poema* evidently had a detailed knowledge of the principles which governed the distribution of booty among victorious troops (see Lacarra, pp.32-50). The account of the arrangements made following the victory at Castejón and the raids along the Henares contains a number of significant points which coincide with details in law codes: the role of responsible officials, the keeping of a precise written record, and the promptness with which the officials act; mention of the fifth share which falls to the Cid (see note to l.515); and the principle which allows the knight double the reward of the foot soldier.

**515** This fifth share is that which would normally fall to the king. After each subsequent battle, the poet again mentions the Cid's *quinta*, thus emphasizing the exile's growing power and independence.

72

"I am very grateful, renowned Battler,
for this share that you have offered me;
it would satisfy Alfonso of Castile himself.                              495
I return it to you and ask nothing of you.
I promise to God on high
that until I have had my fill of fighting
on my fine horse, against the Moors on the plain of battle,
and till I use my lance and wield my sword                                500
and blood flows down to my elbow
in the presence of Ruy Díaz, the celebrated warrior,
I shall not take from you a rotten pennyworth.
Until you gain from me something of true worth,
all this is yours."                                                       505

All this booty had been gathered together.
It occurred to My Cid, the man born in a favoured hour,
that the men of King Alfonso might draw near
and the King with all his troops might make an attack.
He commanded that all this wealth be carefully divided up,              510
and that the officials should give him a written record.
His knights received their share:
to each of them fell a hundred silver marks,
and to each of the footsoldiers exactly half that sum.
My Cid was left with a fifth share;                                      515
but here it could not be sold or given away.
He wanted to take with him no prisoners, neither men nor women;
he negotiated with the people of Castejón and sent messengers
                              to Hita and Guadalajara
to determine what they would pay him for his fifth share:
despite what they paid, they would gain from the deal.                   520
The Moors offered three thousand silver marks
and this sum satisfied My Cid;
on the third day it was paid in full.
My Cid calculated that he and all his troops
would be unable to stay in the fortress;                                 525
it could be easily defended but the water supply would be uncertain.
"The Moors are at peace, there is a written truce;
King Alfonso could pursue us with his entire army.
I want to leave Castejón.   Listen, my men; listen, Minaya.

**527** See note to l.473.

73

26 Lo que yo dixier     non lo tengades a mal.                    530
   En Castejon     non podriemos fincar;
   çerca es el rey Alfonsso     e buscar nos verna.
   Mas el castielo     non lo quiero hermar;
   çiento moros e çiento moras     quiero las quitar,
   por que lo pris dellos     que de mi non digan mal.      535
   Todos sodes pagados     e ninguno por pagar.
   Cras a la mañana     pensemos de cavalgar,
   con Alfonsso mio señor     non querria lidiar.'
   Lo que dixo el Çid     a todos los otros plaz.
   Del castiello que prisieron     todos ricos se parten;      540
   los moros e las moras     bendiziendol estan.
   Vansse Fenares arriba     quanto pueden andar,
   troçen las Alcarias     e ivan adelant,
   por las Cuevas d'Anquita     ellos passando van,
   passaron las aguas,     entraron al campo de Torançio,      545
   por essas tierras ayuso     quanto pueden andar,
   entre Fariza e Çetina     mio Çid iva albergar.
   Grandes son las gananças que priso     por la tierra do va.
   Non lo saben los moros     el ardiment que an.
   Otro dia movios     mio Çid el de Bivar               550
   e passo a Alfama,     la Foz ayuso va,
   passo a Bovierca     e a Teca que es adelant
   e sobre Alcoçer     mio Çid iva posar
   en un otero redondo     fuerte e grand;
   açerca corre Salon,     agua nol pueden(t) vedar.         555
   Mio Çid don Rodrigo     Alcoçer cueda ganar.

27 Bien puebla el otero,     firme prende las posadas,
   los unos contra la sierra     e los otros contra la agua.
   El buen Canpeador     que en buen ora nasco
   derredor del otero,     bien çerca del agua,             560
   a todos sos varones     mando fazer una carcava
   que de dia nin de·noch     non les diessen arebata,
   que sopiessen que mio Çid     alli avie fincança.

---

**538** This statement is sometimes cited as evidence of the Cid's dutiful behaviour towards his lord. On the other hand, as Lacarra points out (pp.20-21), he has already weighed the situation carefully and concluded for strategic reasons that Castejón could not be held (see, for example, l.526) and that he would have little chance in battle against Alfonso's troops.
**545** The Cid has left the valley of the upper Henares and passed across the mountainous region of the Alcarria, reaching the river Tajuña near Anguita. The 'waters' which he crosses are the tributaries of the upper Tajuña.
**553** Alcocer has proved difficult to ientify. It is probable that it corresponds to the town of Castejón de las Armas: as Michael points out ('Geographical Problems: I', pp.122-23), this is the only appropriately situated settlement not mentioned in the *Poema*, and it is understandable that the poet should have changed its name to distinguish it from Castejón de Henares, which featured in the previous episode. Michael also identifies a nearby hill,

Do not misunderstand what I say: 530

we cannot stay at Castejón;

King Alfonso is nearby and will come in pursuit.

But neither do I want to destroy this fortress.

I intend to free two hundred Moors, a hundred men and a
                                        hundred women,

that they shall not speak ill of me for what I have taken from them.

You are all paid; none is without reward.

Tomorrow morning let us ride on our way.

I do not want to fight Alfonso, my lord."

My Cid's men were pleased by his words.

They were all rich men when they left the citadel they had taken.

They were blessed by the Moors.

They moved as quickly as they could up the Henares valley,

advanced across the Alcarria

and passed the caves of Anguita.

They crossed the waters and entered the scrublands of Taranz, 545

and moved as quickly as they could through those lands.

My Cid pitched camp between Fariza and Cetina.

Great was the plunder he took in the lands through which he passed.

The Moors knew nothing of their plan.

Next day, My Cid, the man from Vivar, moved on; 550

he passed Alhama and went down the gorge of La Foz;

passing Bubierca, he rode on to Ateca;

My Cid halted at Alcocer

on a rounded hill, massive and commanding.

Nearby runs the Jalón, ensuring a certain supply of water. 555

My Cid Don Rodrigo plans to take Alcocer.


Firmly establishing his camp, he posted many men on the hill,

some towards the mountains and some down by the river.

The good Battler, born in a favoured hour,

ordered that, round the hill, by the river - bank, 560

all his men should dig a defensive ditch

so that no surprise attack could be made on them by day or
                                        by night,

and that it should be known that My Cid had come to stay.

---

north-west of Castejón, which could correspond to that described in l.554. The account of the taking of Alcocer
has a probable source in the *Strategemata* of Frontinus (see Smith, 'Literary Sources'); the Spanish poet is
unlikely to have known such classical works in their full form, but rather in a *florilegium* or manual.

28 Por todas esas tierras     ivan los mandados
que el Campeador mio Çid     alli avie poblado,     565
venido es a moros,     exido es de christianos.
En la su vezindad     non se treven ganar tanto.
Agardando se va mio Çid     con todos sus vassallos:
el castiello de Alcoçer     en paria va entrando.

29 Los de Alcoçer a mio Çid     yal dan parias de grado     570

e los de Teca     e los de Ter[rer] la casa;
a los de Calatauth     sabet, ma[l] les pesava.
Ali yogo mio Çid     complidas .xv. semanas.
Quando vio mio Çid     que Alcoçer non sele dava
el fizo un art     e non lo detardava:     575
dexa una tienda fita     e las otras levava,
cojo[s] Salon ayuso     la su seña alçada,
las lorigas vestidas     e çintas las espadas
a guisa de menbrado     por sacar los a çelada.
Veyen lo los de Alcoçer.     ¡Dios, commo se alabavan!     580
Falido a a mio Çid     el pan e la çevada.
Las otras abes lieva,     una tienda a dexada;
de guisa va mio Çid     commo si escapasse de arrancada.
Demos salto a el     e feremos grant ganançia
antes quel prendan     los de Ter[rer] [la casa];     585
si non,     non nos daran dent nada:     585b
La paria qu'el a presa     tornar nos la ha doblada.'
Salieron de Alcoçer     a una priessa much estraña;
mio Çid quando los vio fuera     cogios commo de arrancada,
cojos Salon ayuso,     con los sos abuelta [anda].
Dizen los de Alcoçer:     '¡Ya se nos va la ganançia!'     590
Los grandes e los chicos     fuera salto da[va]n,
al sabor del prender     de lo al non pienssan nada;
abiertas dexan las puertas     que ninguno non las guarda.
El buen Campeador     la su cara tornava,
vio que entr'ellos y el castiello     mucho avie grand plaça;     595

**566** These events are taking place within the Moslem kingdom of Saragossa (see note to 1.914).
**570** It is surprising, in view of the fact that the inhabitants of Alcoçer are now paying the Cid tribute – effectively, protection money – that he should continue the siege and proceed to take the town by force. Contrast the point made in ll.940-42.
**575 ff.** For a full explanation of the Cid's tactics and the course of the battle, see H.Ramsden, 'The Taking of Alcoçer', *Bulletin of Hispanic Studies*, 36 (1959), 129-34. The poet is adapting material from Frontinus' account of a major battle to one of a relatively minor encounter, and he has imitated only the broad outline of the battle description, disregarding (or, possibly, misunderstanding) the importance of the tent. In the Frontinus text, that of the commander, Crassus, is left behind, containing hidden troops. The author of the *Poema* does not make clear why the Cid's men leave a tent, and there is no indication that there are soldiers hidden in it; the Christian troops win the town by virtue of the Cid and Álvar Fáñez (accompanied, presumably, by a number of other knights) having ridden swiftly back and placed themselves between the Moors and the gate (l.607).

The news spread throughout those lands
that My Cid the Battler had settled there;                                    565
he had come to the land of Moors, he no longer lived
                                        amongst Christians.
With him so near, the Moors dared not work their lands.
My Cid dug in and waited with his vassals;
the town of Alcocer reached an agreement.

The inhabitants of Alcocer paid tribute willingly,                           570

and so too did the inhabitants of Ateca and of the town of Terrer.
Those of Calatayud, I tell you, were deeply worried.
My Cid stayed there for a full fifteen weeks.
When My Cid saw that Alcocer did not yield to him,
he at once prepared to trick its people:                                     575
he struck camp but left one tent standing,
and moved off down the Jalón, with his standard raised,
his men wearing their armour and with swords girded on;
with cunning, he aimed to draw his enemies into a trap.
The inhabitants of Alcocer saw this. Lord God, how they boasted! 580
"My Cid has run out of bread and fodder;
he can hardly manage his tents; he has left one behind;
My Cid is leaving as if he were fleeing from a rout.
Let us attack him and bring back great booty,
before it is taken by the men of Terrer.                                     585
If we do not, nothing will be left for us.                                   585b
He will give us back twice the tribute he has taken!"
In great haste, they rushed out from Alcocer.
My Cid, seeing them outside the town, rode off as though fleeing
                                        from the field.
Down the Jalón he went, together with his men.
The people of Alcocer said: "Our booty is slipping away from us!"
All hurried out from the town,
lusting for plunder, thinking only of that;
they left the gates open and unguarded.
The good Battler looked round
and saw the great distance between them and the citadel.                    595

---

580 ff. It is characteristic of the author of the *Poema* that he should show the defeat and humiliation of the people
of Alcocer to come as the result of their over-confidence and greed.

mando tornar la seña,    a priessa espoloneavan:
'¡Firid los, cavalleros,    todos sines dubdança,
con la merçed del Criador    nuestra es la ganançia!'
Bueltos son con ellos    por medio de la laña,
¡Dios, que bueno es el gozo    por aquesta mañana!    600
Mio Çid e Albar Fañez    adelant aguijavan,
tienen buenos cavallos    sabet, a su guisa les andan,
entr'ellos y el castiello    en essora entravan.
Los vassallos de mio Çid    sin piedad les davan,
en un ora e un poco de logar    .ccc. moros matan.    605
Dando grandes alaridos    los que estan en la çelada
dexando van los delant,    por el castiello se tornavan,
las espadas desnudas    a la puerta se paravan;
luego legavan los sos    ca fecha es el arrancada.
Mio Çid gaño a Alcoçer,    sabe(n)t, por esta maña.    610

30 Vino Pero Vermuez    que la seña tiene en mano,
metiola en somo    en todo lo mas alto.
Fablo mio Çid Ruy Diaz    el que en buen ora fue nado:
'¡Grado a Dios del çielo    e a todos los sos santos:
ya mejoraremos posadas    a dueños e a cavallos!    615

31 ¡Oid a mi, Albar Fañez    e todos los cavalleros!
En este castiello    grand aver avemos preso;
los moros yazen muertos,    de bivos pocos veo.
Los moros e las moras    vender non los podremos,
que los descabeçemos    nada non ganaremos;    620
cojamos los de dentro,    ca el señorio tenemos,
posaremos en sus casas    e dellos nos serviremos.'

32 Mio Çid con esta ganançia    en Alcoçer esta;
fizo enbiar por la tienda    que dexara alla.
Mucho pesa a los de Teca    e a los de Ter[rer] non plaze,    625
e a los de Calatayuth    [sabet, pesando va].
Al rey de Valençia    enbiaron con mensaje:

---

**611** According to l.2351, Pedro Bermúdez is the Cid's nephew, and in later legend, chronicle and epic, Pedro was to be a prominent figure. However, there is no historical evidence that such an individual was closely associated with the Cid. Though a document of 1085 makes it clear that a Pedro Bermúdez was at the court of Alfonso in that year, the name is quite a common one and the character depicted in the *Poema* cannot be identified with any known individual.

**619** The factors influencing the Cid's decision to act leniently towards the captive Moors are in part practical economic ones. In spite of this, it is the humanitarian aspect of his conduct that the poet is later to emphasize; see, for example, the attitude of the Moors themselves to their conqueror (ll.851-56).

**627** There is no reason why towns of this region (under the domination of Saragossa) should turn for help to the kingdom of Valencia. Such a departure from historical fact is part of the process by which the poet accelerates and

He ordered the ensign to turn back and they spurred on at a
great pace:
"Strike fearlessly, my knights,
with the help of the Creator, the gain is ours!"
They fell to battle in the middle of the plain.
Lord God, how great was the joy on that morning!    600
My Cid and Álvar Fáñez spurred on ahead.
They had good horses, I tell you, which obeyed them willingly.
Now they passed between the Moors and the fortress;
My Cid's vassals attacked the Moors mercilessly,
and in little over an hour they had killed three hundred.    605
Caught in the trap, the Moors shrieked loudly
as the Cid, with his small band, spurred on towards the fortress;
with their swords drawn, they waited by the gate;
soon their fellows arrived, for the victory was complete.
By this trick, I tell you, My Cid won Alcocer.    610

Pedro Bermúdez approached, bearing the standard in his hand,
and placed it on the very highest point.
Then spoke My Cid Ruy Díaz, the man born in a favoured hour:
"Thanks be to God in heaven and to all his saints!
Now riders and horses shall have a better resting place.    615

Listen to me, Álvar Fáñez, and all my knights!
In this fortress we have gained much booty;
the Moors lie dead, I see few alive.
We shall be unable to sell the Moors as slaves, neither men nor
women;
we should gain nothing by beheading them.    620
Let us bring them in, for we are the lords;
we shall stay in their homes and use them as our servants."

My Cid was in Alcocer with all that he had won.
He sent for the tent which he had left nearby.
The inhabitants of Ateca were greatly alarmed, and the people of
Terrer    625
and those of Calatayud, I can tell you, were much troubled.
They sent a message to the King of Valencia

simplifies his narrative in order to introduce and develop as rapidly as possible the account of the conquest of Valencia.

que a uno que dizien     mio Çid Ruy Diaz de Bivar  
airolo el rey Alfonsso,    de tierra echado lo ha,  
vino posar sobre Alcoçer    en un tan fuerte logar,      630  
sacolos a çelada,    el castiello ganado a.  
'Si non das consejo    a Teca e a Ter[rer] perderas,  
perderas Calatayuth    que non puede escapar,  
ribera de Salon    todo ira a mal,  
assi ffera lo de Siloca    que es del otra part.'      635  
Quando lo oyo el rey Tamin    por cuer le peso mal:  
'Tres reyes veo de moros    derredor de mi estar;  
non lo detardedes,    los dos id pora alla,  
tres mill moros levedes    con armas de lidiar,  
con los de la frontera    que vos ayudaran      640  
prendet melo a vida,    aduzid melo deland;  
por que se me entro en mi tierra    derecho me avra a dar.'  
Tres mill moros cavalgan    e pienssan de andar;  
ellos vinieron a la noch    en Sogorve posar.  
Otro dia mañana    pienssan de cavalgar,      645  
vinieron a la noch    a Çelfa posar;  
por los de la frontera    pienssan de enviar,  
non lo detienen,    vienen de todas partes.  
Ixieron de Çelfa    la que dizen de Canal,  
andidieron todo'l dia    que vagar non se dan,      650  
vinieron essa noch    en Calatayu[t]h posar.  
Por todas essas tierras    los pregones dan,  
gentes se ajuntaron    sobejanas de grandes  
con aquestos dos reyes    que dizen Ffariz e Galve;  
al bueno de mio Çid    en Alcoçer le van çercar.      655  

33 Fincaron las tiendas    e prenden(d) las posadas,  
   creçen estos virtos    ca yentes son sobejanas.  
   Las arobdas    que los moros sacan  
   de dia e de noch    enbueltos andan en armas;  
   muchas son las arobdas    e grande es el almofalla.      660  
   A los de mio Çid    ya les tuellen el agua;  
   mesnadas de mio Çid    exir querien a la batalla,  
   el que en buen ora násco    firme gelo vedava.  
   Tovieron gela en çerca    complidas tres semanas.  

34 A cabo de tres semanas,    la quarta querie entrar,      665  
   mio Çid con los sos    tornos a acordar:  

**635** The expression *del otra part* ('on the other side'), used several times in the Poema, has a close parallel in legal formulae which serve to describe the boundaries of a plot of land (see Hook, 'On Certain Correspondences', pp.37-38).  
**636** No King Tamín of Valencia existed, though it is possible that the poet here takes the name from Tamim, an Almoravid general of the early twelfth century and victor at the battle of Uclés.  
**654** Fáriz and Galve are fictitious characters with no known counterparts in history.

that a man called My Cid Ruy Díaz of Vivar
had been outlawed and banished by King Alfonso;
he had camped at Alcocer, in so formidable a place;     630
he had drawn the people into a trap and taken the fortress.
"If you do not help us, you will lose Ateca and Terrer;
you will lose Calatayud, which cannot escape,
and along the valley of the Jalón all will go from bad to worse,
and so too at the other extreme, along the Jiloca."     635
When King Tamín heard this, he was deeply troubled:
"I have three Moorish kings with me.
Two of you go there at once,
and take three thousand Moors armed for battle,
and, together with the people from the frontier who will assist you,
capture him alive for me and bring him here before me.
He will pay for entering my lands!"
Three thousand Moors rode on their way;
at nightfall they halted in Segorbe;
next morning they moved on,     645
and at nightfall halted at Cella.
They sent for the men of the frontier regions,
who quickly gathered together from all around.
They left the town known as Cella del Canal
and rode all day without resting,     650
and that night they halted at Calatayud.
All around, proclamations were made,
and an army, vast beyond reckoning, came together
under the two kings Fáriz and Galve.
They moved forward to besiege My Cid in Alcocer.     655

They pitched tents and established their camp;
the numbers grew — it was a huge army.
The Moors' advance guards, heavily armed,
went out both by night and by day.
There were many patrols; it was a vast force.     660
They cut off the water supply of My Cid's men.
My Cid's troops wanted to go out into battle;
the man born in a favoured hour firmly forbade it.
The siege lasted a full three weeks.

At the end of the third week, at the beginning of the fourth,     665
My Cid again took counsel with his men:

81

'El agua nos an vedada,      exir nos ha el pan;
que nos queramos ir de noche      no nos lo consintran.
Grandes son los poderes      por con ellos lidiar;
dezid me, cavalleros,      commo vos plaze de far.'      670
Primero fablo Minaya      un cavallero de prestar:
'De Castiella la gentil      exidos somos aca;
si con moros non lidiaremos      no nos daran del pan.
Bien somos nos .vi. çientos,      algunos ay de mas;
¡en el nombre del Criador      que non pase por al,      675
vayamos los ferir      en aquel dia de cras!'
Dixo el Campeador:      'A mi guisa fablastes.
Ondrastes vos, Minaya,      ca aver vos lo iedes de far.'
Todos los moros e las moras      de fuera los manda echar
que non sopiesse ninguno      esta su poridad.      680
El dia e la noche      pienssan se de adobar.
Otro dia mañana      el sol querie apuntar,
armado es mio Çid      con quantos que el ha.
Fablava mio Çid      commo odredes contar:
'Todos iscamos fuera,      que nadi non raste      685
si non dos peones solos      por la puerta guardar;
si nos murieremos en campo      en castiello nos entraran,
si vençieremos la batalla      creçremos en rictad.
E vos, Pero Vermuez,      la mi seña tomad;
commo sodes muy bueno      tener la edes sin ar[t]h;      690
mas non aguijedes con ella      si yo non vos lo mandar.'
Al Çid beso la mano,      la seña va tomar.
Abrieron las puertas,      fuera un salto dan;
vieron lo las arobdas de los moros,      al almofalla se van tornar.
¡Que priessa va en los moros!      e tornaron se a armar;      695
ante roido de atamores      la tierra querie quebrar;
veriedes armar se moros,      a priessa entrar en az.
De parte de los moros      dos señas ha cabdales,
e fizieron dos azes de peones mezclados,      ¿qui los podrie
                                              contar?

Las azes de los moros      yas mueven adelant      700
por a mio Çid e a los sos      a manos los tomar.
'Quedas sed, me[s]nadas,      aqui en este logar;

---

**684** Such formulaic expressions of direct address to a listening public are common in French epic poems. For the arguments that the Spanish poet is directly influenced in their use by a French source, see Smith, *The Making* ..., pp.191 ff.
**696** This is the first encounter described in the *Poema* with the war-drums which appeared for the first time with the Almoravid invaders of 1086; the Africans used them both as a means of signalling messages and commands to their massed battle formations and also in order to achieve a powerful psychological effect on their enemy. The terror caused by the drums is again mentioned in ll.1658 ff. and in ll.2345 ff.

82

"They have cut off our water; our bread will run out.
They will not allow us to break out at night;
their numbers are great for us to engage them in battle.
Tell me, my knights, what you think we should do!"                    670
First to speak was Minaya, an excellent knight:
"We have come to this place from our beloved Castile.
If we do not fight with Moors we gain no bread.
There are a good six hundred of us, indeed a few more.
In the name of the Creator, let us take no other way                  675
but to attack them tomorrow!"
The Battler spoke: "What you have said is to my liking.
You have brought honour on yourself Minaya, which I would have
                               expected of you."
He ordered all the Moors, men and women, to be sent out of
                               the city
lest any of them should know this secret.                             680
All day and night they prepared themselves for battle.
The next morning, as day was about to break,
My Cid was armed, together with all his men.
My Cid spoke, as you will hear:
"Let us all go forth and none remain behind                           685
save two footsoldiers to guard the gate.
If we die on the field of battle, the Moors will take the fortress;
and if we win the battle, we shall gain yet more wealth.
And you, Pedro Bermúdez, take my ensign.
As you are an honourable man, you will carry it loyally;              690
but do not ride ahead with it unless at my command."
He kissed the Cid's hand and took the ensign.
They opened the gate and charged out;
the Moorish patrols saw this and returned to their army.
How the Moors rushed to rearm themselves!                             695
At the beating of the drums it seemed that the earth would break
                               open;
you could see the Moors arming themselves and hurrying into their
                               lines of battle.
The Moors had two main standards
and formed two lines of mixed infantry.  Who could count them?
Now the lines of Moors moved ahead                                    700
to join battle with My Cid and his men.
"Be still, my troops, do not move from here;

83

non deranche ninguno    fata que yo lo mande.'
Aquel Pero Vermuez    non lo pudo endurar,
la seña tiene en mano,    conpeço de espolonar:    705
'¡El Criador vos vala,    Çid Campeador leal!
Vo meter la vuestra seña    en aquela mayor az;
¡los que el debdo avedes    veremos commo la acorr[a]des!'
Dixo el Campeador:    '¡Non sea, por caridad!'
Respuso Pero Vermuez:    '¡Non rastara por al!'    710
Espolono el cavallo    e metiol en el mayor az;
moros le reçiben    por la seña ganar.
dan le grandes colpes    mas nol pueden falssar.
Dixo el Campeador:    '¡Valelde, por caridad!'

35 Enbraçan los escudos    delant los coraçones,    715
abaxan las lanças    abue[l]tas de los pendones,
enclinaron las caras    de suso de los arzones,
ivan los ferir    de fuertes coraçones.
A grandes vozes lama    el que en buen hora nasco:
'¡Ferid los, cavalleros,    por amor de caridad!    720
¡Yo so Ruy Diaz el Çid    Campeador de Bivar!'
Todos fieren en el az    do esta Pero Vermuez;
trezientas lanças son,    todos tienen pendones;
seños moros mataron,    todos de seños colpes;
a la tornada que fazen    otros tantos son.    725

36 Veriedes tantas lanças .    premer e alçar,
tanta adagara    foradar e passar,
tanta loriga    falssa[r e] desmanchar,
tantos pendones blancos    salir vermejos en sangre,
tantos buenos cavallos    sin sos dueños andar.    730
Los moros laman '¡Mafomat!'    e los christianos '¡Santi
Yagu[e]!'
Cayen en un poco de logar    moros muertos mill e .ccc. ya.

---

**704** There are a number of parallels between the ensuing account of Pedro Bermúdez's impetuousness and that of
the standard bearer whose eagerness to attack is described by Julius Caesar in the *De Bello Gallico* (IV,25): see
D.Hook, 'Pedro Bermúdez and the Cid's Standard', *Neophilologus*, 63 (1979), pp.45-53.
    Here and on a number of other occasions we have translated *aquel* as if its sense were equivalent to that of the
Latin *ille* ('the well known').
**726-30** The repetition of *tantas* ... ('so many ...') in successive lines is a device used on a number of occasions in the
*Poema* (see, for example, ll.1987 ff., ll.2400 ff., and ll.3242 ff.). It has many parallels in medieval vernacular
literature, and echoes closely practice in a number of French texts, epics in particular, and also courtly romances.
It could be seen as an example of the feature of stylistic ornament which the grammarians defined as *repetitio*, but
it is better viewed as a formula which became a conventional part of battle descriptions and which the poet could
have imitated from any of a large number of sources.

let none break ranks till I give the command."
This same Pedro Bermúdez could not endure it,
and bearing the ensign in his hand he spurred ahead: 705
"May the Creator protect you, Cid, O loyal Battler!
I am going to post your ensign in the main enemy line.
We shall see how you can protect it — those of you who are
responsible!"
The Battler shouted out: "Do not go, for the love of mercy!"
Pedro Bermúdez replied: "There is no other way!" 710
He spurred the horse on and set the ensign in the main enemy line.
Moors rushed forward towards him to seize the ensign;
though they struck him heavy blows, they could not pierce his armour.
The Battler cried out: "Help him, in love of mercy!"

They clasped their shields before their hearts 715
and lowered their lances with their pennants;
they kept their heads low over the saddle - bow
and advanced to strike them with strong hearts.
The man born in a favoured hour cried out at the top of his voice:
"Strike them, my knights, for the love of mercy! 720
I am Ruy Díaz the Cid, the Battler of Vivar!"
They all struck at the battle line, round Pedro Bermúdez;
there were three hundred lances, each with its pennant;
they killed as many Moors, with one blow each,
and as many again in the next charge. 725

You could see so many lances lowered and raised again,
so many shields pierced right through,
so much armour holed and torn,
so many white pennants stained red with blood,
so many fine horses, wandering riderless. 730
The Moors cried out, "Mahomet!" and the Christians, "Santiago!"
In a short time, thirteen hundred Moors lay dead.

---

731 Santiago, the apostle James, was associated in legend with the earliest preaching of Christianity in the Peninsula, and by the beginning of the ninth century there existed a belief that his body had been transported to Spain and buried at a spot in Galicia which became the site of the city of Santiago de Compostela. The shrine quickly began to attract pilgrims from far afield. Saint James, believed to have made at least one appearance in battle to inspire a Christian victory, soon came to be seen by Christian Spain as its special protector. From the tenth century his name was used as a battle cry. He acquired the title of *matamoros* ('the Moor-killer').

37 ¡Qual lidia bien    sobre exorado arzon
   mio Çid Ruy Diaz    el buen lidiador!
   Minaya Albar Fañez    que Çorita mando,       735
   Martin Antolinez    el burgales de pro,
   Muño Gustioz    que so criado fue,
   Martin Muñoz    el que mando a Mont Mayor,
   Albar Albarez    e Albar Salvadorez,
   Galin Garçia    el bueno de Aragon,       740
   Felez Muñoz    so sobrino del Campeador:
   desi adelante    quantos que i son
   acorren la seña    e a mio Çid el Campeador.

38 A Minaya Albar Fañez    mataron le el cavallo,
   bien lo acorren    mesnadas de christianos;    745
   la lança a quebrada,    al espada metio mano,
   mager de pie    buenos colpes va dando.
   Violo mio Çid    Ruy Diaz el Castelano:
   acostos a un aguazil    que tenie buen cavallo,
   diol tal espadada    con el so diestro braço    750
   cortol por la çintura    el medio echo en campo.
   A Minaya Albar Fañez    ival dar el cavallo:
   '¡Cavalgad, Minaya,    vos sodes el mio diestro braço!
   Oy en este dia    de vos abre grand bando;
   firme[s] son los moros,    aun nos van del campo.    755
   Cavalgo Minaya    el espada en la mano,
   por estas fuerças    fuerte mientre lidiando;
   a los que alcança    valos delibrando.
   Mio Çid Ruy Diaz    el que en buen ora nasco
   al rey Fariz    .iii. colpes le avie dado,    760
   los dos le fallen    y el unol ha tomado,
   por la loriga ayuso    la sangre destellando;
   bolvio la rienda    por ir se le del campo.
   Por aquel colpe    rancado es el fonssado.

39 Martin Antolinez    un colpe dio a Galve,    765
   las carbonclas del yelmo    echo gelas aparte,

**733-41** The list of heroes – given three times in the *Poema* (see also ll.1991-96 and ll.3063-71) – is another conventional element of battle descriptions. Legal documents could have provided a convenient source for the information given in this passage; indeed, the poet may well have drawn the names of the Cid's captains from the lists of illustrious figures recorded as confirmers of diplomas of the late eleventh century; see Smith, *The Making* ..., pp.166 ff.

**737** Muño Gustioz is presented here as a vassal of the Cid, brought up in his household. Historically he must have been of higher standing than this, for he is known to have been the Cid's brother-in-law, married to Jimena's sister, Aurovita.

**738** Martín Muñoz was governor of Montemayor in Portugal and count of Coimbra from 1091 to 1094. His name appears in documents over a period of some forty years.

**741** There is no evidence for the historical existence of Félez Muñoz; the fact that he is described as the Cid's nephew would not be incompatible with his being the son of Muño Gustioz, but the latter relationship is not

86

Mounted on his gilded saddle,
Oh how well fought My Cid, the good warrior!
And Minaya Álvar Fáñez, who was lord of Zorita; 735
Martín Antolínez, worthy man of Burgos;
Muño Gustioz, whom the Cid had brought up;
Martín Muñoz, lord of Montemayor;
Álvar Álvarez and Álvar Salvadórez;
Galindo García, good man of Aragón; 740
Félez Muñoz, nephew of the Battler.
The whole army then
went to the aid of the ensign of My Cid the Battler.

Minaya Álvar Fáñez's horse was killed under him
and the Christian troops rushed to his aid. 745
Though his lance was broken he drew his sword,
and though scarcely still standing he delivered valiant blows.
My Cid, Ruy Díaz of Castile, saw this:
he drew close to a Moorish general riding a fine horse,
and with his right arm struck him such a blow with his sword 750
that he severed his body at the waist, throwing half of it to the
                                    ground.
He gave the horse to Minaya Álvar Fáñez:
"Mount, Minaya, you are my right arm!
Today I shall want much help from you;
the Moors are standing firm and have not yet fled the field." 755
Minaya rode, sword in hand,
cutting his way fiercely through the enemy;
those within his reach he killed.
My Cid Ruy Díaz, the man born in a favoured hour,
had delivered three blows at King Fáriz: 760
two had missed but one struck him,
and now blood dripped down his armour.
He pulled at the reins to flee the battle.
With that blow the whole army was defeated.

Martín Antolínez struck Galve a blow 765
which shattered the rubies on his helm,

mentioned by the poet.
**750-51** Such a blow, with its dramatic and grotesque result, is quite credible in view of the sheer size of the sword
which a knight would wield in battle – Menéndez Pidal points out that the blade could be 75 millimetres or more in
thickness.

cortol el yelmo     que lego a la carne;
sabet, el otro     non gel oso esperar.
Arancado es     el rey Fariz e Galve:
¡Tan buen dia     por la christiandad     770
ca fuyen los moros     de la [e de la] part!
Los de mio Cid     firiendo en alcaz,
el rey Fariz     en Ter[rer] se fue entrar,
e a Galve     nol cogieron alla;
para Calatayu[t]h     quanto puede se va.     775
El Campeador     ival en alcaz,
fata Calatayu[t]h     duro el segudar.

40 A Minaya Albar Fañez     bien l'anda el cavallo,
d'aquestos moros     mato .xxxiiii.;
espada tajador,     sangriento trae el braço,     780
por el cobdo ayuso     la sangre destellando.
Dize Minaya:     'Agora so pagado,
que a Castiella     iran buenos mandados
que mio Çid Ruy Diaz     lid campal a [arrancada].'
Tantos moros yazen muertos     que pocos vivos a dexados,     785
ca en alcaz     sin dubda les fueron dando.
Yas tornan     los del que en buen ora nasco.
Andava mio Çid     sobre so buen cavallo,
la cofia fronzida:     ¡Dios, commo es bien barbado!
Almofar a cuestas,     la espada en la mano.     790
Vio los sos     commos van alegando:
'¡Grado a Dios     aquel que esta en alto,
quando tal batalla     avemos arrancado!'
Esta albergada     los de mio Çid luego la an robada
de escudos e de armas     e de otros averes largos;     795
de los moriscos     quando son legados
ffallaron     .dx. cavallos.     796b
Grand alegreya     va entre essos christianos;
mas de quinze de los sos     menos non fallaron.
Traen oro e plata     que non saben recabdo,
refechos son todos esos christianos     con aquesta ganançia.     800
A sos castiellos a los moros     dentro los an tornados;
mando mio Çid     aun que les diessen algo.
Grant a el gozo mio Çid     con todos sos vassalos.

---

777 That is, for at least some fifteen kilometres.
781 This passage recalls Álvar Fáñez's vow in l.501. The groove which ran along the blade would, indeed, when the sword was held aloft after inflicting a wound, cause the blood to flow down onto its bearer's forearm.
802 Such an unusual act does, of course, help to explain the surprising warmth which the inhabitants of Alcocer feel for their conqueror (ll.851-56) and is further evidence of the outstanding generosity which is one of the Cid's most conspicuous characteristics.

and cut through it to the flesh.
I tell you he dared not wait for a second blow.
The kings Fáriz and Galve were defeated:
such a great day for Christendom,                                        770
for on all sides the Moors fled!
My Cid's men continued the attack as they went.

King Fáriz took shelter in Terrer,
but Galve was given no shelter there.
He made for Calatayud as fast as he could.                               775
The Battler followed him closely,
and to Calatayud the pursuit continued.


Minaya Álvar Fáñez's horse proved a swift animal,
and he killed thirty—four of those Moors;
his sword cut sharply, and his arm was bloody,                           780
the blood flowing down to his elbow.
Minaya said: "Now I am satisfied,
for good reports will go to Castile
of how My Cid Ruy Díaz has won a pitched battle."
So many Moors had been killed that few remained alive,                   785
for in their pursuit My Cid's men did not hesitate to attack them.
Now returning are the troops of the man born in a favoured hour.
My Cid rode out on his fine horse,
with his cap rolled back: Lord God, how magnificent a beard!
With the hood of his chain mail around his shoulders, and his sword
                              in his hand,                               790
ne watched his men as they were arriving:
"Thanks be to God on high
for victory in such a battle!"
Then My Cid's men plundered the camp,
taking shields and weapons and many other possessions.                  795
When their booty had been gathered together, they found they had
five hundred and ten horses taken from the Moors.                       796b
There was great joy amongst the Christians;
they missed only fifteen of their number.
They brought so much gold and silver that they had nowhere to
                              keep it;
all the Christians became rich men through these gains.                 800
They took the Moors of Alcocer back into their fortress,
and My Cid ordered that they be given gifts.
Great was the rejoicing of My Cid and all his vassals.

Dio a partir estos dineros     y estos averes largos,
en la su quinta     al Çid caen .c. cavallos;                    805
¡Dios, que bien pago     a todos sus vassallos
a los peones     e a los encavalgados!
Bien lo aguisa     el que en buen ora nasco;
quantos el trae     todos son pagados.
'¡Oid, Minaya,     sodes mio diestro braço!                      810
D'aquesta riqueza     que el Criador nos a dado
a vuestra guisa     prended con vuestra mano.
Enbiar vos quiero     a Castiella con mandado
desta batalla     que avemos arancada.
Al rey Alfonsso     que me a airado                              815
quierol enbiar     en don .xxx. cavallos
todos con siellas     e muy bien enfrenados,
señas espadas     de los arzones colgadas.'
Dixo Minaya Albar Fañez:     'Esto fare yo de grado.'

41 'Evades aqui     oro e plata,                                 820
una uesa leña,     que nada nol minguava:

en Santa Maria de Burgos     quitedes mill missas,
lo que romançiere     daldo a mi mugier e a mis fijas,
que rueguen por mi     las noches e los dias;
si les yo visquier     seran dueñas ricas.'                      825

42 Minaya Albar Fañez     desto es pagado;
por ir con el     omnes son contados.                           826b

Agora davan çevada,     ya la noch era entrada,
mio Çid Ruy Diaz     con los sos se acordava:

43 '¿Hides vos, Minaya,     a Castiella la gentil?
A nuestros amigos     bien les podedes dezir:                   830
Dios nos valio     e vençiemos la lid(it).
A la tornada     si nos fallaredes aqui;
si non, do sopieredes que somos     indos conseguir.
Por lanças e por espadas     avemos de guarir;
si non, en esta tierra angosta     non podriemos bivir.'        835

44 Ya es aguisado,     mañanas fue Minaya,
y el Campeador     con su mesnada.

---

**815-18** The horses are freely sent as a gift, and Alfonso accepts them as such (l.884). Had the Cid acted out of obligation to his feudal lord, the King would have been entitled to one fifth of all the booty.
**837** Menéndez Pidal, not satisfied with the length or sense of this line, emends it to mean 'and the Battler remained behind with all his troops.'

The Cid ordered this money and great booty to be shared out;
in his fifth share there fell to him a hundred horses.      805
Lord God, how well he paid all his vassals,
both footsoldiers and horsemen!
The man born in a favoured hour conducted this so well
that all his men were well satisfied.
"Listen, Minaya, my right arm!                              810
Of this wealth that the Creator has given us,
take with your own hand as much as you like.
I intend to send you to Castile with news
of this battle that we have won.
To King Alfonso who has banished me                         815
I want to send a gift of thirty horses,
all equipped with saddles and bridles
and with a sword hanging from the saddle - bow."
Minaya Álvar Fáñez said: "I will do this willingly."

"Here is gold and fine silver                               820
contained in a boot, full to overflowing.
Pay for a thousand masses in Santa María de Burgos
and give what is left to my wife and daughters,
that they may pray for me by day and by night.
If I live long enough, they shall be rich ladies."          825

Minaya Álvar Fáñez was pleased at this;
men were chosen to accompany him.                           826b

Now, at nightfall, they gave fodder to the horses;
My Cid Ruy Díaz took counsel with his men:

"You are going, Minaya, to our beloved Castile.
You can surely tell our friends                             830
that God helped us and we won the battle.
On your return you may find us here;
if not, go and look for us where you are directed.
We must defend ourselves with the lance and the sword;
if we did not in this barren land, we would not survive."    835

All was now ready; next day Minaya set off,
and so did the Battler with his troops.

La tierra es angosta     e sobejana de mala.
Todos los dias    a mio Çid aguardavan
moros de las fronteras    e unas yentes estrañas;    840
sano el rey Fariz,    con el se consejavan.
Entre los de Techa    e los de Ter[rer] la casa
e los de Calatayut    que es mas ondrada
asi lo an asmado    e metudo en carta:
vendido les a Alcoçer    por tres mill marchos de plata.    845

45  Mio Cid Ruy Diaz    a Alco(l)çer [ha] ven[d]ido;
    ¡que bien pago    a sus vassalos mismos!
    A cavalleros e a peones    fechos los ha ricos,
    en todos los sos    non fallariedes un mesquino.
    Qui a buen señor sirve    siempre bive en deliçio.    850

46  Quando mio Çid    el castiello quiso quitar
    moros e moras    tomaron se a quexar:
    '¿Vaste, mio Çid?    ¡Nuestras oraçiones vayante delante!
    Nos pagados finca[m]os    señor, de la tu part.'
    Quando quito a Alcoçer    mio Çid el de Bivar    855
    moros e moras    compeçaron de lorar.
    Alço su seña,    el Campeador se va;
    paso Salon ayuso,    aguijo cabadelant,
    al exir de Salon    mucho ovo buenas aves.
    Plogo a los de Terer    e a los de Calatayut mas;    860
    peso a los de Alcoçer    ca pro les fazie grant.
    Aguijo mio Çid,    ivas cabadelant
    y ffinco en un poyo    que es sobre Mont Real;
    alto es el poyo,    maravilloso e grant,
    non teme gerra.    sabet, a nulla part.    865
    Metio en paria    a Daroca enantes,
    desi a Molina    que es del otra part,
    la terçera Teruel    que estava delant;
    en su mano tenie    a Çelfa la de Canal.

47  ¡Mio Çid Ruy Diaz    de Dios aya su graçia!    870
    Ido es a Castiella    Albar Fañez Minaya;
    treinta cavallos    al rey los enpresentava.

---

**844-45** It is significant that there should be mention of the legal formalities of the sale: the calculation of the sum to be paid and the drawing up of legal documents. Such details give a pointer to the nature of the poet's own background and outlook and underline the Cid's careful observance of the correct legal procedure (see Hook, 'On Certain Correspondences', p.42).Compare the account of the negotiations for the sale of Castejón (ll.518 ff.).

**863** The Cid has ridden eastwards, down the Jalón valley, and then south along the Jiloca. The hill on which he camps is probably the Cerro de Esteban, near the present-day village of Monreal del Campo (see Michael, 'Geographical Problems: I', p.124).

Poor and harsh was the land, beyond telling.
Every day My Cid was spied upon
by Moors of the frontier lands and some from other regions.          840
King Fáriz grew well, and they took counsel with him.
With the people of Ateca and of the town of Terrer,
and those of Calatayud, a greater city,
a sum was fixed and an agreement was set down in writing,
by which My Cid sold them Alcocer for three thousand silver marks.

When My Cid Ruy Díaz had sold Alcocer,
how well he paid his vassals!
He gave riches both to knights and to those on foot,
and you could not have found a poor man amongst his company.
One who serves a good lord will always live in happiness!          850

When My Cid decided to leave the fortress
the Moors began to lament, men and women alike.
"Are you going, My Cid?  Let our prayers go before you!
We are very grateful to you, our lord, for what you have done."
When My Cid, the man from Vivar, left Alcocer,          855
the Moors began to weep, men and women alike.
The Battler raised his ensign and set off;
he passed down the Jalón and spurred on;
when he left the Jalón valley, the birds gave him very good omens.
The people of Terrer were well pleased that he left, and those of
                                        Calatayud even more so;          860
the people of Alcocer were saddened, for he had done them much
                                        good.
My Cid spurred on ahead
and camped on a hill near to Monreal.
High is the hill, wondrous and imposing,
safe from attack on all sides.          865
First he imposed a tribute on Daroca,
and then on Molina, in the other direction,
thirdly on Teruel, which lay further away.
He also had under his domination Cella del Canal.

May God give His grace to My Cid, Ruy Díaz!          870
Álvar Fáñez Minaya has gone to Castile,
to make a gift of thirty horses to the King.

Violos el rey,      fermoso sonrrisava:
'¿Quin los dio estos?      ¡Si vos vala Dios, Minaya!'
'Mio Çid Ruy Diaz      que en buen ora çinxo espada      875
vençio dos reyes de moros      en aquesta batalla;
sobejana es, señor      la su ganançia.
A vos, rey ondrado,      enbia esta presentaja;
besa vos los pies      e las manos amas
quel ay[a]des merçed,      ¡si el Criador vos vala!'      880
Dixo el rey:      'Mucho es mañana
omne airado      que de señor non ha graçia
por acogello      a cabo de tres semanas.
Mas despues que de moros fue      prendo esta presentaja;
aun me plaze de mio Çid      que fizo tal ganançia.      885
Sobr'esto todo      a vos quito, Minaya,
honores e tierras      avellas condonadas;
hid e venit,      d'aqui vos do mi graçia;
mas del Çid Campeador      yo non vos digo nada.

48 Sobre aquesto todo      dezir vos quiero, Minaya:      890

de todo mio reino      los que lo quisieren far
buenos e valientes      por a mio Çid huyar
suelto les los cuerpos      e quito les las heredades.'
Beso le las manos      Minaya Albar Fañez:
'¡Grado e graçias, rey,      commo a señor natural!      895
Esto feches agora,      al feredes adelant.'

49 'Hid por Castiella      e dexen vos andar, Minaya;
si[n] nulla dubda      id a mio Çid buscar ganançia.'
Quiero vos dezir      del que en buen ora (nasco e) çinxo
                                                            espada:
aquel poyo      en el priso posada;      900
mientra que sea el pueblo de moros      e de la yente christiana
el Poyo de mio Çid      asil diran por carta.

Estando alli      mucha tierra preava,
el [val] de rio Martin      todo lo metio en paria.
A Saragoça      sus nuevas legavan,      905
non plaze a los moros,      firme mientre les pesava.
Ali sovo mio Çid      conplidas .xv. semanas.

---

**883** The King talks loosely of 'three weeks', meaning 'a very short time'. To judge from what we have been told about the length of the campaigns at Alcocer, the Cid must now have been in exile for several months.
**884** The fact that Alfonso accepts the Cid's gift is sufficient to imply that he will ultimately be prepared to welcome back his vassal into his service when the latter has given further proof of his loyalty.
**902** This seems to be an allusion to the appearance of the village of El Poyo de Mio Cid in a twelfth-century charter, the *Fuero de Molina*, though Russell (*Temas*, pp.176-77) suggests that the phrase *por carta* simply has the sense of 'in writing' and that the reference is to a written account of the Cid's campaigns. Hook ('On Certain Correspondences', pp.42-43) points out that l.901 offers a further parallel with the language of the law codes.
**904** The Martín is a tributary of the Ebro, rising some twenty kilometres to the east of El Poyo.

The King saw them and smiled broadly:
"Who has given me these?   May God protect you, Minaya!"
"My Cid Ruy Díaz, who girded his sword in a favoured hour,      875
has defeated two Moorish kings in this battle;
great, my lord, is his booty.

To you, noble King, he sends this gift.
He kisses your feet and both hands,
begging you to have pity on him.   May the Creator protect you!" 880
The King spoke: "It is very soon
for an exile, out of favour with his king,
to be received back after just three weeks.
But, since it was won from Moors, I accept this gift.
I am indeed pleased that My Cid has won this booty.      885
Above all, Minaya, I pardon you
and restore to you your incomes and your lands.
I give you my permission to come and go as you please;
but of the Cid, the Battler, I say nothing to you.

And in addition, I want to say to you, Minaya,      890

that to all those of my subjects, good and valiant,
wishing to go and join the Cid,
I give permission and I allow them to keep their property."
Minaya Álvar Fáñez kissed his hands in thanks:
"I offer you gratitude and thanks, my King, as my natural lord! 895
This you do now, in due course you will do more."

"Go at liberty through Castile, Minaya; may you not be hindered on
                                  your way;
do not fear to go to My Cid in search of greater wealth."
I want to tell you of the man who girded his sword in a favoured
                                  hour:
he had established his camp on the hill;      900
whether it be in the hands of Moors or Christians,
it will always be rightly known as El Poyo de Mio Cid.
While he was there, he made raids in all directions,
and imposed a tribute throughout the valley of the Martín.
News of his deeds reached Saragossa.      905
The Moors were much troubled and deeply disturbed.
My Cid remained there for a full fifteen weeks.

Quando vio el caboso     que se tardava Minaya
con todas sus yentes     fizo una trasnochada;
dexo el Poyo,     todo lo desemparava,                    910
alen de Teruel     don Rodrigo passava,
en el pinar de Tevar     don Roy Diaz posava.
Todas essas tierras     todas las preava,
a Saragoça     metuda l'a en paria.
Quando esto fecho ovo     a cabo de tres semanas     915
de Castiella     venido es Minaya,
dozientos con el     que todos çiñen espadas;
non son en cuenta     sabet, las peonadas.
Quando vio mio Çid     asomar a Minaya
el cavallo corriendo     valo abraçar sin falla;     920
beso le la boca     e los ojos de la cara,
todo gelo dize     que nol encubre nada.
El Campeador     fermoso sonrrisava:
'¡Grado a Dios     e a las sus vertudes santas!
¡Mientra vos visquieredes     bien me ira a mi, Minaya!'     925

50 ¡Dios, commo fue alegre     todo aquel fonssado
que Minaya Albar Fañez     assi era legado,
diziendo les saludes     de primos e de hermanos
e de sus compañas     aquelas que avien dexadas!

51 ¡Dios, commo es alegre     la barba velida     930
que Albar Fañez     pago las mill missas
e quel dixo saludes     de su mugier e de sus fijas!
¡Dios, commo fue el Çid pagado     e fizo grant alegria!
'¡Ya Albar Fañez     bivades muchos dias!'

52 Non lo tardo     el que en buen ora nasco:     935
tierras d'Alcañ[i]z     negras las va parando
e a derredor     todo lo va preando.
Al terçer dia     don ixo i es tornado.

53 Hya va el mandado     por las tierras todas.
Pesando va a los de Monçon     e a los de Huesca;     940
por que dan parias     plaze a los de Saragoça,
de mio Çid Ruy Diaz     que non temien ninguna fonta.

**910-12** The route described here is an unlikely one, for Teruel is a long way to the south-east of El Poyo and the Cid's subsequent route promptly takes him back towards the north. The Cid continues to push eastwards: his new encampment is situated in the north-east of the present-day province of Teruel, some thirty kilometres south of the town of Alcañiz (see l.936).

**914** Saragossa (Zaragoza) was one of the largest and most prosperous Moorish kingdoms in Spain, and the poet's statement that the Cid was rapidly able to force it to pay him tribute is unconvincing from a historical point of view. In fact, the Cid spent several months in the service of the rulers of Saragossa, al-Muqtadir and subsequently his son al-Mu'tamin, playing a prominent and successful role in the campaign against al-Mu'tamin's brother, al-Hachib (see note to l.957).

**917** These are men who, by virtue of their wealth, have the right to fight on horseback and bear a sword, but have not been formally knighted and do not have the legal privileges of knighthood (see Lacarra, p.161).

When the noble Battler saw that Minaya was a long time in returning,
he marched by night with all his men,
leaving El Poyo abandoned and deserted.                                  910
Don Rodrigo passed beyond Teruel.
In the pine grove at Tévar camped Don Ruy Díaz.
He raided throughout these lands
and imposed a tribute on Saragossa.
When he had done this, three weeks later,                                915
Minaya returned from Castile,
bringing with him two hundred fighting men,
and footsoldiers, I tell you, beyond reckoning.
When My Cid saw Minaya appear,
he galloped out to embrace him warmly,                                   920
kissing his mouth and his eyes.
Minaya told him everything, keeping nothing from him.
The Battler smiled broadly:
"Thanks be to God and His divine grace!
As long as you live, Minaya, all will be well with me!"                 925

Lord God, how happy was all the army
that Minaya had returned so safely,
passing on to them greetings of cousins and brothers
and of the loved ones that they had left behind!

Lord God, how happy was the man of the fine beard                        930
that Álvar Fáñez had paid for the thousand masses
and given him greetings from his wife and daughters!
Lord God, how delighted was the Cid and how he rejoiced!
"May you live long, Álvar Fáñez!"

At once, the man born in a favoured hour rode off;                       935
he left desolate the lands of Alcañiz
and raided all the surrounding area.
On the third day he returned to his base.

Now the news of this spread throughout the land;
the people of Monzón and Huesca were troubled,                           940
but those of Saragossa were relieved — as they were paying tribute,
they feared no harm from My Cid Ruy Díaz.

54 Con estas ganançias    a la posada tornando se van;
   todos son alegres,    ganançias traen grandes.
   Plogo a mio Çid    e mucho a Albar Fañez.    945
   Sonrrisos el caboso    que non lo pudo endurar:
   '¡ Hya cavalleros!    dezir vos he la verdad:
   qui en un logar mora siempre    lo so puede menguar;
   cras a la mañana    penssemos de cavalgar,
   dexat estas posadas    e iremos adelant.'    950
   Estonçes se mudo el Çid    al puerto de Alucat,
   dent corre mio Çid    a Hues(c)a e a Mont Alvan;
   en aquessa corrida    .x. dias ovieron a morar.
   Fueron los mandados    a todas partes
   que el salido de Castiella    asi los trae tan mal.    955
   Los mandados son idos    a todas partes.

55 Llegaron las nuevas    al conde de Barçilona
   que mio Çid Ruy Diaz    quel corrie la tierra toda;
   ovo grand pesar    e tovos lo a grand fonta.

56 El conde es muy folon    e dixo una vanidat:    960
   '¡Grandes tuertos me tiene    mio Çid el de Bivar!
   Dentro en mi cort    tuerto me tovo grand:
   firiom el sobrino    e non lo enmendo mas.
   Agora correm las tierras    que en mi enpara estan;
   non lo desafie    nil torne enemistad,    965
   mas quando el melo busca    ir gelo he yo demandar.'
   Grandes son los poderes    e a priessa se van legando;
   gentes se le alegan grandes    entre moros e christianos.
   Adeliñan tras mio Çid    el bueno de Bivar,
   tres dias e dos noches    penssaron de andar,    970
   alcançaron a mio Çid    en Tevar y el pinar;
   asi viene esforçado    que el conde a manos sele cuido tomar.
   Mio Çid don Rodrigo    trae ganançia grand;
   diçe de una sierra    e legava a un val.
   Del conde don Remont    venido l'es mensaje;    975

**943** The camp mentioned here is the one at Tévar and not the earlier one at El Poyo (abandoned in 1.910). However, the Cid's next change of base takes him back much closer to his earlier encampment (see Michael, 'Geographical Problems: 1', pp.124-25).

**957** The Cid did in fact twice encounter in battle, and defeat each time, Count Berenguer Ramón II of Barcelona (known as the Fratricide). The first encounter took place in 1082 while the Cid was in the service of al-Mu'tamin of Saragossa, during the conflict with al-Hachib, ruler of Lérida and Tortosa. Al-Hachib turned for support and protection to the Count of Barcelona and also to Sancho Ramírez of Navarre and Aragón; the Count was heavily defeated and taken prisoner at Almenar. Eight years later, Berenguer Ramón, again fighting in alliance with al-Hachib, for a second time suffered defeat and capture at the Cid's hands, this time at Tévar. The *Historia Roderici* (see note to ll.1-2) gives an account of both episodes: that of the battle at Tévar is much the longer and may well have suggested to the poet several details of his version of the Count's humiliation.

**958** These are not the Count's own lands, but rather territory under his domination and from which he would expect to exact tribute in return for protection.

My Cid's men returned to the camp with their booty;
all were joyful, for they brought great booty.
My Cid was pleased, and Álvar Fáñez overjoyed.                    945
The noble Battler smiled, and could not contain his pleasure:
"Now, my knights, I shall tell you the truth:
anyone who stays for ever in the same place may find his fortunes on
                         the wane.
Let us ride on tomorrow,
leave this camp and be on our way."                               950
Then My Cid moved to the pass of Gallocanta,
from where he made raids towards Huesa and Montalbán.
These raids lasted for ten days.
The news spread to all parts
that the man who had left Castile was treating the people so harshly.
The news was heard in all parts.


A report came to the ears of the Count of Barcelona
that My Cid Ruy Díaz was ravaging all his lands;
he was greatly troubled and considered himself offended.


The Count was boastful and spoke vain words:                     960
"My Cid, the man from Vivar, has greatly wronged me!
In my court he wronged me greatly.
He wounded my nephew and has done nothing to make amends,
and now he is ravaging lands under my protection.
I have never challenged him or ceased to be friendly towards him,
but since he seeks trouble with me I must go and demand redress."
His forces were great and assembled rapidly;
he gathered together many men, both Moors and Christians.
They went in search of My Cid, good man of Vivar.
They rode for three days and two nights                          970
and they reached My Cid in the pine wood at Tévar.
The Count came with so great a force that he expected to take the
                         Cid prisoner.
My Cid Don Rodrigo carried great booty with him;
he rode down from a hill into a valley.
A messenger came to him from Count Don Ramón,                    975

---

**960** The poet is quick to let us know how we are to react to his portrait of a vain, blustering, and foppish individual, viewed with no small measure of Castilian intolerance towards an effete Catalan nobleman.
**961-63** It is recorded that early in his period of exile the Cid stayed briefly in Barcelona, but we have no information as to the identity of the nephew mentioned here or the nature of the insult.

mio Çid quando lo oyo    enbio pora alla:
'Digades al conde    non lo tenga a mal;
de lo so non lievo nada,    dexem ir en paz.'
Respuso el conde:    '¡Esto non sera verdad!
Lo de antes e de agora    todom lo pechara;      980
¡sabra el salido    a quien vino desondrar!'
Tornos el mandadero    quanto pudo mas;
essora lo connosçe    mio Çid el de Bivar
que a menos de batalla    nos pueden den quitar.

57 '¡Hya cavalleros.    apart fazed la ganançia!    985
A priessa vos guarnid    e metedos en las armas;
el conde don Remont    dar nos ha grant batalla,
de moros e de christianos    gentes trae sobejanas,
a menos de batalla    non nos dexarie por nada.
Pues adellant iran tras nos,    aqui sea la batalla;    990
apretad los cavallos    e bistades las armas.
Ellos vienen cuesta yuso    e todos trahen calças,
e las siellas coçeras    e las çinchas amojadas;
nos cavalgaremos siellas gallegas    e huesas sobre caiças.
¡Çiento cavalleros    devemos vençer aquelas mesnadas!    995
Antes que ellos legen a[l] laño    presentemos les las lanças;
por uno que firgades    tres siellas iran vazias.
¡Vera Remont Verengel    tras quien vino en alcança
oy en este pinar de Tevar    por toler me la ganançia!'

58 Todos son adobados    quando mio Çid esto ovo fablado;  1000
las armas avien presas    e sedien sobre los cavallos.
Vieron la cuesta yuso    la fuerça de los francos;
al fondon de la cuesta,    çerca es de[l] laño,
mando los ferir mio Çid    el que en buen ora nasco;
esto fazen los sos    de voluntad e de grado,    1005
los pendones e las lanças    tan bien las van enpleando
a los unos firiendo    e a los otros derrocando.
Vençido a esta batalla    el que en buen ora nasco;
al conde don Remont    a preson le an tomado.

**992-94** The Catalan troops have little idea of how to prepare for battle; it is indicative of the poet's attitude to the Count and his men that he shows them not to wear boots, which, although they give a firm advantage to a horseman in battle, are inelegant; compare the Count's scornful description of the Cid's men as *malçalcados* (literally 'ill-shod') in l.1023.

and when he heard him, he sent the following reply:
"Tell the Count not to take things badly;
I am taking nothing of his, and he should allow me to go in peace."
The Count replied: "That cannot be!
He will make amends to me for his past and present deeds;     980
the exile will know who it is that he has come to dishonour!"
The messenger returned as fast as he could.
Now My Cid, the man from Vivar, realized
that there was no other way but to fight.

"Now, my knights, put the booty to one side.     985
Be quick to equip and arm yourselves;
Count Don Ramón is to engage us in a great battle;
he has a vast army of Moors and Christians,
and he would not leave us in peace without a battle.
Since they will pursue us wherever we go, let the battle be fought here.
Tighten the saddle - girths and arm yourselves.
They are coming downhill and are all wearing breeches
and riding light saddles with the girths slack.
We shall be using strong saddles and wearing boots over our breeches.
With a hundred knights we could not fail to beat those men.    995
Let us attack them with our lances before they reach level ground,
and for every one that you strike three saddles will be emptied.
Ramón Berenguer will soon see what sort of man he has come to seek,
today in the pine wood of Tévar, intending to deprive me of my booty."

When My Cid had finished speaking, they all made ready;    1000
they had taken up their arms and mounted their horses.
Up the slope they saw the Frankish force;
when the enemy neared the foot of the slope, close to the level ground,
My Cid, the man born in a favoured hour, commanded his men to
attack;
they did so eagerly and with great courage.    1005
The lances with their pennants were used to great effect,
striking some and unseating others.
The man born in a favoured hour won the battle
and took Count Don Ramón as his prisoner.

---

**1002** Catalonia was reconquered from the Moslems by the Franks in the late eighth century and for a number of
centuries was ruled by Frankish counts. The Catalans continued to be quite commonly known as Franks, and it is
not surprising that the Castilian poet, seeing them as an alien people, hostile to his hero, should refer to them in
this way.

59 Hi gaño a Colada     que mas vale de mill marcos de plata,   1010
   i bençio esta batalla     por o ondro su barba;
   priso lo al conde,     pora su tie[nd]a lo levava,
   a sos creenderos     guardar lo mandava.
   De fuera de la tienda     un salto dava,
   de todas partes     los sos se ajunta[va]n;     1015
   plogo a mio Çid     ca grandes son las ganançias.
   A mio Çid don Rodrigo     grant cozinal adobavan;
   el conde don Remont     non gelo preçia nada,
   aduzen le los comeres,     delant gelos paravan,
   el non lo quiere comer,     a todos los sosañava:     1020
   '¡Non combre un bocado     por quanto ha en toda España,
   antes perdere el cuerpo     e dexare el alma
   pues que tales malcalçados     me vençieron de batalla!'

60 Mio Çid Ruy Diaz     odredes lo que dixo:
   'Comed, conde, deste pan     e beved deste vino;     1025
   si lo que digo fizieredes     saldredes de cativo,
   si non, en todos vuestros dias     non veredes christianismo.'

61 Dixo el conde don Remont:     'Comede, don Rodrigo, e
                            penssedes de folgar,
   que yo dexar m'e morir,     que non quiero comer.'
   Fasta terçer dia     nol pueden acordar;     1030
   ellos partiendo     estas ganançias grandes
   nol pueden fazer comer     un muesso de pan.

62 Dixo mio Çid:     'Comed, conde, algo,
   ca si non comedes     non veredes christianos;     1033b
   e si vos comieredes     don yo sea pagado
   a vos     e dos fijos dalgo     1035
   quitar vos he los cuerpos     e darvos e de mano.'     1035b
   Quando esto oyo el conde     yas iva alegrando:
   'Si lo fizieredes, Çid,     lo que avedes fablado,
   tanto quanto yo biva     sere dent maravillado.'
   'Pues comed, conde,     e quando fueredes yantado
   a vos e a otros dos     dar vos he de mano;     1040
   mas quanto avedes perdido     e yo gane en canpo

1010 The name of the sword is probably derived from the verb meaning 'to cast' (a metal). The value placed on Colada is almost certainly exaggerated, for a thousand marks represents an immense sum. It is, however, revealing that the poet should choose to emphasize the cash value of the sword rather than, for example, its beauty or special attributes; Hook points to the contrast in this respect with the description of swords in other medieval epic poems ('On Certain Correspondences', pp.37-39).
1019 The Count is being asked to take part in a banquet to celebrate his own defeat.
1023 For the sense of *malcalçados*, see note to ll.992-94. We can imagine how the comic effect of this and the

There My Cid gained Colada, worth more than a thousand silver marks.
There he won this battle, by which he brought honour upon himself.
He captured the Count, took him to his tent, a prisoner,
and ordered his servants to guard him.
When he emerged from the tent,
his men were assembling from all directions.                              1015
My Cid was pleased, for the booty was great.
A great banquet was prepared for My Cid Don Rodrigo,
but Don Ramón did not appreciate it at all.
Food was brought and set before him,
but he would not eat, refusing every dish:                               1020
"I will not eat a mouthful, for all the wealth in Spain;
I would rather die and give up my soul,
since such ill - shod ruffians have defeated me in battle!"

You will hear how My Cid Ruy Díaz replied:
"Come, Count, eat this bread and drink this wine.                        1025
If you do what I say you will be set free;
if not, in all your days you will never again see Christian lands."

Count Don Ramón said: "You eat, Don Rodrigo, and take your rest,
for I shall let myself die; I will not eat."
Till the third day, they could not persuade him;                        1030
they were sharing out the huge amounts of booty
and they could not make him eat a mouthful of bread.

My Cid spoke: "Come, come, Count, eat something,
for if you do not you will never again see your people;                 1033b
but if you eat enough to please me,
both you and two of your noblemen                                       1035
will be set free and sent on your way."                                 1035b
When the Count heard this, his spirits revived.
"Cid, if you do what you have said,
my amazement will last as long as I live."
"Well, eat, Count, and when you have feasted
I shall release you and two others.                                     1040
but of all that you have lost and I have won on the field of battle,

ensuing speeches could be maximized in performance.
**1035-1035b** The Cid again displays his exceptional generosity: he might have been expected to demand a large
ransom for his illustrious prisoner and his two companions.

sabet, non vos dare    a vos un dinero malo,
mas quanto avedes perdido    non vos lo dare
ca huebos melo he    e pora estos mios vassallos
que conmigo andan lazrados,    ¡e non vos lo dare!    1045
Prendiendo de vos e de otros    ir nos hemos pagando;
abremos esta vida    mientra plogiere al Padre santo,
commo que ira a de rey    e de tierra es echado.'
Alegre es el conde    e pidio agua a las manos,
e tienen gelo delant    e dieron gelo privado.    1050
Con los cavalleros    que el Çid le avie dados
comiendo va el conde    ¡Dios, que de buen grado!
Sobr'el sedie    el que en buen ora nasco:
'Si bien non comedes, conde,    don yo sea pagado
aqui feremos la morada,    no nos partiremos amos.'    1055
Aqui dixo el conde:    '¡De voluntad e de grado!'
Con estos dos cavalleros    a priessa va yantando;
pagado es mio Çid    que lo esta aguardando
por que el conde don Remont    tan bien bolvie las manos.
'Si vos ploguiere, mio Çid,    de ir somos guisados;    1060
mandad nos dar las bestias    e cavalg[a]remos privado.
Del dia que fue conde    non yante tan de buen grado,
el sabor que dend e    non sera olbidado.'
Dan le tres palafres    muy bien ensellados
e buenas vestiduras    de peliçones e de mantos.    1065
El conde don Remont    entre los dos es entrado;
fata cabo del albergada    escurriolos el Castelano:
'¡Hya vos ides, conde,    a guisa de muy franco!
¡En grado vos lo tengo    lo que me avedes dexado!
Si vos viniere emiente    que quisieredes vengalo    1070
si me vinieredes buscar    fallar me podredes;
e si non, mandedes buscar;    o me dexaredes
de lo vuestro    o de lo mio levaredes algo.'
'¡Folgedes, ya mio Çid,    sodes en vuestro salvo!
Pagado vos he    por todo aqueste año,    1075
de venir vos buscar    sol non sera penssado.'

63 Aguijava el conde    e penssava de andar;
   tornando va la cabeça    e catandos atras,

---

1049 Though the Count has not eaten for three days and is presumably consumed by hunger, he still insists on washing his hands before he will eat; the poet mocks his refined and affected manners, inappropriate in a true warrior.
1064 A palfrey is a saddle-horse for ordinary riding, as opposed to a charger ridden in battle.
1068 The Cid's jibe plays on two meanings of the word *franco*: 'free', but also 'Frankish'.

104

I tell you I shall not give you a rotten pennyworth;
no, all that you have lost I shall not give back,
for I need it for these my vassals,
who suffer hardship with me; I shall not give it back!                  1045
We shall satisfy ourselves by taking from you and others;
and we shall lead this life while it pleases the heavenly Father,
as befits one who has incurred the King's anger and been sent
                              into exile."
Joyful was the Count; he asked for water for his hands;
quickly it was brought and set before him.                              1050
With the knights that the Cid had brought to him,
the Count began to eat — Lord God with what pleasure!
Over him sat the man born in a favoured hour:
"If you don't eat well, Count, sufficiently to satisfy me,
we shall stay here and the two of us will never part."                  1055
At this the Count answered: "I will eat most willingly."
With his two knights he made haste to eat.
My Cid, watching him, was well pleased
that Count Don Ramón was setting to so heartily.
"If you are willing, My Cid, we are ready to leave;                     1060
order the horses to be given to us, and we shall ride quickly on
                              our way.
since I became count, never did I have so pleasant a meal;
I shall never forget its good taste."
He was given three palfreys, with very fine saddles,
and fine clothes, fur capes and cloaks.                                 1065
Count Don Ramón took his place between the other two,
and the Castilian escorted him as far as the edge of the camp.
"You are on your way, Count, a free man!
I am grateful to you for what you have left me!
If it should occur to you to seek vengeance,                            1070
if you come and look for me you will be able to find me;
otherwise you can send men out to look for me; either you will
                              leave me
some of your possessions or you will take away some of mine!"
"Do not worry, My Cid, you are safe from that!
I have paid you sufficient for all this year,                           1075
and it will not even occur to me to come and seek you out again."

The Count spurred on his way,
turning his head and glancing behind him,

105

miedo iva aviendo    que mio Çid se repintra,
lo que non ferie el caboso    por quanto en el mundo ha   1080
—una deslea[l]tança—    ca non la fizo alguandre.
Hido es el conde,    tornos el de Bivar;
juntos con sus mesnadas,    conpeçolas de legar
de la ganançia que an fecha    maravillosa e grand.

---

**1083-84** The MS reading, preserved by Smith, means 'he began to gather them (his troops) together', and leaves l.1084 making little sense. Menéndez Pidal and Michael correct *llegar* to *alegrar* and *pagar* respectively, both readings conveying the sense of rejoicing.

106

afraid that My Cid would change his mind;
but the noble Battler would not do that for all the wealth in the world;
for never did he commit a dishonourable act.
The Count had gone on his way and the man from Vivar turned back.
He rejoined his troops and began to rejoice
at the booty they had taken, which was wonderful and great of value.

*The* Puerta del Sol *in Toledo was built in the fourteenth century, over two hundred years after the Cid's death, but, with its large horseshoe arch, it shows clearly the influence which Moorish culture still exerted in Spain (courtesy Spanish National Tourist Office).*

# CANTAR II

64 Aquis conpieça la gesta de mio Çid el de Bivar. 1085
 Tan ricos son los sos que non saben que se an.
 Poblado ha mio Çid el puerto de Aluca(n)t,
 dexado a Saragoça e las tierras duca
 e dexado a Hues(c)a e las tierras de Mont Alvan.
 Contra la mar salada conpeço de guerrear. 1090
 A orient exe el sol e tornos a essa part.
 Mio Çid gaño a Xerica e a Onda e Almenar,
 tierras de Borriana todas conquistas las ha.

65 Ayudol el Criador, el Señor que es en çielo.
 El con todo esto priso a Murviedro; 1095
 ya vie mio Çid que Dios le iva valiendo.
 Dentro en Valençia non es poco el miedo.

66 Pesa a los de Valençia sabet, non les plaze;
 prisieron so consejo quel viniessen çercar;
 trasnocharon de noch. al alva de la man 1100
 açerca de Murviedro tornan tiendas a fincar.
 Violo mio Çid, tomos a maravillar:
 '¡Grado a ti Padre spiritall! 1102<sup>b</sup>
 En sus tierras somos e femos les todo mal,
 bevemos so vino e comemos el so pan;
 si nos çercar vienen con derecho lo fazen. 1105
 A menos de lid aquesto nos partira.
 Vayan los mandados por los que nos deven ayudar:
 los unos a Xerica e los otros a Alucad,
 desi a Onda e los otros a Almenar,
 los de Borriana luego vengan aca. 1110
 Conpeçaremos aquesta lid campal

---

**1085** The Spanish text tells us just that the tale of the Cid's deeds is beginning. The manuscript does not indicate any break between l.1084 and l.1085, and the assonance in *a (-e)* continues from *tirada* 63 into 64.

**1087** This is Olocau de Liria, within about twenty-five kilometres of the city of Valencia, and possibly confused by the poet with the pass of Gallocanta mentioned in l.951 – the two toponyms appear in the text as Alucat and Alucant respectively. The inaccuracios and vagueness over detail which characterize the geography of this section of the *Poema* suggest that its author had no first-hand knowledge of the area around Valencia.

**1095** In the *Poema*, the Cid continues to use Murviedro (the present-day city of Sagunto) as his base in the campaign leading to the taking of Valencia. Though Murviedro occupied an important strategic position, its role here has no historical basis: in reality, the Cid's campaign was based on Cebolla (now Puig), eighteen kilometres north of Valencia, whilst Murviedro was not conquered till 1098. The poet's account of the capture of Valencia dwells on the raiding, the siege and famine, and the eventual truce, and gives the impression of a rapid and progressive military conquest. It makes no mention of the complex process by which the Cid formed alliances, imposed tribute and steadily tightened his grip on the city. For an examination of the poet's approach to this part of his narrative, see D. Hook, 'The Conquest of Valencia in the *Cantar de Mio Cid*', *Bulletin of Hispanic Studies*.

# CANTAR II

Here begins again the story of My Cid of Vivar.                    1085
His men are so rich that they can no longer tell their wealth.
My Cid has occupied the pass of Olocau,
having left behind Saragossa and its lands,
and Huesa and the lands of Montalbán.
He began to make war by the salt sea;                              1090
then he set off eastwards towards the sunrise.
My Cid took Jérica and Onda and Almenar,
and overran all the lands of Burriana.

He was guided by the Creator, our Lord in heaven;
and thus it was he captured Murviedro.                             1095
Now My Cid saw that God was protecting him.
Inside Valencia there was great fear.

The people of Valencia were in distress, I tell you.
They decided in counsel to besiege him;
they marched through the night, and at dawn                        1100
they pitched camp near Murviedro.
My Cid saw this and marvelled:
"I thank you, Holy Father!
We are in their lands and are doing them all possible wrong,
we are drinking their wine and eating their bread;
if they come and besiege us, they have every right to do so.       1105
This will not be settled without a battle.
Let messengers go to those towns whose duty it is to support us;
some to Jérica, others to Olocau,
after that to Onda, and others to Almenar;
then let the men of Burriana come to me.                           1110
We shall fight a pitched battle.

50 (1973), 120-26.
**1102b** Confident of victory, the Cid offers thanks for the fresh challenge, accepting this new development as part
of God's providential scheme.
**1103** Hook ('On Certain Correspondences', p.45) discerns a very close similarity here to terms used in formal
treaties at the end of the twelfth century.
    It is, perhaps, surprising that the poet should show his hero to recognize that his adversaries have right on
their side. This comment reminds us that, in moving into the territory of others and bringing them misfortune, the
Cid is acting not of his own free will but as a result of the action of his lord.
**1107** That is, to those towns of the region which he now dominates and which pay him tribute.

```
      yo fio por Dios      que en nuestro pro eñadran.'
      Al terçer dia       todos juntados s'[a]n.
      El que en buen ora nasco      compeço de fablar:
      '¡Oid, mesnadas!      ¡Si el Criador vos salve!                1115
      Despues que nos partiemos      de la linpia christiandad
      —non fue a nuestro grado      ni nos non pudiemos mas—
      grado a Dios      lo nuestro fue adelant.
      Los de Valençia      çercados nos han:
      si en estas tierras      quisieremos durar                     1120
      firme mientre son estos      a escarmentar.
```

```
   67 Passe la noche      e venga la mañana,
      aparejados me sed      a cavallos e armas.
      Hiremos ver      aquela su almofalla;
      commo omnes exidos      de tierra estraña                      1125
      ¡ali pareçra      el que mereçe la soldada!'
```

```
   68 Oid que dixo      Minaya Albar Fañez:
      'Campeador,      fagamos lo que a vos plaze.
      A mi dedes .c. cavalleros,      que non vos pido mas;
      vos con los otros      firades los delant,                     1130
      bien los ferredes,      que dubda non i avra;
      yo con los çiento      entrare del otra part.
      ¡Commo fio por Dios      el campo nuestro sera!'
      Commo gelo a dicho      al Campeador mucho plaze.
      Mañana era      e pienssan se de armar;                        1135
      quis cada uno dellos      bien sabe lo que ha de far.
      Con los alvores      mio Çid ferir los va:
      '¡En el nombre del Criador      e del apostol Santi Yague
      ferid los, cavalleros,      d'amor e de grado e de grand voluntad
      ca yo so Ruy Diaz      mio Çid el de Bivar!'                   1140
      Tanta cuerda de tienda      i veriedes quebrar,
      arancar se las estacas      e acostar se a todas partes los tendales.
      Moros son muchos,      ya quieren reconbrar.
      Del otra part      entroles Albar Fañez,
      mager les pesa      ovieron se a dar e a arancar.              1145
      Grand es el gozo      que va por es logar.
      Dos reyes de moros      mataron en es alcaz,
      fata Valençia      duro el segudar.
```

---

**1115-26** In this speech, the Cid makes clear the motives which drive him and his men into battle: there is no mention of a crusade against the forces of Islam, but rather the emphasis is on the practical need to establish a right to live in these hostile lands.

**1141-42** This detail is repeated in almost identical terms in the account of the battle against Búcar (ll.2401-02). Deyermond and Hook show that it represents a motif which occurs in several French epics: 'The Afrenta de Corpes and Other Stories', *La Corónica*, 10 (1981-82), 12-37 (pp.26-28).

**1145-55** Some editors reorder these lines to produce a more coherent account, but Smith preserves the

I trust in God that they will give us even greater advantage."
By the third day they had all gathered together.
The man born in a favoured hour began to speak:
"Listen, my men!  May the Creator save you!                    1115
Since we departed from our pure Christian lands —
it was not through desire, for we had no choice —
thanks be to God, our affairs have prospered.
The men of Valencia are besieging us;
if we wish to remain in these lands,
these men must be taught a tough lesson.                       1120

Let the night pass and the morning come:
be then ready, mounted and armed!
We shall go and engage their army in battle;
since you are exiles, estranged from your homeland,            1125
now it may be seen who deserves his pay!"

Hear the words of Minaya Álvar Fáñez:
"Battler, let us do what you wish.
Give me one hundred knights, I ask no more of you;
you with the others attack them from the front,                1130
striking resolutely and without fear;
I with the hundred will attack from behind.
As I trust in God, the field of battle will be ours."
His words greatly pleased the Battler.
The next day came and they took up their arms;                 1135
each knew well what he had to do.
At dawn My Cid rode out to attack his enemies:
"In the name of the Creator and Saint James the Apostle,
strike them, my knights, with all your heart and strength and will,
for I am Ruy Díaz, My Cid of Vivar!"                           1140
You could see so many ropes cut,
stakes pulled up and on all sides tent poles thrown to the ground.
There were many Moors and now they tried to rally their forces.
From the rear Álvar Fáñez advanced amongst them.
To their sorrow, they had to surrender and acknowledge defeat.  1145
Great was the joy that spread throughout the field.
They killed two Moorish kings in that pursuit,
and the chase extended to Valencia.

manuscript order, commenting that 'The *MS* makes fair sense, and one must allow for the poet's abrupt and
elliptical style and capacity for switching subjects (as in l.1151).'

111

Grandes son las ganançias    que mio Çid fechas ha,
prisieron Çebola    e quanto que es i adelant,    1150
de pies de cavallo    los ques pudieron escapar;
robavan el campo    e pienssan se de tornar,
entravan a Murviedro    con estas ganançias que traen grandes.
Las nuevas de mio Çid    sabet, sonando van;
miedo an en Valençia    que non saben que se far.    1155
Sonando van sus nuevas    alent parte del mar.

69 Alegre era el Çid    e todas sus compañas
que Dios le ayudara    e fiziera esta arrancada.
Davan sus corredores    e fazien las trasnochadas,
legan a Gujera    e legan a Xativa,    1160
aun mas ayusso    a Deyna la casa;
cabo del mar tierra de moros    firme la quebranta,
ganaron Peña Cadiella    las exidas e las entradas.

70 Quando el Cid Campeador    ovo Peña Cadiella
ma[l] les pesa en Xativa    e dentro en Gujera;    1165
non es con recabdo    el dolor de Valençia.

71 En tierra de moros    prendiendo e ganando
e durmiendo los dias    e las noches tranochando
en ganar aquelas villas    mio Çid duro .iii. años.

72 A los de Valençia    escarmentados los han,    1170
non osan fueras exir    nin con el se ajuntar;
tajava les las huertas    e fazia les grand mal;
en cada uno destos años    mio Çid les tolio el pan.
Mal se aquexan los de Valençia    que non saben(t) ques far;
de ninguna part que sea    non les vinie pan,    1175
nin da conssejo padre a fijo    nin fijo a padre,
nin amigo a amigo    nos pueden consolar.
Mala cueta es    señores, aver mingua de pan,
fijos e mugieres    ver lo murir de fanbre.
Delante veyen so duelo,    non se pueden huviar,    1180

**1161** The Cid's forces probe extensively through the coastal area: Denia lies about a hundred kilometres south of Valencia.
**1163** Literally, '(both) the exits and points of entry' (see also l.1572); this phrase reflects terminology used in legal documents in both Latin and the vernacular (see Smith, *Estudios cidianos* (Madrid, 1977), pp.197-98).
   The poet refers here to the mountains of Benicadell. In 1091 the Cid rebuilt the castle of Benicadell, which dominated the southern approaches to Játiva and to the plain of Valencia. From a watch-tower on the nearby peak it was possible to see as far as Valencia itself, seventy kilometres away.
**1172** The *Huerta* of Valencia was, and remains, a highly fertile and intensively cultivated area, benefiting from an elaborate system of irrigation and producing a wide range of crops, most notably citrus fruits and rice.

112

Great was the booty captured by My Cid.
They took El Puig and all the lands beyond it.　　　　　1150
Those Moors who could escaped on horseback.
My Cid's men plundered the battlefield and returned to their camp.
They entered Murviedro with the great booty they carried with them.
I tell you the fame of My Cid was carried far and wide;
there was such fear in Valencia, the people knew not what to do. 1155
His fame was carried beyond the sea.

Joyful was the Cid, and all his troops,
that God had helped him and granted him this victory.
Raiding parties were sent out and the men marched by night.
They reached Cullera, they reached Játiva,　　　　　1160
and farther south they came to the town of Denia.
My Cid despoiled the Moorish lands along the coast.
They took the whole territory of Benicadell.

Since My Cid the Battler had Benicadell in his possession,
there was anxiety among all the people of Játiva and those of Cullera;
the sorrow of Valencia was beyond reckoning ...

In the domain of the Moors, taking and conquering,
sleeping by day and marching by night,
My Cid spent three years overcoming those towns.

The people of Valencia had been taught a lesson;　　　　1170
they dared not leave the city or engage My Cid in battle.
He cut down their plantations and did them great harm;
each year My Cid deprived them of their food.
The people of Valencia bitterly lamented — they knew not what to do;
from nowhere could they get food.　　　　　1175
Father could not aid son nor son help father,
nor could friend bring consolation to friend.
It is a harsh fate, my lords, to have not enough to eat,
and to see women and children dying of hunger.
Though they saw their sorrow all too clearly, they could not help
　　　　　　　　　　　　themselves.　　　　　1180

1178-79 In his description of the siege of Valencia, the poet appears to take a number of details from the *Historia
Roderici*, though modifying the latter account in important respects (see Smith, *The Making* ..., pp.146-48).
Moslem chronicles (not known by the poet) give a more graphic account of the horrors of the siege and the awful
sufferings of the starving inhabitants of Valencia

113

por el rey de Marruecos    ovieron a enbiar;
con el de los Montes Claros    avien guerra tan grand
non les dixo consejo    nin los vino huviar.
Sopolo mio Çid,    de coraçon le plaz;
salio de Murviedro    una noch en trasnochada,    1185
amaneçio a mio Çid    en tierras de Mon Real.
Por Aragon e por Navarra    pregon mando echar,
a tierras de Castiella    enbio sus menssajes:
'Quien quiere perder cueta    e venir a rritad
viniesse a mio Çid    que a sabor de cavalgar;    1190
¡çercar quiere a Valençia    por a christianos la dar!'

73 'Quien quiere ir comigo    çercar a Valençia
todos vengan de grado,    ninguno non ha premia,
tres dias le sperare    en Canal de Çelfa.'

74 .Esto dixo mio Çid    el que en buen ora nasco.    1195
Tornavas a Murviedro    ca el se la a ganada.

Andidieron los pregones    sabet, a todas partes;
al sabor de la ganançia    non lo quieren detardar,
grandes yentes se le acojen    de la buena christiandad.
Creçiendo va riqueza    a mio Çid el de Bivar.    1200
Quando vio mio Çid las gentes juntadas    compeços de pagar.
Mio Çid don Rodrigo    non lo quiso detardar;
adeliño pora Valençia    e sobr'ellas va echar,
bien la çerca mio Çid,    que non i avia hart,
viedales exir    e viedales entrar.    1205
Sonando van sus nuevas    todas a todas partes;
mas le vienen a mio Çid    sabet, que nos le van.
Metiola en plazo    si les viniessen huviar;
nueve meses complidos    sabet, sobr'ella yaz,
quando vino el dezeno    ovieron gela a dar.    1210
Grandes son los gozos    que van por es logar
quando mio Çid gaño a Valençia    y entro en la çibdad;

---

**1181** This is Yusuf ibn Tashufin, Emperor of the Almoravids, who in fact entered Spain for the first time in 1086, in answer to a request from al-Mu'tamid of Seville and other Moslem rulers of the Peninsula, and in the same year won a massive victory over Alfonso at Sagrajas. The Almoravids were a fanatical sect, whose African empire was in 1086 already four times the size of Spain; for some forty years they were to dominate Moslem Spain and pose a severe threat to the Christian kingdoms. By the third decade of the twelfth century, however, their position had begun to weaken, and in particular their power in Africa was being threatened by another, equally fanatical sect, the Almohads. It is the Almohads who are alluded to in l.1182, anachronistically, for this conflict was not to begin until some thirty years after the events that the poet is describing.
**1185-86** Michael ('Geographical Problems: I', p.127) points out that this would be impossible to achieve in a night's march, for Murviedro (Sagunto) is a hundred and seventy-eight kilometres from Monreal.

They appealed to the Emir of Morocco;
he was engaged in a great conflict with the lord of the Atlas Mountains,
and so he neither sent them aid nor came himself.
My Cid heard this, and was greatly pleased.
He left Murviedro on a night march.                   1185
Daybreak found My Cid in the lands of Monreal.
He ordered it to be proclaimed throughout Aragón and Navarre,
and sent messengers into the lands of Castile:
"Whoever wishes to escape poverty and find wealth
should come to My Cid, for he desires to ride into battle;       1190
My Cid plans to lay siege to Valencia and place it in Christian hands!

Let all those who wish to go with me to besiege Valencia
come of their own free will, none under compulsion;
I shall await them for three days at Cella del Canal."

These were the words of My Cid, the man born in a favoured hour.
He returned to Murviedro, as that town was already his.

Messengers travelled throughout the land, I tell you;
with the attraction of the booty, men came without delay;
great numbers came to join him from the fair lands of the Christians.
My Cid, the man from Vivar, was acquiring yet greater wealth.    1200
When My Cid saw the forces that had gathered, he began to rejoice.
My Cid Don Rodrigo did not wish to delay;
he made straight for Valencia ready to launch an attack on the city.
My Cid encircled it so tightly that there was no way through;
he stopped the people going out and stopped them entering.      1205
News of My Cid's deeds spread everywhere;
more men joined him, none left, I tell you.
He granted the city a period of respite in case any aid should come;
he waited there for a full nine months, I tell you,
and when the tenth month came the city surrendered.        1210
Great was the joy that spread around
when My Cid took possession of Valencia and entered the city;

**1208** This was quite common practice. An Arab historian states that before Valencia finally surrendered the Cid had given its inhabitants a truce of fifteen (or possibly twenty-five) days in order that they might appeal for help to the kings of Saragossa and Murcia.
**1210** Valencia finally surrendered on 16 June 1094, having been in a state of siege for much of the time since October 1092. Some six years had elapsed since the Cid had set about the process of establishing for himself a protectorate over the Levante and some thirteen years since his departure into exile.

los que fueron de pie      cavalleros se fazen,
el oro e la plata      ¿quien vos lo podrie contar?
Todos eran ricos      quantos que alli ha.      1215
Mio Çid don Rodrigo      la quinta mando tomar;
en el aver monedado      .xxx. mill marcos le caen
e los otros averes      ¿quien los podrie contar?
Alegre era el Campeador      con todos los que ha

quando su seña cabdal      sedie en somo del alcaçar.      1220

75 Ya folgava mio Çid      con todas sus conpañas.
[A] aquel rey de Sevilla      el mandado legava
que presa es Valençia,      que non gela enparan;
vino los ver      con .xxx. mill de armas.
Apres de la uerta      ovieron la batalla,      1225
arrancolos mio Çid      el de la luenga barba;
fata dentro en Xativa      duro el arrancada,
en el passar de Xucar      i veriedes barata,
moros en aruenço      amidos bever agua;
aquel rey de [Sevilla]      con tres colpes escapa.      1230
Tornado es mio Çid      con toda esta ganançia.
Buena fue la de Valençia      quando ganaron la casa,
mas mucho fue provechosa      sabet, esta aranca(n)da;
a todos los menores      cayeron .c. marcos de plata.
Las nuevas del cavallero      ya vedes do legavan.      1235

76 Grand alegria es      entre todos essos christianos
con mio Çid Ruy Diaz      el que en buen ora nasco.
Yal creçe la barba      e vale allongando.
Dixo mio Çid      de la su boca atanto:
'Por amor del rey Alffonsso      que de tierra me a echado      1240
nin entrarie en ela tigera      ni un pelo non avrie tajado,
e que fablassen desto      moros e christianos.'
Mio Çid don Rodrigo      en Valençia esta folgando,
con el Minaya Albar Ffañez      que nos le parte de so braço.
Los que exieron de tierra      de ritad son abondados,      1245
a todos les dio en Valençia      casas y heredades de que son
                                          pagados;

**1213** This is a striking expression of the gains made by the Cid's vassals: material wealth brings them higher social standing. For an explanation of the status of these men, see note to l.917.

**1222** By 1094 Seville had no king, as such, for though King al-Mu'tamid had invited the Almoravids to enter Spain, he had himself been dethroned and sent as a prisoner to Morocco. The commander of the Moslem army is likely to be the Almoravid governor of Seville, though here (as at a number of points in this section of the *Poema*) the poet is rather vague in his presentation of historical detail.

**1238-42** The practice of allowing the beard to grow as a sign of grief is a common one, not restricted to medieval Spain. The poet wishes to underline the fact that the Cid, even at a time of triumph and great power, is mindful of the importance of his relationship with his feudal lord and wishes to make public his longing to be received back into Alfonso's service.

those who had fought on foot now rode on horseback,
and who could reckon the value of the silver and the gold they seized?
All My Cid's troops were now wealthy men.                                        1215
My Cid ordered his fifth share to be collected;
in money, thirty thousand marks fell to his lot,
and who could reckon the value of the other goods he gained?
Full of joy were the Battler and all his men

when his standard was flown from the citadel.                                    1220

Now, while My Cid was resting with his troops,
word reached the renowned King of Seville
that Valencia had been taken as it could no longer be defended;
he came to fight My Cid's men with thirty thousand warriors.
Near to the plantations the battle was fought;                                   1225
the day was won by My Cid with the flowing beard;
the rout extended as far as Játiva.
At the crossing of the Júcar you could see great confusion —
the Moors struggling against the current and drinking the water
                                                    against their will.
The renowned King of Seville escaped, having suffered just three blows.
My Cid returned with all his booty;
great was that taken at Valencia when the city fell,
but even greater gains, I tell you, were brought by this new victory.
Even the most lowly soldier received one hundred silver marks.
Now you can see how the Knight's fame spread.                                    1235

There was great happiness amongst all those Christians
with My Cid Ruy Díaz, the man born in a favoured hour.
Now his beard grew long and flowing.
These words were on My Cid's lips:
"For love of King Alfonso, who has exiled me,                                     1240
I would not take shears to it or cut a single hair;
let this be the talk of Moors and Christians."
My Cid Don Rodrigo is resting in Valencia
with Minaya Álvar Fáñez, who does not leave his side.
Those who went with him into exile are showered with riches:                     1245
he has given them all houses and estates, and with this they are
                                                    well pleased.

**1245** The Cid shows special favour to those who, in spite of Alfonso's threats, accompanied him when he first left
Castile.

el amor de mio Çid    ya lo ivan provando.
Los que fueron con el e los de despues    todos son pagados;
veelo mio Çid    que con los averes que avien tomados
que sis pudiessen ir    fer lo ien de grado.                    1250
Esto mando mio Çid,    Minaya lo ovo consssejado:
que ningun omne de los sos    ques le non spidies o nol besas la
                                                              mano,

sil pudiessen prender    o fuesse alcançado
tomassen le el aver    e pusiessen le en un palo;
afevos todo aquesto    puesto en buen recabdo.                  1255
Con Minaya Albar Fañez    el se va consegar:
'Si vos quisieredes    Minaya, quiero saber recabdo
de los que son aqui    e comigo ganaron algo;
meter los he en escripto    e todos sean contados,
que si algunos furtare    o menos le fallaren                   1260
el aver me avra a tornar    [a] aquestos mios vassalos
que curian a Valençia    e andan arobdando.'                   1261b
Ali dixo Minaya:    'Consejo es aguisado.'

77 Mando los venir a la corth    e a todos los juntar.
Quando los fallo    por cuenta fizo los nonbrar;
tres mill e seis çientos    avie mio Çid el de Bivar.          1265
Alegras le el coraçon    e tornos a sonrrisar:
'¡Grado a Dios, Minaya,    e a Santa Maria madre!
Con mas pocos ixiemos    de la casa de Bivar;
agora avemos riquiza,    mas avremos adelant.
Si a vos ploguiere, Minaya,    e non vos caya en pesar,        1270
enbiar vos quiero a Castiella    do avemos heredades,
al rey Alfonsso    mio señor natural;
destas mis gananças    que avemos fechas aca
dar le quiero .c. cavallos    e vos id gelos levar.
Desi por mi besalde la mano    e firme gelo rogad              1275
por mi mugier e mis fijas    quenlas dexe sacar.               1276-7
Enbiare por ellas,    e vos sabed el mensage:
la mugier de mio Çid    e sus fijas las iffantes
de guisa iran por ellas    que a grand ondra vernan            1280
a estas tierras estrañas    que nos pudiemos ganar.'
Essora dixo Minaya:    '¡De buena voluntad!'

---

**1252-54** Any of the Cid's vassals who leave with their gains are formally to sever their bond with him and forfeit his protection. The Cid guards against a sudden weakening of his army through unexpected departures: generosity and fairness are combined with rigorous enforcement of laws essential for the security of both the lord and his vassals.

Now they knew the love of My Cid.
Payment was given both to those who had left with him and to
                                    those who joined him later.
My Cid saw that, with the possessions they had gained,
if they had the chance to go they would do so willingly.          1250
This is what My Cid commanded, as Minaya had advised:
that no man should leave without seeking permission and formally
                                    severing his allegiance,
and that if any did so, were he to be seized or captured,
he should be hanged from the gallows and his possessions confiscated.
Now all of this had been carefully dealt with.                    1255
My Cid went to take counsel with Minaya Álvar Fáñez:
"If you are willing, Minaya, I wish to have an account
of those who are here and have made gains under me;
I will have them all counted and their names recorded in writing,
so that if any of them should steal away or be missed            1260
their gains shall be returned to me and handed over to those
                                    vassals of mine
who are guarding Valencia outside the city."                     1261b
Then Minaya said: "It is a wise plan."

He ordered them all to assemble in the court.
When he came in to them he had them all recorded by name.
My Cid, the man from Vivar, had three thousand six hundred men.
His heart was filled with joy and he smiled again.
"Thanks be to God, Minaya, and to Saint Mary the Holy Mother!
We left the village of Vivar with fewer men than this!
Now we are rich; in time to come we shall be richer still.
If you are willing, Minaya, and it does not trouble you,          1270
I want to send you to Castile, where we have our estates,
to King Alfonso, my natural lord.
From this booty which we have taken here
I want to give him one hundred horses, and I want you to take
                                    them to him.
Then on my behalf kiss his hand and ask him resolutely           1275
to allow me to bring out from Castile my wife and daughters.     1276−7
I shall send for them; listen, this is my message:
the wife of My Cid, and his daughters, noble of birth,
will be sent an escort to conduct them with great honour         1280
into these foreign lands which we have been able to conquer."
Then Minaya said: "I am most willing."

119

Pues esto an fablado     pienssan se de adobar.
Çiento omnes le dio     mio Çid a Albar Fañez
por servirle en la carrera     [a toda su voluntad],     1284b
e mando mill marcos de plata     a San Pero levar     1285

e que los [.d.] diesse     al abbat don Sancho.

78 En estas nuevas     todos se(a) alegrando
de parte de orient     vino un coronado:
el obispo don Jeronimo     so nombre es lamado,
bien entendido es de letras     e mucho acordado,     1290
de pie e de cavallo     mucho era areziado.
Las provezas de mio Çid     andava las demandando,
sospirando (el obispo) ques viesse     con moros en el campo,
que sis fartas lidiando     e firiendo con sus manos
a los dias del sieglo     non le lorassen christianos.     1295
Quando lo oyo mio Çid     de aquesto fue pagado:
'¡Oid, Minaya Albar Fañez:     por aquel que esta en alto,
quando Dios prestar nos quiere     nos bien gelo gradescamos!
En tierras de Valençia     fer quiero obispado
e dar gelo     a este buen christiano.     1300
Vos quando ides a Castiella     levaredes buenos mandados.'

79 Plogo a Albar Fañez     de lo que dixo don Rodrigo.
A este don Jeronimo     yal otorgan por obispo,
dieron le en Valençia     o bien puede estar rico;
¡Dios, que alegra era     todo christianismo     1305
que en tierras de Valençia     señor avie obispo!
Alegre fue Minaya     e spidios e vinos.

80 Tierras de Valençia     remanidas en paz,
adeliño pora Castiella     Minaya Albar Fañez;
dexare vos las posadas,     non las quiero contar.     1310
Demando por Alfonsso     do lo podrie fallar;

---

**1286** For the destination of the other five hundred marks, see ll.1423 ff. The manuscript reading, probably through a scribal error, states that the thousand marks were all to be given to the abbot, but Smith (with most other editors) emends to give the sense demanded by ll.1422-23.
**1288** Literally, 'came from the east' – from a Castilian point of view. Jerónimo (Jérôme de Périgord), a French Cluniac, came to Spain possibly as late as 1097. In the document of 1098 which confirms the Cid's endowment of the Cathedral of Santa María (a converted mosque) the bishop is several times mentioned by name. When Valencia was abandoned, Jerónimo accompanied Jimena to Toledo and was subsequently made Bishop of Salamanca and Zamora. He is, then, a solid historical figure, but there is no known factual basis for his military exploits (l.1291). The inspiration for this aspect of his portrait could well be a literary one – see Introduction, V (c).
**1299** The creation of a bishopric and the choice of bishop were a royal prerogative. Historically, Pope Urban II and the Archbishop of Toledo lent their authority to the consecration of Jerónimo.

After this conversation, they began to make preparations:
My Cid gave a hundred men to Álvar Fáñez
to attend to his needs on the journey,                              1284b
and ordered that one thousand silver marks be taken to San Pedro

and that five hundred should be given to Abbot Don Sancho.

While all rejoiced at the news of this event,
a priest arrived from France —
his name was Bishop Don Jerónimo.
He had studied widely and was very wise,                            1290
and fought well both on foot and on horseback.
He asked about My Cid's deeds,
longing to encounter Moors on the field of battle,
for so long as he were to have his fill of fighting hand to hand
no Christian ever need weep for his death.                         1295
When My Cid heard this he was pleased:
"Listen, Minaya Álvar Fáñez! By our Father on high,
since God wishes to favour us we are grateful to Him.
I wish to create a bishopric in the lands of Valencia
and give it to this good Christian.                                 1300
When you go to Castile, you will carry good news."

Álvar Fáñez was pleased by Don Rodrigo's words.
Now Don Jerónimo was consecrated bishop
and was granted the see of Valencia, through which he could
                                        become very rich.
Lord God, how happy were all Christians                            1305
that in the land of Valencia there was a lord bishop!
In joy, Minaya took his leave and went on his way.

Leaving the land of Valencia in peace,
Minaya Álvar Fáñez made for Castile.
I shall not describe the stages of his journey — I do not wish to
                                        tell of them.               1310
He asked where he could find Alfonso.

fuera el rey a San Fagunt      aun poco ha,
tornos a Carrion,      i lo podrie fallar.
Alegre fue de aquesto      Minaya Albar Fañez;
con esta present[a]ja      adeliño pora alla.      1315

81 De missa era exido      essora el rey Alfonsso;
¡afe Minaya Albar Fañez      do lega tan apuesto!
Finco sos inojos      ante tod el pueblo,
a los pies del rey Alfonsso      cayo con grand duelo,
besava le las manos      e fablo tan apuesto:      1320

82 '¡Merçed, señor Alfonsso,      por amor del Criador!
Besava vos las manos      mio Çid lidiador
los pies e las manos      commo a tan buen señor
quel ayades merçed,      ¡si vos vala el Criador!
Echastes le de tierra,      non ha la vuestra amor;      1325
mager en tierra agena      el bien faze lo so:
ganada a Xerica      e a Ond(r)a por nombre,
priso a Almenar      e a Murviedro que es miyor,
assi fizo Çebolla      e adelant Castejon,
e Peña Cadiella      que es una peña fuert;      1330
con aquestas todas      de Valençia es señor,
obispo fizo de su mano      el buen Campeador
e fizo çinco lides campales      e todas las arranco.
Grandes son las ganançias      quel dio el Criador,
fevos aqui las señas,      verdad vos digo yo:      1335
çient cavallos      gruessos e corredores,
de siellas e de frenos      todos guarnidos son;
besa vos las manos      (e) que los prendades vos,
razonas por vuestro vassallo      e a vos tiene por señor.'
Alço la mano diestra,      el rey se santigo:      1340
'De tan fieras ganançias      commo a fechas el Campeador
¡si me vala Sant Esidro!      plazme de coraçon,
e plazem de las nuevas      que faze el Campeador;
reçibo estos cavallos      quem enbia de don.'

**1312** The king had no fixed court. Alfonso has been staying at the abbey of Sahagún (situated sixty-six kilometres south-east of the city of León) and now has returned to what is represented as being his customary base, at Carrión, capital of the county governed by the powerful Vani-Gómez family (see note to l.1372). It is significant that Alfonso should be shown to have this close association with the home of the Infantes, whose conduct and whose standing with the King are both to be of great importance in the second half of the poem.
**1333** The poet has not described five pitched battles. In the campaign in the Levante the Cid has fought only two – against the people of Valencia and against the King of Seville – and Álvar Fáñez had already told Alfonso of the two earlier victories. It is probable that this is a conventional expression of great military achievement. Compare the detail of the five squires in l.187.
**1342** The remains of Saint Isidore of Seville were transferred to León in 1063 and deposited in the basilica previously dedicated to St John the Baptist; a royal pantheon was constructed, where Fernando I himself agreed to be buried and in which were placed the remains of a number of monarchs including Sancho the Great of

122

The King had gone to Sahagún shortly before
and had returned to Carrión; there he could now be found.
At this, Minaya Álvar Fáñez was filled with joy.
Taking his gifts with him, he went straight to Carrión.          1315

King Alfonso had just come out from mass.
Behold Minaya Álvar Fáñez, arriving in such fine style!
He knelt before all the people,
and fell at King Alfonso's feet in a great show of sorrow;
he kissed his hands and spoke such fine words:                    1320

"A favour, Lord Alfonso, for the love of the Creator!
My Cid the Warrior kisses your hands
and feet, requesting you, as a good lord,
to grant him a favour, may the Creator protect you!
You sent him into exile, and he does not enjoy your love:        1325
though in alien lands he is acting worthily.
He has captured Jérica and the town of Onda;
he has taken Almenar and Murviedro, which is still greater;
and likewise Puig and, further on, Castellón,
and Benicadell on its formidable rock;                           1330
and, still more, he is lord of Valencia.
The good Battler, by his own authority, has created a bishop;
he has fought five pitched battles and won them all.
Great is the booty which the Creator has granted him.
Here is the proof that what I say is true —                      1335
one hundred horses, swift and strong,
all equipped with saddles and bridles;
he humbly asks that you accept them;
he considers himself your vassal and accepts you as his lord.
Raising his right hand, the King made the sign of the cross:     1340
"With the huge gains won by the Battler,
by Saint Isidore, I am profoundly pleased,
and I am delighted to hear of the Battler's deeds;
I accept from him the gift of these horses."

Navarre. The presence of this centre (of both spiritual and secular significance) gave the old imperial city of León
a fresh prestige. It is striking that Alfonso – king originally of León, and against whom the Cid had fought in the
service of the king of Castile – should at this moment invoke the name of this saint; but revealingly, here as at
other points at which St Isidore is mentioned, the context is one in which Alfonso is acting with fairness and
impartiality towards his Castilian vassal – see Introduction, V (c).
**1344** Again it is made clear that the horses are a gift and not a payment due as from vassal to lord.

Mager plogo al rey     mucho peso a Garçi Ordoñez:    1345
'¡Semeja que en tierra de moros     non a bivo omne
quando assi faze a su guisa     el Çid Campeador!'
Dixo el rey al conde:     'Dexad essa razón,
que en todas guisas     mijor me sirve que vos.'
Fablava Minaya i     a guisa de varon:     1350
'Merçed vos pide el Çid,     si vos cayesse en sabor,
por su mugier doña Ximena     e sus fijas amas a dos:
saldrien del monesterio     do elle las dexo
e irien pora Valençia     al buen Campeador.'
Essora dixo el rey:     'Plazme de coraçon;     1355
hyo les mandare dar conducho     mientra que por mi tierra
                                         fueren.
de fonta e de mal     curial[l]as e de desonor;
quando en cabo de mi tierra     aquestas dueñas fueren
catad commo las sirvades     vos y el Campeador.
¡Oid me, escuellas     e toda la mi cort!     1360
Non quiero que nada pierda     el Campeador;
a todas las escuellas     que a el dizen señor
por que los deserede     todo gelo suelto yo;
sirvan le[s] sus her[e]dades     do fuere el Campeador.
Atrego les los cuerpos     de mal e de ocasion,     1365
por tal fago aquesto     que sirvan a so señor.'
Minaya Albar Fañez     las manos le beso;
sonrrisos el rey,     tan velido fablo:
'Los que quisieren ir     se[r]vir al Campeador
de mi sean quitos     e vayan a la graçia del Criador;     1370
mas ganaremos en esto     que en otra desonor.'
Aqui entraron en fabla     los iffantes de Carrion:
'Mucho creçen las nuevas     de mio Çid el Campeador;

---

**1345** García Ordóñez, a Castilian nobleman, was, for a time, commander of King Alfonso's army; he had a distinguished career in the royal service until his death at Uclés in 1108. In 1080, as the result of a conflict over the exaction of tribute from the king of Seville, he had met the Cid in battle, and had been defeated and captured at Cabra. The incident was a celebrated one and is mentioned in the *Carmen Campidoctoris* and recounted in the *Historia Roderici*; it is alluded to later in the *Poema* (ll.3287 ff. and it may well be that the missing opening section of the work tells of how the influence of García Ordóñez, in the months following his humiliation at Cabra, was partly responsible for the banishment of the Cid. Accounts of later events in the two men's careers suggest that there was a lasting hostility between them, and the fame of the Cabra episode in itself furnishes a good reason for the Count's role in the poem as the Cid's adversary. Lacarra (p.147) points out that a marriage in the early years of the twelfth century was to link García Ordóñez's family with the Vani-Gómez clan, of which the Poema's other villains are members.

**1349** The open declaration of warmth towards the Cid, followed by this sharp rebuke to García Ordóñez, is of great significance: the poet has strongly implied that the King's judgement has till now been far from impartial and just, but henceforth Alfonso is to be seen to break free from the influence of his loyal vassal's enemies.

124

Though the King was pleased, García Ordóñez was greatly annoyed.
"It seems that in the land of the Moors there is no one left living,
since our Cid the Battler has everything his own way."
The King said to the Count: "Be silent!
For in any case, he serves me better than you."
Minaya spoke in a noble fashion:                                    1350
"The Cid begs a favour of you, if you are willing to grant it,
on behalf of his wife, Doña Jimena, and their two daughters,
that they may be allowed to depart from the monastery where he
                                        left them
and go to join the good Battler in Valencia."
Then the King said: "Most happily I give my consent.               1355
I shall order them to be provided for as long as they are in my
                                        kingdom,
and shall protect them from all harm, outrage and dishonour.
When these ladies reach the frontier of my kingdom,
see to it that you and the Battler look after them.
Hear me, my vassals and all my court:                              1360
I wish the Battler to lose nothing;
to all vassals who call him their lord
I now return all that I confiscated;
wherever they may go with the Battler, let them remain in
                                        possession of their estates.
I pledge to protect them against all injury.                       1365
I do this that they may serve their lord."
Minaya Álvar Fáñez kissed his hands in thanks;
the king smiled and spoke with such eloquence:
"Those who wish to leave to serve the Battler
I make free of their obligation to me; let them go with the grace
                                        of God;                      1370
we shall gain more from this than by further dishonour."
Then the Infantes of Carrión began to talk together:
"The prestige of My Cid the Battler is increasing greatly;

1372 Rather like the Jews, Raquel and Vidas, the two Infantes are seen huddled together in furtive discussion;
they rarely act independently of each other. Their historical existence and link with the royal court are attested by
the appearance of their names in a number of documents, from 1090 to 1109. They were members of the
illustrious Vani-Gómez (Beni-Gómez or 'sons of Gómez') family, and their uncle, Pedro Ansúrez, was one of the
outstanding generals of his age. Scholars have emphasized the Leonese origins of the Infantes, but Lacarra
(pp.150-57) argues that the Vani-Gómez were essentially a Castilian family, whose descendants in the later
twelfth century were to earn a reputation for treachery by their Leonese alliances.
    The title *Infante* is used here simply to mean a young man of noble family, though in the course of the
thirteenth century it came to be used almost exclusively for those of the royal line.

bien casariemos con sus fijas     pora huebos de pro.
Non la osariemos acometer     nos esta razon;                    1375
¡mio Çid es de Bivar     e nos de los condes de Carrion!'
No lo dizen a nadi     e finco esta razon.
Minaya Albar Fañez     al buen rey se espidio:
'¿Hya vos ides, Minaya?     ¡Id a la graçia del Criador!
Levedes un portero,     tengo que vos avra pro;                  1380
si levaredes las dueñas     sirvan las a su sabor,
fata dentro en Medina     denles quanto huebos les fuer;
desi adelant     piensse dellas el Campeador.'
Espidios Minaya     e vasse de la cort.

83 Los iffantes de Carrion     dando ivan conpaña a Minaya
                                                    Albar Fañez:
'En todo sodes pro,     en esto assi lo fagades:                 1386
saludad nos     a mio Çid el de Bivar,
somos en so pro     quanto lo podemos far;
el Çid que bien nos quiera     nada non perdera.'
Respuso Minaya:     'Esto non me a por que pesar.'               1390
Hido es Minaya,     tornansse los iffantes.
Adeliño pora San Pero     o las dueñas estan,
tan grand fue el gozo     quandol vieron assomar;
deçido es Minaya,     a Ssan Pero va rogar.
Quando acabo la oraçion     a las dueñas se [fue] torn[ar]:      1395
'Omilom, doña Ximena;     ¡Dios vos curie de mal!
¡Assi ffaga     a vuestras fijas amas!
Saluda vos mio Çid     alla ond(d)e elle esta,
sano lo dexe     e con tan grand rictad.
El rey por su merçed     sueltas me vos ha                       1400
por levaros a Valençia     que avemos por heredad.
Si vos viesse el Çid     sanas e sin mal
todo serie alegre     que non avrie ningun pesar.'
Dixo doña Ximena:     '¡El Criador lo mande!'
Dio tres cavalleros     Minaya Albar Fañez,                      1405
enviolos a mio Çid     a Valençia do esta:

---

1375-76 The Infantes wish to keep their intention secret because of their acute awareness of the difference
between their origins and those of the Cid. They stress the contrast between the Cid's estates in the village of
Vivar and their family's much more distinguished inheritance in the town of Carrión. They are impressed by the
signs of the Cid's wealth, but there is already a strong hint of their excessive pride in their own exalted birth.
1382 The city of Medinaceli, commanding the descent into the Ebro valley, had recently been conquered by
Alfonso and marked the limit of his kingdom.
1401 Valencia is seen as the permanent possession of the Cid and his family, a source of income and a token of
their future security. For the terminology used here there is a parallel in a document summarized in the *Historia
Roderici*, conceding lands to the Cid *iure hereditario*.

we would do well to marry his daughters for our own gain.          1375
We would not dare broach this affair,
for My Cid is from Vivar and we are of the line of Carrión."
They told no one and the matter rested.
Minaya Álvar Fáñez took leave of the good King.
"Are you leaving now, Minaya?  May the grace of the Creator go
                          with you!
Take with you an official of the court, I think he will be of service
                          to you.          1380
While you accompany the ladies, ensure that they are given every
                          attention;
until you reach Medinaceli, they are to be given all they need;
from there on, let the Battler take responsibility for them."
Minaya took his leave and departed from the court.

The Infantes of Carrión rode out with Minaya Álvar Fáñez:          1385
"You are obliging in all things, be so in this matter:
give our greetings to My Cid of Vivar,
we will both do for him all that we can.
If the Cid gives us his friendship it will not be to his disadvantage."
Minaya replied: "This will be no trouble."          1390
He rode off and the Infantes turned back.
Minaya made straight for San Pedro, where the ladies were to be
                          found;
so great was the joy on his appearance.
Minaya dismounted and went in to pray to Saint Peter.
On finishing his prayer, he went to meet the ladies:          1395
"I offer my humble respect, Doña Jimena; may God keep you
                          from harm!
And so too may he protect your two daughters!
From Valencia, My Cid offers you greeting.
I left him in good health and enjoying great riches.
The King, in his mercy, has granted that I take you with me,          1400
and accompany you to Valencia which is ours to be an inheritance.
If the Cid saw you healthy and unharmed
he would be so happy that his troubles would be no more."
Doña Jimena replied: "May the Creator be pleased that it should
                          be so!"
Minaya Álvar Fáñez sent three knights          1405
to My Cid waiting in Valencia:

'Dezid al Canpeador    —¡que Dios le curie de mal!—
que su mugier e sus fijas    el rey sueltas me las ha;
mientra que fueremos por sus tierras    conducho nos mando
dar.
De aquestos .xv. dias    —si Dios nos curiare de mal—    1410
seremos yo e su mugier    e sus fijas que el a
hy todas las dueñas con ellas    quantas buenas ellas han.'
Hidos son los cavalleros    e dello penssaran;
remaneçio en San Pero    Minaya Albar Fañez.
Veriedes cavalleros    venir de todas partes,    1415
hir se quieren a Valençia    a mio Çid el de Bivar,
que les toviesse pro    rogavan a Albar Fañez;
diziendo est[a] Mi(a)naya:    'Esto fere de veluntad.'
A Minaya .lxv. cavalleros    acreçidol han
y el sẽ tenie c.    que aduxiera d'alla;    1420
por ir con estas dueñas    buena conpaña se faze.
Los quinientos marcos    dio Minaya al abbat;
de los otros quinientos    dezir vos he que faze:
Minaya a doña Ximina    e a sus fijas que ha
e a las otras dueñas    que las sirven delant    1425
el bueno de Minaya    pensolas de adobar
de los mejores guarnimientos    que en Burgos pudo falar,
palafres e mulas,    que non parescan mal.
Quando estas dueñas    adobadas las han
el bueno de Minaya    penssar quiere de cavalgar.    1430
Afevos Rachel e Vidas    a los pies le caen:
'¡Merçed, Minaya,    cavallero de prestar!
Desfechos nos ha el Çid    sabet, si no nos val;
soltariemos la ganançia    que nos diesse el cabdal.'
'Hyo lo vere con el Çid    si Dios me lieva ala;    1435
por lo que avedes fecho    buen cosiment i avra.'
Dixo Rachel e Vidas:    '¡El Criador lo mande!
Si non, dexaremos Burgos,    ir lo hemos buscar.'
Hido es pora San Pero    Minaya Albar Fañez;
muchas yentes sele acogen,    pensso de cavalgar.    1440
Grand duelo es    al partir del abbat:
'¡Si vos vala el Criador    Minaya Albar Fañez!
Por mi al Campeador    las manos le besad;

"Tell the Battler — May God protect him from harm! —
that his wife and daughters have been released by the King into
my care.
He has commanded that we be provided for as long as we are
within his kingdom.
Within fifteen days, if God protects us from harm,                    1410
I shall be at his side, with his wife and daughters
and all the good ladies who accompany them."
The knights left to carry out the task entrusted to them;
Minaya Álvar Fáñez remained at San Pedro.
You could see knights arriving from all directions,                   1415
wanting to go to Valencia to My Cid, the man from Vivar.
They begged Álvar Fáñez to give them his support,
and he replied: "I will do so willingly."
Sixty - five more knights had joined Minaya,
and he also had the hundred that he had brought from Valencia.   1420
They formed a fine escort for the ladies.
Minaya gave the abbot the five hundred marks;
I shall tell you what he did with the other five hundred.
For Doña Jimena and her daughters
and the other ladies who served them,                               1425
good Minaya set about providing
the richest garments and trimmings that he could find in Burgos,
together with palfreys and mules, that they should appear in proper
dignity.
When the ladies had been prepared for the journey,
good Minaya made ready to ride on his way.                           1430
Look, here are Raquel and Vidas falling at his feet!
"A favour, Minaya, worthy knight!
Unless he helps us now, the Cid has ruined us;
we would forget about the interest, if only he would give us back
the capital."
"I will ask the Cid about it, if God takes me safely to him;          1435
there will be a good reward for what you have done!"
Raquel and Vidas said: "May the Creator be willing!
If not, we shall leave Burgos and go in search of him."
Minaya Álvar Fáñez set off for San Pedro.
Many men came and joined his company; he prepared to ride off.
Great was the sorrow of the abbot when they left:
"May the Creator protect you, Minaya Álvar Fáñez!
Ask the Cid a favour on my behalf —

129

aqueste monesterio    no lo quiera olbidar,
todos los dias del sieglo    en levar lo adelant    1445
el Çid    siempre valdra mas.'
Respuso Minaya :    '¡Fer lo he de veluntad !'
Hyas espiden    e pienssan de cavalgar,
el portero con ellos    que los ha de aguardar;
por la tierra del rey    mucho conducho les dan.    1450

De San Pero fasta Medina    en .v. dias van;
felos en Medina    las dueñas e Albar Fañez.
Direvos de los cavalleros    que levaron el menssaje :
al ora que lo sopo    mio Çid el de Bivar
plogol de coraçon    e tornos a alegrar,    1455
de la su boca    conpeço de fablar :
'¡Qui buen mandadero enbia    tal deve sperar !
Tu, Muño Gustioz    e Pero Vermuez delant
e Martin Antolinez    un burgales leal,
el obispo don Jeronimo    coronado de prestar,    1460
cavalg edes con çiento    guisados pora huebos de lidiar;
por Santa Maria    vos vayades passar,
vayades a Molina    que yaze mas adelant,
tienela Avengalvon    —mio amigo es de paz—
con otros çiento cavalleros    bien vos conssigra;    1465
hid pora Medina    quanto lo pudieredes far;
mi mugier e mis fijas    con Minaya Albar Ffañez
asi commo a mi dixieron    hi los podredes falar,
con grand ondra    aduzid melas delant.
E yo fincare en Valençia    que mucho costadom ha,    1470
gran locura serie    si la desenparas;
yo ffincare en Valençia    ca la tengo por heredad.'
Esto era dicho,    pienssan de cavalgar
e quanto que pueden    non fincan de andar.
Troçieron a Santa Maria    e vinieron albergar a Fron[chales],
y el otro dia vinieron    a Molina posar.    1476
El moro Avengalvon    quando sopo el menssaje
saliolos reçebir    con grant gozo que faze :
'¿Venides, los vassallos    de mio amigo natural?
¡A mi non me pesa    sabet, mucho me plaze !'    1480
Fablo Muño Gustioz,    non spero a nadi :
'Mio Çid vos saludava    e mandolo recabdar

1464 Molina was in Moorish hands until at least 1126 and the name of Abengalbón seems to coincide with that of the last (Ibn Galbūn) of its Moslem rulers – kings in their own right, but paying tribute to Valencia. No historical account, however, mentions an association between the Cid and any of the lords of Molina. Lacarra (pp.197-201) explains the prominent role of this city in the *Poema* by further reference to the struggles between the Laras and the Castros in the twelfth century (see Introduction, II, and note 6), pointing out that in 1164 a Castilian lord of Molina was killed by a member of the Castro family, and that by the end of the century the city was in the hands of the Laras.
1482-86 Though Abengalbón has been described as the Cid's friend, it is clear that he is in fact his tributary.

130

that he does not forget this monastery.
In continuing to give it for ever his protection, 1445
the Cid will always increase his own prestige."
Minaya replied: "I will do so willingly!"
Now they took their leave and rode off,
with them the court official who was to ensure their safety;
throughout the King's lands they were richly provided for. 1450
They went from San Pedro to Medinaceli in five days.
Now here are the ladies and Álvar Fáñez in Medinaceli.
I shall tell you about the knights who carried the message:
when My Cid of Vivar learned what had happened,
he was filled with happiness and rejoiced again; 1455
these words were on his lips:
"The man who sends a good messenger must expect such success!
You, Muño Gustioz, and you too, Pedro Bermúdez,
and Martín Antolínez, loyal man of Burgos,
and Bishop Don Jerónimo, worthy priest, 1460
ride out with a hundred men equipped for battle;
pass through the town of Albarracín
and carry on as far as Molina,
governed by Abengalbón, my friend, with whom I am at peace,
and he will accompany you with a further one hundred knights. 1465
Ride towards Medinaceli, as fast as you can;
meet my wife and daughters with Minaya Álvar Fáñez,
as I have been told you will be able to find them there,
and escort them to me in great honour.
And I shall remain in Valencia, which I won only after a great struggle.
It would be great folly were I to abandon it.
I shall remain in Valencia, for I consider it my property."
When these words were spoken, they set off,
and for as long as they could, they rode without a halt.
They passed through Albarracín and rested that night at Bronchales,
and the following day they halted at Molina.
The Moor Abengalbón, when he learned of their mission,
went out to meet them, rejoicing greatly.
"So, you are vassals of my close friend?
I feel not sorrow at this, I can tell you, but great joy!" 1480
Muño Gustioz spoke immediately:
"My Cid greets you and commands us to arrange

obeying a command. See also ll. 1523-26, which indicate that the Moor is motivated not only by friendship but also by other, more pragmatic, concerns.

131

con çiento cavalleros    que privadol acorrades.
Su mugier e sus fijas    en Medina estan;
que vayades por ellas,    adugades gelas aca      1485
e ffata en Valençia    dellas non vos partades.'
Dixo Avengalvon:    '¡Fer lo he de veluntad!'
Essa noch    conducho les dio grand;
a la mañana    pienssan de cavalgar;
çientol pidieron    mas el con dozientos va.      1490
Passan las montañas    que son fieras e grandes,
passaron Mata de Toranz    de tal guisa que ningun miedo
non han,
por el val de Arbux[uel]o    pienssan a deprunar.
Y en Medina    todo el recabdo esta:
envio dos cavalleros Minaya Albar Fañez    que sopiessen la
verdad,
esto non detardan    ca de coraçon lo han;      1496
el uno finco con ellos    y el otro torno a Albar Fañez:
'Virtos del Campeador    a nos vienen buscar;
Afevos aqui Pero Vermuez e Muño Gustioz    que vos quieren
sin hart,
e Martin Antolinez    el burgales natural      1500
y el obispo don Jeronimo    cor[o]nado leal,
y el alcayaz Avengalvon    con sus fuerças que trahe
por sabor de mio Çid    de grand ondral dar;
todos vienen en uno,    agora legaran.'
Essora dixo Minaya:    '¡Vay[a]mos cavalgar!'      1505
Esso ffue a priessa fecho    que nos quieren detardar;
bien salieron den çiento    que non pareçen mal,
en buenos cavallos    a petrales e a cascaveles
e a cuberturas de çendales    y escudos a los cuellos
y en las manos lanças    que pendones traen,      1510
que sopie(n)ssen los otros    de que seso era Albar Fañez
o cuemo saliera de Castiella    Albar Fañez con estas dueñas
que trahe.
Los que ivan mesurando    e legando delant
luego toman armas    e tomanse a deportar;
por çerca de Salon    tan grandes gozos van.      1515
Don legan los otros    a Minaya Albar Fañez se van homilar.
Quando lego Avengalvon    dont a ojo [lo] ha
sonrrisando se de la boca    hivalo abraçar,
en el ombro lo saluda    ca tal es su husaje:
'¡Tan buen dia con vusco    Minaya Albar Fañez!      1520
Traedes estas dueñas    por o valdremos mas,
mugier del Çid lidiador    e ssus ffijas naturales;

---

**1509** A knight's shield, large and cumbersome, would be fitted with straps so that it might be carried from the neck. In battle it would be held in the hand, but it would remain fastened to the neck.

that you accompany us at once with one hundred knights;
his wife and daughters are in Medinaceli.
He wishes you to go to them and escort them here                    1485
and then remain with them till you reach Valencia."
Abengalbón said: "I will do so willingly."
That night he gave them a great feast;
the next morning they rode on their way;
they had asked him for a hundred men, but he took two hundred. 1490
They passed through the forests, dense and forbidding,
crossed fearlessly the scrublands of Taranz,
and began to descend through the valley of the Arbujuelo.
In Medinaceli, every precaution was being taken;
Minaya Álvar Fáñez sent two knights to find out what was going on.
They wasted no time, for their hearts were in what they did;
one remained with the escort and the other returned to Álvar Fáñez:
"Soldiers from the Battler have come to fetch us.
Here come Pedro Bermúdez and Muño Gustioz, who sincerely love you,
Martín Antolínez, native of Burgos,                                 1500
and Bishop Don Jerónimo, loyal priest,
and the governor, Abengalbón, who brings his troops,
such is his desire to honour My Cid.
They are all coming together, and will very soon arrive."
Then Minaya said: "Let us ride to meet them!"                       1505
It was quickly done — they wanted to waste no time.
A good hundred of them rode out, elegant in appearance,
mounted on fine horses with armour and bells,
draped in fine silk; they carried shields from their necks,
and in their hands were lances bearing pennants;                    1510
Álvar Fáñez intended that the others should see what he could
                                        accomplish,
and in what style he was bringing these ladies from Castile.
Then the men who went ahead, surveying the land,
took up their arms to display their prowess,
so great was the rejoicing along the Jalón.                         1515
As soon as the others arrived, they humbled themselves before Minaya;
once Abengalbón had come within sight of Minaya,
he smiled and drew near to embrace him,
kissing him on the shoulder, as was his custom.
"Praised be the day on which I have met you, Minaya Álvar Fáñez!
Because you have brought these ladies, the wife of the warrior Cid
and his natural daughters, we gain in honour.

ondrar vos hemos todos     ca tal es la su auze,
mager que mal le queramos     non gelo podremos f[a]r,
en paz o en gerra     de lo nuestro abra;     1525
muchol tengo por torpe     qui non conosçe la verdad.'

84  Sorrisos  de la boca     Minaya Albar Fañez:

'¡Hy[a] Avengalvon     amigol sodes sin falla!
Si Dios me legare al Çid     e lo vea con el alma
desto que avedes fecho     vos non perderedes nada.     1530
Vayamos posar     ca la çena es adobada.'
Dixo Avengalvon:     'Plazme desta presentaja,
antes deste te[r]çer dia     vos la dare doblada.'
Entraron en Medina,     sirvialos Minaya;
todos fueron alegres     del çervicio que tomar[a]n.     1535
El portero del rey     quitar lo mandava;
ondrado es mio Çid     en Valençia do estava
de tan grand conducho     commo en Medinal sacar[a]n:
el rey lo pago todo     e quito se va Minaya.
Passada es la noche,     venida es la mañana,     1540
oida es la missa     e luego cavalgavan;
salieron de Medina     e Salon passavan,
Arbuxuelo arriba     privado aguijavan,
el campo de Torançio     luegol atravessavan,
vinieron a Molina     la que Avengalvon mandava.     1545
El obispo don Jheronimo     —buen christiano sin falla—
las noches e los dias     las dueñas aguarda[va],
e buen cavallo en diestro     que va ante sus armas,
entre el e Albar Fañez     hivan a una compaña.
Entrados son a Molina,     buena e rica casa;     1550
el moro Avengalvon     bien los sirvie sin falla,
de quanto que quisieron     non ovieron falla,
aun las ferraduras     quitar gelas mandava;
a Minaya e a las dueñas     ¡Dios, commo las ondrava!
Otro dia mañana     luego cavalgavan;     1555
faṭa en Valençia     sirvialos sin falla,
lo so despendie el moro     que del[l]os non tomava nada.
Con estas alegrias     e nuevas tan ondradas
apres son de Valençia     a tres leguas contadas.

1536 Alfonso, by his attention to the Cid's family and those who accompany them, has made quite clear the
warmth with which he now regards his exiled subject, and has prepared the way for the reconciliation which is
soon to take place.
1548 The bishop has a team of three horses: the palfrey, on which he rides, the war-horse, which is led along on his
right-hand side by a squire, and a pack-animal carrying his arms.

134

We shall all honour you, for such is his prestige.
Even if we had no love for him we could do him no harm;
he will have a share of what is ours in time of peace or of war. 1525
I consider very foolish anyone who does not recognize the truth of this."

Minaya Álvar Fáñez smiled:

"Abengalbón, you are a devoted friend to him.
If God brings me back into the presence of the Cid and I live to
                              see him again,
by what you have done, you will not lose.                         1530
Let us go and rest, the meal has been prepared."
Abengalbón said: "I am grateful for this welcome;
before three days have passed I shall repay it twice over."
They entered Medinaceli and Minaya saw their needs were met;
all were grateful for the attention they received.              1535
The King's official ordered it all to be paid for.
My Cid, who had remained in Valencia, was honoured
by the great banquet that was served to his men in Medinaceli.
The King paid for it all, and Minaya suffered no expense.
Night had passed and morning had come;                          1540
after hearing mass, they rode on their way;
they left Medinaceli and crossed the river Jalón,
spurring on rapidly up the valley of the Arbujuelo;
then they crossed the scrublands of Taranz,
and came to Molina, where Abengalbón was governor.             1545
Bishop Don Jerónimo, a fine and true Christian,        —— crusadyr
was watching over the ladies night and day,                    pruest
a fine war horse to his right, his arms carried after him.
He and Álvar Fáñez rode together.
They entered Molina, a fine, rich town.                         1550
The Moor Abengalbón served them impeccably
and saw that they wanted for nothing;
he even paid for the horses to be reshod.
Lord God, what honour he paid to Minaya and the ladies!
The next morning they rode on their way again.                 1555
As far as Valencia, Abengalbón attended them faithfully;
the Moor paid for everything and took nothing from them.
Amidst this joy and honour
they came within just three leagues of the city of Valencia.

85 A mio Çid    el que en buen ora nasco       1560
    dentro a Valençia    lievan le el mandado;
    alegre fue mio Çid    que nunqua mas nin tanto
    ca de lo que mas amava    yàl viene el mandado.
    Dozi[en]tos cavalleros    mando exir privado
    que reçiban a Mi(a)naya    e a las dueñas fijas dalgo;   1565
    el sedie en Valençia    curiando e guardando
    ca bien sabe que Albar Fañez    trahe todo recabdo.

86 Afevos todos aquestos    reçiben a Minaya
    e a las dueñas e a las niñas    e a las otras conpañas.
    Mando mio Çid    a los que ha en su casa      1570
    que guardassen el alcaçar    e las otras torres altas
    e todas las puertas    e las exidas e las entradas,
    e aduxiessen le a Bavieca    —poco avie quel ganara,
    aun non sabie mio Çid    el que en buen ora çinxo espada
    si serie corredor    o ssi abrie buena parada—;   1575
    a la puerta de Valençia    do fuesse en so salvo
    delante su mugier e de sus fijas    querie tener las armas.
    Reçebidas las dueñas    a una grant ondrança
    el obispo don Jheronimo    adelant se entrava,
    i dexava el cavallo,    pora la capiella adeliñava;   1580
    con quantos que el puede    que con oras se acordar[a]n,
    sobrepeliças vestidas    e con cruzes de plata,
    reçibir salien las dueñas    e al bueno de Minaya.
    El que en buen ora nasco    non lo detardava;
    ensiellan le a Bavieca,    cuberturas le echavan,   1585
    mio Çid salio sobr'el    e armas de fuste tomava;
    vistios el sobregonel;    luenga trahe la barba;
    por nombre el cavallo    Bavieca cavalga;   1589
    fizo una corrida;    esta fue tan estraña   1588
    quando ovo corrido    todos se maravillavan;   1590
    des dia se preçio Bavieca    en quant grant fue España.
    En cabo del cosso    mio Çid desca[va]lgava,
    adeliño a su mugier    e a sus fijas amas.
    Quando lo vio doña Ximena    a pies se le echava:

---

**1566** The Cid's caution reminds us that Valencia is a conquered and occupied city and that there may still be danger for the Christians. See also the strict precautions taken before the Cid's departure for Castile (ll. 1999 ff.)
**1573** It is natural that an epic hero should be shown to possess an outstanding mount. Nothing is recorded of any of the horses which in history belonged to the Cid, and there is no known mention of Babieca in any work, historical or literary, before his appearance in the *Poema*. However, he is said to have been buried at Cardeña; and certainly he figures quite prominently in later legend and in ballad tradition.
**1581** The sense of this line is not clear. We have taken *oras* as an allusion to the canonical hours, the daily routine of prayer requiring the presence of a certain number of priests. Menéndez Pidal, however, interprets the meaning as 'those priests who had made ready in time'.

To My Cid, the man born in a favoured hour,                          1560
came the message into Valencia.
Joyful was My Cid, more so than ever before,
for now news had come of the matter so dear to him.
He commanded two hundred knights to ride out quickly
to welcome Minaya and the noble ladies.                             1565
He remained in Valencia to ensure that all was well.
He knew that Álvar Fáñez had the situation well in hand.

Now see how they all greet Minaya,
the ladies, the girls and the rest of the company.
My Cid commanded that his followers                                 1570
should keep guard over the citadel and the other tall towers,
and all the gates, and the ways in and out,
and that they should bring him Babieca, whom he had recently won.
My Cid, who girded his sword in a favoured hour, did not yet know
how swift he would be or if he would respond well to the bit.       1575
At the gate of Valencia, where he could be in safety,
he wanted to give a display of arms to his wife and daughters.
When the ladies had been received with great honour,
Bishop Don Jerónimo rode ahead
and, dismounting, made for the chapel:                              1580
with all those priests who could be free from their devotions,
wearing surplices and carrying silver crosses,
he went out to welcome the ladies and good Minaya.
The man born in a favoured hour did not delay.
Babieca was saddled and given full harness;                        1585
My Cid rode out on him and took up wooden jousting weapons.
He wore a tunic and allowed his beard to flow freely.
On the horse called Babieca                                         1589
he rode at a gallop; the speed of the horse was so wonderful       1588
that when the ride was finished all were filled with amazement;    1590
from that day on, Babieca's worth was known throughout all Spain.
At the end of the ride, My Cid dismounted,
and went towards his wife and their two daughters.
When Doña Jimena saw him she threw herself at his feet:

'¡Merçed, Campeador    en buen ora çinxiestes espada!  1595
Sacada me avedes    de muchas verguenças malas;
afe me aqui, señor,    yo [e] vuestras fijas amas,
con Dios e con vusco    buenas son e criadas.'
A la madre e a las fijas    bien las abraçava,
del gozo que avien    de los sos ojos loravan.    1600
Todas las sus mesnadas    en grant dele[i]t estavan,
armas teniendo    e tablados quebrantando
Oid que dixo    el que en buen ora nasco:
'Vos [doña Ximena]    querida mugier e ondrada,
e amas mis fijas    mi coraçon e mi alma,    1605
entrad comigo    en Valençia la casa,
en esta heredad,    que vos yo he ganada.'
Madre e fijas    las manos le besavan;
a tan grand ondra    ellas a Valençia entravan.

87  Adeliño mio Çid    con ellas al alcaçar    1610
    ala las subie    en el mas alto logar.
    Ojos velidos    catan a todas partes,
    miran Valençia    commo yaze la çibdad
    e del otra parte    a ojo han el mar;
    miran la huerta    espessa es e grand;    1615
    alçan las manos    por a Dios rogar
    desta ganançia    commo es buena e grand.
    Mio Çid e sus compañas    tan a grand sabor estan.
    El ivierno es exido    que el março quiere entrar.
    Dezir vos quiero nuevas    de alent partes del mar,    1620
    de aquel rey Yuçef    que en Marruecos esta.

88  Pesol al rey de Marruecos    de mio Çid don Rodrigo:
    '¡Que en mis heredades    fuerte mientre es metido
    y el non gelo gradeçe    si non a Jhesu Christo!'
    Aquel rey de Marruecos    ajuntava sus virtos,    1625
    con .l. vezes mill de armas    todos fueron conplidos;
    entraron sobre mar,    en las barcas son metidos,

1596 There is no indication in the *Poema* of the nature of this dishonour, but the *Historia Roderici* furnishes a possible explanation, telling how, on the occasion of the Cid's second banishment, the King ordered Jimena to be 'cruelly imprisoned'.

1602 The *tablados* consisted of scaffolding covered with boards, against which the knights would tilt. This was a very popular pastime during such celebrations and is mentioned in a number of medieval Spanish texts.

1610 ff. Smith has argued that a number of details in this scene were suggested to the poet by the French epic *Berte aus grans piés* (see *The Making* ..., pp.161-62 and *Estudios cidianos*, pp.141-42).

1620 ff. Following the capture of Valencia, Spanish Moslems, notably those of the cities of the Levante, again asked Yusuf for help. In late summer 1094, a huge army, reinforced by troops from the cities of Andalusia, marched on Valencia. This was not, however, the Africans' first intervention in the affairs of Valencia, which had been in Almoravid hands for some months in 1092-93. Indeed, before the capture of the city by the Cid, a force sent from Africa had come within fifteen kilometres and withdrawn in the face of the Christian army.

138

"I thank you, Battler, who girded your sword in a
                                    favoured hour!                          1595
You have saved me from very great dishonour.
Behold myself, my lord, and your two daughters,
fine girls, well instructed to serve you and God."
He embraced warmly both the mother and the daughters;
such was their joy that tears flowed from their eyes.              1600
All My Cid's vassals were overjoyed;
they jousted and attacked the mock castles.
Hear what was said by the man who girded his sword in a
                                    favoured hour:
"You, Doña Jimena, my dear and honoured wife,
and my two daughters, my heart and my soul,                      1605
come with me into the city of Valencia,
into this inheritance which I have won for you."
Mother and daughters kissed his hands in thanks,
and in such great honour they entered Valencia.

My Cid goes with them to the citadel                                     1610
and takes them up to the highest point.
Their beautiful eyes gaze about them;
they see how the city of Valencia lies,
and in the opposite direction they look upon the sea.
They see the plantations, thick and extensive,                       1615
and raise their hands to praise God
for all that they have gained, so rich and plentiful.
My Cid and his followers are well satisfied.
Winter is over, it is the beginning of March.
I want to tell you of events beyond the sea,                          1620
of the renowned Emir Yusuf in Morocco.

The Emir of Morocco was aggrieved at the deeds of My Cid
                                    Don Rodrigo:
"That he should strike so deeply into my lands
and praise only Jesus Christ for his success!"
The renowned Emir of Morocco gathered his forces,              1625
and with a full fifty thousand soldiers
embarked and set sail

van buscar a Valençia     a mio Çid don Rodrigo.
Arribado an las naves,     fuera eran exidos.

89 Legaron a Valençia     la que mio Çid a conquista;     1630
fincaron las tiendas     e posan las yentes descreidas.
Estas nuevas     a mio Çid eran venidas:

90 '¡Grado al Criador     e a[l] Padre espirital!
Todo el bien que yo he     todo lo tengo delant;
con afan gane a Valençia     y ela por heredad,     1635
a menos de muert     no la puedo dexar.
¡Grado al Criador     e a Santa Maria madre
mis fijas e mi mugier     que las tengo aca!
Venidom es deliçio     de tierras d'alent mar;
entrare en las armas,     non lo podre dexar;     1640
mis fijas e mi mugier     verme an lidiar,
en estas tierras agenas     veran las moradas commo se fazen,
¡afarto veran por los ojos     commo se gana el pan!'
Su mugier e sus fijas     subiolas al alcaçar,
alçavan los ojos,     tiendas vieron fincadas:     1645
'¿Ques esto, Çid?     ¡Si el Criador vos salve!'
'¡Ya mugier ondrada     non ayades pesar!
Riqueza es que nos acreçe     maravillosa e grand;
¡a poco que viniestes     presend vos quieren dar;
por casar son vuestras fijas:     aduzen vos axuvar!'     1650
'¡A vos grado, Çid,     e al Padre spirital!'
'Mugier, sed en este palaçio,     e si quisieredes en el alcaçar.
Non ayades pavor     por que me veades lidiar;
con la merçed de Dios     e de Santa Maria madre
creçem el córaçon     por que estades delant;     1655
¡con Dios aquesta lid     yo la he de arrancar!'

91 Fincadas son las tiendas     e pareçen los alvores,
a una grand priessa     tañien los atamores;
alegravas mio Çid e dixo:     '¡Tan buen dia es oy!'
Miedo a su mugier     e quierel quebrar el coraçon,     1660
assi ffazie a las dueñas     e a sus fijas amas a dos;
del dia que nasquieran     non vieran tal tremor.

---

1657 The Moslem army camped on the plain of Cuarte, five kilometres to the west of Valencia. The battle of
Cuarte was to prove the first defeat of an Almoravid army in pitched battle in Spain.

140

and made for Valencia in search of My Cid Don Rodrigo.
The ships reached the shore and the army disembarked.

They came to Valencia which My Cid had conquered;       1630
the infidels pitched camp and waited.
News of this came to My Cid:

"Thanks be to God, to the heavenly Father!
All that I possess I have before me:
after a great struggle I won Valencia, and I hold it as my inheritance.
Unless I die, I shall not relinquish it.
thanks be to the Creator and to Saint Mary the Holy Mother
that I have my daughters and my wife here with me!
Good fortune has come to me from beyond the sea;
I shall take up arms, it must be so.       1640
My daughters and my wife will see me fight.
They will see what life is like in these alien lands.
With their own eyes they shall see full well how we earn our bread."
He took his wife and daughters up to the citadel;
they looked out and saw the land covered with tents.       1645
"What is this, Cid?  May the Creator save you!"
"Now, do not be alarmed, by noble wife!
We are to gain wonderful and great riches;
you have hardly arrived and they want to make you gifts!
Your daughters are of age to be married and they are bringing
                    you a dowry!"       1650
"I thank you, Cid, and the Holy Father as well!"
"My wife, stay in the palace and, if you wish, go up into the tower.
Do not be afraid to see me fight;
with God's mercy and that of Saint Mary the Holy Mother,
my heart swells with pride because you are present.       1655
With God's aid I shall win this battle."


The tents had been pitched; dawn broke;
the drums beat furiously.
My Cid spoke joyfully: "What a day this is!"
His wife was so terrified it seemed her heart would burst,       1660
and so too were her ladies and her two daughters.
Since the day of their birth they had never heard such a
                    thunderous noise.

141

Prisos a la barba     el buen Çid Campeador:
'Non ayades miedo     ca todo es vuestra pro;
antes destos .xv. dias     si plogiere a[l] Criador     1665
aquelos atamores a vos los pondran delant     e veredes
                                                    qua(n)les son,
desi an a sser     del obispo don Jheronimo,
colgar los han en Santa Maria     madre del Criador.'
Vocaçion es que fizo     el Çid Campeador.
Alegre[s] son las dueñas,     perdiendo van el pavor.     1670
Los moros de Marruecos     cavalgan a vigor
por las huertas adentro     estan sines pavor.

92 Violo el atalaya     e tanxo el esquila;
prestas son las mesnadas     de las yentes christianas,
adoban se de coraçon     e dan salto de la villa;     1675
dos fallan con los moros     cometien los tan aina,
sacan los de las huertas     mucho a fea guisa,
quinientos mataron dellos     conplidos en es dia.

93 Bien fata las tiendas     dura aqueste alcaz;
mucho avien fecho,     pienssan de cavalgar;     1680
Albar Salvadorez     preso finco alla.
Tornados son a mio Çid     los que comien so pan,
el selo vio con los ojos,     cuentan gelo delant.
Alegre es mio Çid     por quanto fecho han:
'¡Oid me, cavalleros,     non rastara por al!     1685
Oy es dia bueno     e mejor sera cras;
por la mañana prieta     todos armados seades,
el obispo don Jheronimo     soltura nos dara,     1689
dezir nos ha la missa,     e penssad de cavalgar.     1688
¡Hir los hemos fferir     en el nombre del Criador e del apostol
                                                    Santi Yague;     1690
mas vale que nos los vezcamos     que ellos cojan el pan!'
Essora dixieron todos:     '¡D'amor e de voluntad!'
Fablava Minaya,     non lo quiso detardar:
'Pues esso queredes     Çid, a mi mandedes al:
dadme cxxx. cavalleros     pora huebos de lidiar;     1695
quando vos los fueredes ferir     entrare yo del otra part,
o de amas o del una     Dios nos valdra.'
Essora dixo el Çid:     '¡De buena voluntad!'

1682 The Cid's vassals are described literally as 'those who ate his bread', an expression with numerous parallels in other literary works and also in contemporary legal documents.

142

The Cid, the good Battler, stroked his beard:
"Do not fear, for all is in your favour;
before fifteen days are over, if the Creator wills it so,      1665
those drums will be set before you that you may see what they
                                        are like.
Then they will be given to Bishop Don Jerónimo,
and will be hung in the church of Saint Mary Mother of the Creator."
My Cid the Battler made this vow.
The ladies, in their joy, gradually lost their fear.            1670
The Moors of Morocco rode swiftly in
through the plantations; they were without fear.


The look—out saw them come and rang the alarm,
The Christian troops made ready;
bravely they armed and marched out from the city.              1675
When they encountered the Moors, they were quick to attack.
In brutal conflict they drove them out of the plantations,
killing a full five hundred of them that day.


That pursuit extended as far as the tents;
they had achieved much and rode back.                          1680
Álvar Salvadórez remained behind, a captive.
The vassals of My Cid, sharers of his food, returned to their lord.
They told him of the fight, though he had seen it with his own eyes.
My Cid was delighted with all that they had done:
"Hear me, my knights, the only way is by fighting.             1685
Today is a good day and tomorrow will be better still.
You are all to be armed before day breaks.
Bishop Don Jerónimo will give us absolution;                   1689
he will say mass for us, then you are to ride out.             1688
We shall go and strike them in the name of the Creator and Saint
                                James the Apostle.             1690
It is better that we defeat them than allow them to take our food."
Then they all said: "So be it, we wish it with all our heart."
Minaya spoke, wishing to waste no time:
"Since that is what you want, My Cid, give me a different task.
Give me a hundred and thirty knights to fight with me;         1695
when you go to strike the enemy, I shall attack from the other
                                direction;
either on one side or on both, God will give us his aid."
Then the Cid replied: "Willingly."

**94** El dia es salido     e la noche entrada es.

> Nos detardan de adobasse     essas yentes christianas.     1700
> A los mediados gallos     antes de la mañana
> el obispo don Jheronimo     la missa les cantava;
> la missa dicha     grant sultura les dava:
> 'El que aqui muriere     lidiando de cara
> prendol yo los pecados     e Dios le abra el alma.     1705
> A vos, Çid don Rodrigo     —¡en buen ora çinxiestes espada!—
> hyo vos cante la missa     por aquesta mañana;
> pido vos un don     e seam presentado:
> las feridas primeras     que las aya yo otorgadas.'
> Dixo el Campeador:     'Des aqui vos sean mandadas.'     1710

> Salidos son todos armados     por las torres de Va[le]nçia.

**95** Mio Çid a los sos vassalos     tan bien los acordando,
> dexan a las puertas     omnes de grant recabdo.
> Dio salto mio Çid     en Bavieca el so cavallo,
> de todas guarnizones     muy bien es adobado.     1715
> La seña sacan fuera,     de Valençia dieron salto,
> quatro mill menos .xxx.     con mio Çid van a cabo,
> a los cinquaenta mill     van los ferir de grado.
> Alvar Alvarez     e Minaya Albar Fañez
> entraron les     del otro cabo;     1720
> plogo al Criador     e ovieron de arrancarlos.
> Mio Çid enpleo la lança,     al espada metio mano,
> atantos mata de moros     que non fueron contados,
> por el cobdo ayuso     la sangre destellando;
> al rey Yuçef     tres colpes le ovo dados,     1725
> salios le de sol espada     ca muchol andido el cavallo,
> metios le en Gujera,     un castiello palaçiano;
> mio Çid el de Bivar     fasta alli lego en alcaz
> con otros quel consigen     de sus buenos vassallos.
> Desd'alli se torno     el que en buen ora nasco;     1730
> mucho era alegre     de lo que an caçado.
> Ali preçio a Bavieca     de la cabeça fasta a cabo:
> toda esta ganançia     en su mano a rastado.
> Los .l. mill     por cuenta fueron notados;
> non escaparon     mas de çiento e quatro.     1735

---

**1709** The right to strike the first blows of a battle, seen as a great privilege and mark of distinction, is mentioned in several other epic poems.
**1718** The poet probably does not greatly exaggerate the size of the Almoravid army; the *Historia Roderici* simply states that the Moslem troops were innumerable. The account of the casualties in l.1735, however, is less convincing.
**1719** In the manuscript Álvar Salvadórez is also mentioned, but his name is deleted by a later hand (see note to l.1994).

144

Day drew to a close and night fell.

The Christian men wasted no time in making ready;                    1700
at three in the morning, before day had broken,
Bishop Don Jerónimo sang mass for them,
and when the mass was over he gave a full absolution:
"If any man dies here face to face with the enemy
I absolve him of his sins and God will receive his soul.            1705
For you, Cid Don Rodrigo, who girded your sword in a favoured hour,
for you I have sung mass this morning.
I beg to be granted this favour which I now ask of you:
that I be given the right to strike the first blows."
The Battler replied: "Let it here be granted."                      1710

They all marched out amidst the towers of Valencia armed for battle.

My Cid instructed his vassals well,
and they left at the gates men of great good sense.
My Cid rode forth on Babieca, his horse,
fully dressed in all his armour.                                    1715
Carrying the ensign, they marched out from Valencia.
Four thousand men, all but thirty, following My Cid,
went forth eagerly to strike the fifty thousand.
Álvar Álvarez and Minaya Álvar Fáñez
came among them from the rear;                                      1720
it pleased the Creator that the enemy should be routed.
My Cid wielded his lance and then drew his sword;
he killed Moors beyond reckoning,
as their blood flowed down to his elbow.
The Emir Yusuf received three blows from him;                       1725
he ducked under My Cid's sword, for his horse moved swiftly,
and fled to Cullera, a fine castle.
My Cid of Vivar pursued him there,
accompanied by some of his good vassals.
From there the man born in a favoured hour returned;               1730
he was very pleased with what had been captured.
Now he knew the true worth of Babieca — in all, a fine beast.
all the booty remained in his possession.
The fifty thousand Moors were accounted for;
only one hundred and four had escaped.                              1735

145

Mesnadas de mio Çid    robado an el canpo,
entre oro e plata    fallaron tres mill marcos,
[de] las otras ganançias    non avia recabdo.
Alegre era mio Çid    e todos sos vassallos
que Dios le ovo merçed    que vençieron el campo.      1740
Quando al rey de Marruecos    assi lo an arrancado
dexo [a] Albar Fañez    por saber todo recabdo.
Con .c. cavalleros    a Valençia es entrado:
fronzida trahe la cara,    que era desarmado,
assi entro sobre Bavieca    el espada en la mano.      1745
Reçibien lo las dueñas    que lo estan esperando,
mio Çid finco ant'ellas,    tovo la rienda al cavallo;
'¡A vos me omillo, dueñas!    Grant prez vos he gañado,
vos teniendo Valençia    e yo vençi el campo;
esto Dios se lo quiso    con todos los sos santos      1750
quando en vuestra venida    tal ganançia nos an dada.
Vedes el espada sangrienta    e sudiento el cavallo,
¡con tal cum esto    se vençen moros del campo!
Roga(n)d al Criador    que vos biva algunt año,
entraredes en prez    e besaran vuestras manos.'      1755
Esto dijo mio Çid    diçiendo del cavallo;
quandol vieron de pie,    que era descavalgado,
las dueñas e las fijas    e la mugier que vale algo
delant el Campeador    los inojos fincaron:
'¡Somos en vuestra merçed    e bivades muchos años!'      1760
En buelta con el    entraron al palaçio
e ivan posar con el    en unos preçiosos escaños:
'¡Hya mugier d[o]ña Ximena!    ¿Nom lo aviedes rogado?
Estas dueñas que aduxistes    que vos sirven tanto
quiero las casar    con de aquestos mios vassallos;      1765
a cada una dellas    do les .cc. marcos (de plata),
que lo sepan en Castiella    a quien sirvieron tanto.
Lo de vuestras fijas    venir se a mas por espaçio.'
Levantaron se todas    e besaron le las manos;
grant fue el alegria    que fue por el palaçio,      1770
commo lo dixo el Çid    assi lo han acabado.
Minaya Albar Fañez    fuera era en el campo

---

**1748** *Omillarse*, to bow, is used in a common expression of greeting.

146

My Cid's men plundered the field of battle;
they found gold and silver worth three thousand marks,
and the other booty was beyond reckoning.
Joyful was My Cid, and all his vassals too,
that God had allowed them to win the day.                              1740
Now that such a victory had been won over the Emir of Morocco,
My Cid left Álvar Fáñez to reckon all the gains.
With one hundred knights he entered Valencia;
he had rolled back his cap and taken off his helmet and cowl of
                                                    chain mail,
and thus he rode in on Babieca, with his sword in his hand.            1745
He was welcomed by the ladies, who were waiting for him;
My Cid stopped before them, holding the reins of his horse:
"I offer my humble respect, ladies! I have won you great renown;
for, while you held Valencia, I was victorious in battle.
This was the will of God, with all his saints,                         1750
that on your arrival he has offered us such gains.
You can see that my sword is bloody and my horse sweating;
that is how Moors are defeated on the field of battle!
Pray to the Creator to grant me a long life,
for through me you will acquire honour and men will do homage
                                            to you."                    1755
The Cid spoke these words as he dismounted.
When they saw the Battler standing there,
the ladies, his daughters, and his noble wife
knelt down before him:
"We depend upon you; may you live many years!"                         1760
They went into the palace at his side
and went to sit with him on rich couches.
"Now, Doña Jimena, my wife! Did you not ask this of me?
These ladies you brought with you, who give such
                                    loyal service,
I wish to marry to some of my vassals.                                 1765
I give to each one of them two hundred silver marks,
that it may be known in Castile to whom they have given such
                                    loyal service.
I shall deal with the future of your daughters later."
They all arose and kissed his hands in thanks;
great was the joy throughout the palace,                               1770
and just as My Cid had said, so it was done.
Minaya Álvar Fáñez was outside the city on the field of battle

con todas estas yentes    escriviendo e contando;
entre tiendas e armas    e vestidos preçiados
tanto fallan desto    que es cosa sobejana.    1775
Quiero vos dezir    lo que es mas granado:
non pudieron ellos saber    la cuenta de todos los cavallos
que andan arriados    e non ha qui tomalos,
los moros de las tierras    ganado se an i algo;
mager de todo esto    el Campeador contado    1780
de los buenos e otorgados    cayeron le mill e .d. cavallos;
quando a mio Çid    cayeron tantos
los otros bien pueden    fincar pagados.    1782<sup>b</sup>
¡Tanta tienda preçiada    e tanto tendal obrado
que a ganado mio Çid    con todos sus vassallos!
La tienda del rey de Marruecos    que de las otras es cabo    1785
dos tendales la sufren,    con oro son labrados;
mando mio Çid Ruy Diaz    que fita soviesse la tienda
e non la tolliesse    dent christiano:
'Tal tienda commo esta    que de Maruecos es passada
enbiar la quiero    a Alfonsso el Castellano    1790
que croviesse sos nuevas    de mio Çid que avie algo.'
Con aquestas riquezas tantas    a Valençia son entrados.
El obispo don Jheronimo    caboso coronado
quando es farto de lidiar    con amas las sus manos
non tiene en cuenta    los moros que ha matados;    1795
lo que caye a el    mucho era sobejano.
Mio Çid don Rodrigo    el que en buen ora nasco
de toda la su quinta    el diezmo l'a mandado.

96 Alegres son por Valençia    las yentes christianas,
tantos avien de averes    de cavallos e de armas;    1800
alegre es doña Ximena    e sus fijas amas
e todas la[s] otras dueñas    que[s] tienen por casadas.
El bueno de mio Çid    non lo tardo por nada:
'¿Do sodes, caboso?    Venid aca, Minaya:
de lo que a vos cayo    vos non gradeçedes nada;    1805
desta mi quinta    —digo vos sin falla—
prended lo que quisieredes,    lo otro remanga;
e cras ha la mañana    ir vos hedes sin falla
con cavallos desta quinta    que yo he ganada
con siellas e con frenos    e con señas espadas;    1810

---

**1785** The poet might have been expected to make more of the opportunity to describe this tent – see Introduction VII (c).

**1789-91** In fact, the poet, probably through an oversight, fails to mention the tent again.

148

with all his men, making out a detailed account.
With the tents and weapons and precious garments,
what they found amounted to a vast sum.                                    1775
I want to tell you about the best part of it:
they could not reckon the number of all the horses,
for they were wandering about fully harnessed and could not be caught;
the Moors of those lands took some for themselves;
but, in spite of all this, to the lot of the illustrious Battler            1780
there fell one thousand five hundred fine, sound horses;
since My Cid received so many,
the others could well rest happy.                                          1782b
How many rich tents and how many finely—worked tent poles
My Cid and all his vassals had gained!
The tent of the Emir of Morocco, which was the finest of all,              1785
was supported by two poles worked in gold;
My Cid Ruy Díaz commanded that the tent should remain standing,
and that no Christian should remove it from there:
"This fine tent has been brought from Morocco
and I want to send it to Alfonso of Castile,                               1790
that he may believe the reports of the great wealth won by My Cid."
They entered Valencia with these great riches.
Bishop Don Jerónimo, the worthy priest,
had grown tired through fighting with both his hands
and could not count the Moors he had killed;                               1795
the booty which fell to his lot was immense.
My Cid Don Rodrigo, the man born in a favoured hour,
granted him his tithe out of his own fifth share.


Joyful were the Christian people throughout Valencia;
so great were their gains in money, in horses, and in arms.                1800
Joyful was Doña Jimena and likewise her two daughters
and all the other ladies, who saw themselves as married.
The good Cid did not delay:
"Where are you, my noble Minaya?  Come here.
You have every right to your share, without thanks;                        1805
from my fifth part, I tell you solemnly
to take what you wish; the rest will remain for me;
and tomorrow morning you will leave for certain,
with horses from my own share,
with saddles, bridles, and each with a sword.                              1810

por amor de mi mugier    e de mis fijas amas
por que assi las enbio    dond ellas son pagadas
estos dozientos cavallos    iran en presentajas
que non diga mal el rey Alfonsso    del que Valençia manda.'
Mando a Pero Vermuez    que fuesse con Minaya.    1815
Otro dia mañana    privado cavalgavan
e dozientos omnes    lievan en su conpaña
con saludes del Çid    que las manos le besava;
desta lid    que ha arrancada
.cc. cavallos    le enbiava en presentaja:    1819b
'¡E servir lo he sienpre    mientra que ovisse el alma!'    1820

97 Salidos son de Valençia    e pienssan de andar;
talles ganançias traen    que son a aguardar.
Andan los dias e las noches    [que vagar non se dan]
e passada han la sierra    que las otras tierras parte;
por el rey don Alfonsso    toman sse a preguntar.    1825

98 Passando van las sierras    e los montes e las aguas,
legan a Valadolid    do el rey Alfonsso estava.
Enviava le mandado    Pero Vermuez e Minaya
que mandasse reçebir    a esta conpaña,
mio Çid el de Valençia    enbia su presentaja.    1830

99 Alegre fue el rey,    non viestes atanto;
mando cavalgar a priessa    to(s)dos sos fijos dalgo,
hi en los primeros    el rey fuera dio salto
a ver estos mensajes    del que en buen ora nasco.
Los ifantes de Carrion    sabet, is açertaron,    1835
[y] el conde don Garçia    so enemigo malo;
a los unos plaze    e a los otros va pesando.
A ojo lo avien    los del que en buen ora nasco,
cuedan se que es almofalla    ca non vienen con mandado;
el rey don Alfonsso    seyse santiguando.    1840
Minaya e Per Vermuez    adelante son legados;
firieron se a tierra,    deçendieron de los cavalos,
ant' el rey Alfonsso    los inojos fincados
besan la tierra    e los pies amos:
'¡Merçed, rey Alfonsso,    sodes tan ondrado!    1845

**1839** It is not clear from the text who caught sight of whom. There seems to be a contradiction between the statement here that no messengers have been sent on ahead and, on the other hand, what we have been told in l.1828. The reaction of the King (l.1840) makes it clear, however, that it is the appearance of the Cid's men, bringing a large number of horses, and thus in the distance resembling an army, that causes the shock.

For the love of my wife and my two daughters,
because he sent them where they can be happy,
these two hundred horses will go as a gift
to King Alfonso, that he may not speak ill of the man who rules
                                        Valencia."
He commanded Pedro Bermúdez to accompany Minaya.                    1815
The next morning they rode swiftly on their way,
taking two hundred men with them
and carrying the Cid's compliments and affection to the King;
and a message that from this battle which he had won
he sent two hundred horses as a gift,                               1819b
and that he would serve him always, as long as he lived.           1820

They left Valencia and rode on their way,
taking with them such great wealth that it had to be well guarded.
They rode by night and day, giving themselves no respite.
They crossed the mountains which separated them from the
                                    kingdom of Castile,
and began to ask after King Alfonso.                                1825

They crossed the mountains, the forests, and the rivers,
and reached Valladolid, where King Alfonso was to be found.
Pedro Bermúdez and Minaya sent word to him
that he should grant permission for their company to be received,
for My Cid, the man from Valencia, was sending gifts.              1830

Joyful was The King, more so than you have ever seen him;
he ordered all of his nobles to ride out in haste,
and there, among the first, the King himself went forth
to see these messengers from that man born in a favoured hour.
But listen!  The Infantes of Carrión were present,                 1835
and Count Don García, evil enemy of My Cid.
Some of them were pleased, and others dismayed.
Catching sight of those from the man born in a favoured hour,
they thought them an army, for they came without warning.
the King, Don Alfonso, made the sign of the cross.                 1840
Minaya and Pedro Bermúdez drew close, ahead;
they set foot to ground, dismounting from their horses.
Before King Alfonso, kneeling down,
they both kissed the ground and his feet.
"A favour, King Alfonso, you who are so honoured!                   1845

Por mio Çid el Campeador      todo esto vos besamos;
a vos lama por señor      e tienes por vuestro vassallo;
mucho preçia la ondra      el Çid quel avedes dado.
Pocos dias ha, rey,      que una lid a arrancado;
a aquel rey de Marruecos      Yuçeff por nombrado      1850
con çinquaenta mill      arrancolos del campo;
las gananças que fizo      mucho son sobejanas,
ricos son venidos      todos los sos vassallos;
y embia vos dozientos cavallos      e besa vos las manos.'
Dixo el rey don Alfonsso:      'Reçibolos de grado;      1855
gradescolo a mio Çid      que tal don me ha enbiado,
aun vea ora      que de mi sea pagado.'
Esto plogo a muchos      e besaron le las manos.
Peso al conde don Garçia      e mal era irado,
con .x. de sus parientes      a parte davan salto:      1860
'¡Maravilla es del Çid      que su ondra creçe tanto!
En la ondra que el ha      nos seremos abiltados;
¡por tan biltada mientre      vençer reyes del campo,
commo si los falasse muertos      aduzir se los cavallos!
Por esto que el faze      nos abremos enbargo.'      1865

100 Fablo el rey don Alfonsso      e dixo esta razon:
'Grado al Criador      e al señor Sant Esidro el de Leon
estos dozientos cavallos      quem enbia mio Çid.
Mio reino adelant      mejor me podra servir.
A vos, Minaya Albar Fañez      e a Pero Vermuez aqui      1370
mando vos los cuerpos      ondrada mientre servir e vestir
e guarnir vos de todas armas      commo vos dixieredes aqui,
que bien parescades      ante Ruy Diaz mio Çid;
dovos .iii. cavallos      e prended los aqui.
Assi commo semeja      e la veluntad melo diz      1875
todas estas nuevas      a bien abran de venir.'

101 Besaron le las manos      y entraron a posar;
bien los mando servir      de quanto huebos han.
De los iffantes de Carrion      yo vos quiero contar,
fablando en su conssejo,      aviendo su poridad:      1880
'Las nuevas del Çid      mucho van adelant;
demandemos sus fijas      pora con ellas casar;
creçremos en nuestra ondra      e iremos adelant.'

1857 Alfonso promises fitting reward for his vassal's loyalty. It is ironic, however, that the marriages which are meant to form part of this reward in fact threaten to bring dishonour.
1863 The jealous Count considers the Cid's triumphs to be 'base' not only because they seem to have been achieved with such ease as to suggest trickery but also because they are the work of a social inferior.
1874 Probably three horses each: palfrey, war-horse, and pack-animal (see note to l.1548).

For My Cid the Battler we ask all this of you:
he acknowledges you his lord and calls himself your vassal;
the Cid holds in great worth the honour you have paid him.
A few days ago, O King, he won a great battle.
The mighty Emir of Morocco, Yusuf by name,                          1850
with fifty thousand men he drove from the field.
The booty that he took is very great of value
and all of his vassals have become rich men;
he sends two hundred horses and offers his humble respect."
King Alfonso answered: "Willingly I accept them.                    1855
I am grateful to My Cid who has sent me such a gift.
May the time come when he receives recompense from me."
Many were delighted, and they kissed his hands in gratitude.
But this grieved Count Don García, who was very angry;
with ten of his kinsmen he drew to one side:                        1860
"It is a marvel that the Cid's reputation grows so much.
By his increasing honour, we shall lose our credit.
In so basely overcoming kings on the field of battle.
as if he found them dead he brings their horses as evidence.
Because of what he does, there will be trouble for us."            1865

King Alfonso spoke and said these words:
"Thanks be to the Creator and to Saint Isidore of León
for these two hundred horses which My Cid sends me.
In future he can perform yet greater service to my kingdom.
You, Minaya Álvar Fáñez, and you, Pedro Bermúdez, here and
                              now I order                            1870
that you equip and dress yourselves worthily,
and fit yourselves with such weapons as you may choose
that you may appear befittingly before Ruy Díaz My Cid.
I give you three horses; take them now.
It seems to me — my heart tells me too —                           1875
that all these events will end favourably."

They kissed his hands and went in to rest.
He ordered them to be provided with all that they needed.
I now want to tell you about the Infantes of Carrión,
talking of their plan in secret:                                    1880
"For the Cid things are going very well;
let us ask for his daughters in marriage;
we shall grow in honour by it and so we shall prosper."

153

Vinien al rey Alfonsso    con esta poridad:

102 '¡Merçed vos pidimos    commo a rey e a señor natural! 1885

Con vuestro conssejo    lo queremos fer nos
que nos demandedes    fijas del Campeador;
casar queremos con ellas    a su ondra e a nuestra pro.
Una grant ora    el rey pensso e comidio:
'Hyo eche de tierra    al buen Campeador,                1890
e faziendo yo ha el mal    y el a mi grand pro
del casamiento    non se sis abra sabor;
mas pues bos lo queredes    entremos en la razon.'
A Minaya Albar Fañez    e a Pero Vermuez
el rey don Alfonso    essora los lamo,                   1895
a una quadra    ele los aparto:
'Oid me, Minaya,    e vos, Per Vermuez:
sirvem    mio Çid el Campeador,
el lo mereçe    e de mi abra perdon;                     1898ᵇ
viniessem a vistas    si oviesse dent sabor.
Otros mandados ha    en esta mi cort:                    1900
Diego e Ferrando    —los iffantes de Carrion—
sabor han de casar    con sus fijas amas a dos.
Sed buenos menssageros    e ruego vos lo yo
que gelo digades    al buen Campeador;
abra i ondra    e creçra en onor                         1905
por conssagrar    con los iffantes de Carrion.'
Fablo Minaya    e plogo a Per Vermuez:
'Rogar gelo emos    lo que dezides vos;
despues faga el Çid    lo que oviere sabor.'
'Dezid a Ruy Diaz    el que en buen ora nasco           1910
quel ire a vistas    do fuere aguisado;
do el dixiere    i sea el mojon,
andar le quiero    a mio Çid en toda pro.'
Espidiensse al rey,    con esto tornados son.
van pora Valençia    ellos e todos los sos.             1915
Quando lo sopo    el buen Campeador

---

**1884** *Poredad* or *puridad* denotes the feudal right to resolve a question by direct and secret consultation with one's superior in the social hierarchy. To deny this right is equivalent to breaking off the relationship between lord and vassal.

**1889** Compare the reaction of the Cid (l.1932), and those of the Cid and Alfonso on learning of the Corpes outrage (l.2828 and l.2953). See Introduction, VII (c).

**1905** On a number of occasions the King alludes to the honour which the Cid and his family will gain from these marriages. There have already been hints – particularly in the way that the Infantes' characters have been presented – that this will not be the case, and we are led to suspect that in this matter Alfonso's judgement is still unsound.

154

They came to King Alfonso with this confidence.

"We ask a favour of you as our king and natural lord!                1885

If you will grant your permission, we want you
to ask on our behalf for the Battler's daughters in marriage;
we want to marry them, to their greater honour and our advantage."
For a good hour the King thought and reflected on this:
"I sent the good Battler into exile;                1890
I have done him wrong and he has done me much good,
and I do not know if he will be pleased by the proposals of marriage.
But, since you wish it, let us discuss the matter."
Minaya Álvar Fáñez and Pedro Bermúdez
were then summoned by King Don Alfonso,                1895
and he took them into another room:
"Listen, Minaya, and you, Pedro Bermúdez,
My Cid the Battler does me good service.
He will have my pardon — he deserves it;                1898b
let him come to meet me, if he is willing.
There is further news here in my court:                1900
Diego and Fernando, the Infantes of Carrión,
wish to marry his two daughters.
Be good messengers: I ask you
to tell the good Battler of this.
He will gain honour and greater wealth                1905
by becoming related to the Infantes of Carrión."
Minaya spoke, with Pedro Bermúdez in agreement:
"We shall ask him about what you have said;
then let the Cid do what he will."
"Tell Ruy Díaz, the man born in a favoured hour,                1910
that I shall go and meet with him wherever he finds convenient;
let the audience take place wherever he says;
I wish to help My Cid in every way I can."
They took their leave of the King, and with this returned;
with all their company they made their way to Valencia.                1915
When the good Battler knew of this,

**1907** Pedro Bermúdez prefers to remain silent. This detail is consistent with the way that his character is presented elsewhere in the poem. Thus it is that the Cid, punning on his surname, is to goad him into action in the court by calling him 'Pedro the Mute'.
**1913** In this the King shows his vassal exceptional favour. In fact, the Cid chooses the place for the audience, and Alfonso the time (l.1962).

a priessa cavalga,      a reçebir los salio;
sonrrisos mio Çid       e bien los abraço:
'¿Venides, Minaya,      e vos, Per Vermuez?
¡En pocas tierras       a tales dos varones!                    ·020
¿Commo son las saludes      de Alfonsso mio señor?
¿Si es pagado      o reçibio el don?'
Dixo Minaya:        'D'alma e de coraçon
es pagado,      e davos su amor.'
Dixo mio Çid:      '¡Grado al Criador!'                         1925
Esto diziendo      conpieçan la razon
lo quel rogava      Alfonsso el de Leon
de dar sus fijas      a los ifantes de Carrion,
quel connosçie i ondra      e creçie en onor,
que gelo conssejava      d'alma e de coraçon.                   1930
Quando lo oyo      mio Çid el buen Campeador
una grant ora      pensso e comidio:
'¡Esto gradesco a Christus      el mio señor!
Echado fu de tierra      e tollida la onor,
con grand afan gane      lo que he yo;                          1935
a Dios lo gradesco      que del rey he su [amor]
e piden me mis fijas      pora los ifantes de Carrion.
Ellos son mucho urgullosos      e an part en la cort,
deste casamiento      non avria sabor;
mas pues lo conseja      el que mas vale que nos                1940
f(l)ablemos en ello,      en la poridad seamos nos.
Afe Dios del çiello:      ¡que nos acuerde en lo mijor!'
'Con todo esto      a vos dixo Alfonsso
que vos vernie a vistas      do oviessedes sabor;
querer vos ie ver      e dar vos su amor,                       1945
acordar vos iedes despues      a todo lo mejor.'
Essora dixo el Çid:      '¡Plazme de coraçon!'
'Estas vistas      o las ayades vos'
—dixo Minaya—      'Vos sed sabidor.'
'Non era maravilla      si quisiesse el rey Alfonsso,           1950
fasta do lo fallassemos      buscar lo iremos nos
por dar le grand ondra      commo a rey [e señor];
mas lo que el quisiere      esso queramos nos.
Sobre Tajo      que es una agua [mayor]
ayamos vistas      quando lo quiere mio señor.'                 1955
Escrivien cartas,      bien las sello,
con dos cavalleros      luego las enbio.

**1924** That is, the Cid's banishment is now at an end.
**1936-42** The poet leaves us in no doubt here that Alfonso bears the responsibility for the ill-fated marriages. The Cid is quick to see the essential problem – the Infantes' pride in their superior birth – but he is bound to submit to the judgement of his king and lord.
**1956-57** These lines reflect accurately procedure in the chancery of an important nobleman. See Russell, 'Some Problems of Diplomatic'. p.346.

quickly he rode out to welcome them.
My Cid smiled, and embraced them warmly:
"So you have returned, Minaya, and you, Pedro Bermúdez.
In few lands are there two such men!                                1920
How is Alfonso, my lord?
Was he pleased by my gift, and did he accept it?"
Minaya said: "In both heart and soul
he is pleased, and he grants you his love."
My Cid replied: "Thanks be to the Creator!"                         1925
When he had said this, they began to put to him
the request made by Alfonso of León
that he give his daughters in marriage to the Infantes of Carrión.
The King, seeing that My Cid would gain honour and greater wealth,
with both heart and soul advised him to consent.                    1930
When My Cid, the good Battler, heard this,
for a good hour he thought and reflected:
"I am grateful for this to Christ, my lord!
I was sent into exile and my possessions were confiscated,
and my gains have been made only with a great struggle.            1935
I thank God that the King has granted me his love and that
I am asked for the hands of my daughters for the Infantes of Carrión.
They are very proud and powerful members of the court;
I would not agree to this marriage,
but, since it is proposed by one worth more than us,               1940
let us talk of this matter, and let us do so in private.
Let God in heaven guide us as to what is best!"
"Apart from this matter, Alfonso sent word to you
that he would come to meet you wherever you wished —
he would like to see you and give you his love —                   1945
and afterwards you would be able to decide what is best."
Then the Cid spoke: "By this I am pleased in my heart."
"Where this audience is to take place,"
said Minaya, "you are to decide."
"It would be no wonder if the King wished to name the place,       1950
for we would search and go to him where we found him,
in order to do him great honour as our king and lord;
but let our wish and his be one.
By the Tagus, which is a great river,
let the audience take place, since that is the wish of our lord."  1955
Letters were written and he sealed them carefully
and sent them with two knights.

157

Lo que el rey quisiere    esso fera el Campeador.

103  Al rey ondrado    delant le echaron las cartas;
     quando las vio    de coraçon se paga:                           1960
     'Saludad me a mio Çid    el que en buen ora çinxo espada;
     sean las vistas    destas .iii. semanas;
     s'yo bivo so    ali ire sin falla.'
     Non lo detardan,    a mio Çid se tornavan.
     Della part e della    pora la[s] vistas se adobavan:            1965
     ¿quien vio por Castiella    tanta mula preçiada
     e tanto palafre    que bien anda,
     cavallos gruessos    e coredores sin falla,
     tanto buen pendon    meter en buenas astas,
     escudos boclados    con oro e con plata,                        1970
     mantos e pielles    e buenos çendales d'Andria?
     Conduchos largos    el rey enbiar mandava
     a las aguas de Tajo    o las vistas son aparejadas.
     Con el rey    atantas buenas conpañas.
     Los iffantes de Carrion    mucho alegres andan,                1975
     lo uno adebdan    e lo otro pagavan;
     commo ellos tenien    creçer les ia la ganançia,
     quantos quisiessen    averes d'oro o de plata.
     El rey don Alfonsso    a priessa cavalgava,
     cuendes e podestades    e muy grandes mesnadas;                 1980
     los ifantes de Carrion    lievan grandes conpañas.
     Con el rey van leoneses    e mesnadas galizianas;
     non son en cuenta    sabet, las castellanas.
     Sueltan las riendas,    a las vistas se van adeliñadas.

104  Dentro en Vallençia    mio Çid el Campeador                     1985
     non lo detarda,    pora las vistas se adobo:
     ¡tanta gruessa mula    e tanto palafre de sazon,
     tanta buena arma    e tanto buen cavallo coredor,
     tanta buena capa    e mantos e pelliçones!
     Chicos e grandes    vestidos son de colores.                   1990
     Minaya Albar Fañez    e aquel Pero Vermuez,
     Martin Muñoz    e Martin Antolinez el burgales de pro.

---

**1971** The Greek island of Andros was famous for the production of silk.
**1976** The Infantes are characterized as spendthrifts. Thus, when at the court they are required to repay the money given them by the Cid, they suffer acute embarrassment, for they have already spent it (ll.3236 ff.).
**1980** A count was a governor of a region, responsible, for example, for military and judicial matters. He drew his authority from the king, who, although the office was not hereditary, would usually keep it within a particular family. The 'noblemen' mentioned here (*podestades*) might have charge of a town and its district, but with less extensive powers. The *condes* and *podestades* were classed as *ricos omnes* (see note to l.3546), the highest category of the nobility.
**1982-83** By mentioning Castile, Leon and Galicia, the poet stresses Alfonso's authority over a unified kingdom.

What the King wishes, the Battler will do.

The letters were brought to the King, great in honour.
When he saw them, his heart rejoiced:                                1960
"I send greetings to My Cid, who girded his sword in a favoured hour.
Let the audience be three weeks from now;
so long as I still live, I shall go there without fail."
Without delay they returned to My Cid.
Both parties made ready for the meeting.                             1965
Who had ever seen in Castile so many valuable mules,
so many palfreys, fine of bearing,
chargers well - fed and swift;
so many rich pennants carried on fine shafts,
bossed shields adorned with gold and silver,                         1970
and cloaks and furs and fine silks of Andros?
The King ordered abundant provisions to be sent
to the banks of the Tagus, where preparations were being made.
With the King was so great and fine a following.
The Infantes of Carrión were filled with great joy,                  1975
now borrowing, now paying out,
for they believed their income should increase,
and that they would have all the gold and silver they wished.
King Don Alfonso rode swiftly,
and with him counts and noblemen and great numbers of his vassals.
The Infantes of Carrión took a great company with them.
With the King went men of León and vassals from Galicia,
and the Castilians, I tell you, were beyond reckoning.
They slackened the reins, and headed straight for the place of meeting.

In Valencia, My Cid the Battler                                      1985
did not delay but made ready for the audience:
so many stout mules and so many palfreys in prime condition,
so much fine armour and so many fine, swift war - horses,
so many fine cloaks, robes and furs!
All men, great and low, dressed in richly - coloured clothes.        1990
Minaya Álvar Fáñez and the notable Pedro Bermúdez,
Martín Muñoz and Martín Antolínez, worthy man of Burgos,

See too his insistence on this point in ll.2923 ff., when the Cid sends his appeal to Alfonso as the impartial
dispenser of justice.
**1987-89** The parallel with the description of Alfonso's retinue (ll.1966 ff.) serves to emphasize that, as regards
wealth and power, the Cid can now approach Alfonso on an equal footing.

el obispo don Jeronimo     cor[o]nado mejor,
Alvar Alvarez     e Alvar Sa[l]vadorez,
Muño Gustioz     el cavallero de pro,                                              1995
Galind Garçiaz     el que fue de Aragon:
estos se adoban     por ir con el Campeador
e todos los otros     que i son.
Alvar Salvadorez     e Galind Garçiaz el de Aragon
a aquestos dos     mando el Campeador                                           2000
que curien a Valençia     d'alma e de coraçon                                    2000<sup>b</sup>
e todos los que     en poder dessos fossen;
las puertas del alcaçar     que non se abriessen de dia nin de
                                                                                                        noch,

dentro es su mugier     e sus fijas amas a dos
en que tiene su alma     e su coraçon,
e otras dueñas     que las sirven a su sabor;                                      2005
recabdado ha     —commo tan buen varon—
que del alcaçar     una salir non puede
fata ques torne     el que en buen ora na[çi]o.
Salien de Valençia,     aguijan [a] espolon:
tantos cavallos en diestro     gruessos e corredores                            2010
mio Çid selos gañara,     que no gelos dieran en don.
Hyas va pora las vistas     que con el rey paro.
De un dia es legado antes     el rey don Alfonsso;
quando vieron que vinie     el buen Campeador
reçebir lo salen     con tan grand onor.                                              2015
Don  lo ovo a ojo     el que en buen ora na[çi]o
a todos los sos     estar los mando
si non a estos cavalleros     que querie de coraçon;
con unos .xv.     a tierras firio
commo lo comidia     el que en buen ora naçio;                                   2020
los inojos e las manos     en tierra los finco,
las yerbas del campo     a dientes las tomo
lorando de los ojos,     tanto avie el gozo mayor,
asi sabe dar omildança     a Alfonsso so señor.
De aquesta guisa     a los pies le cayo.                                              2025
Tan grand pesar     ovo el rey don Alfonsso:
¡Levantados en pie     ya Çid Campeador!
Besad las manos,     ca los pies no;

**1994** Álvar Salvadórez reappears here in spite of his capture by the Moslems in 1.1681.
**1999** The poet seems to err here, for, having just declared that Galindo García and Álvar Salvadórez are to
accompany the Cid, he now tells us that they are to be left in charge of the force guarding Valencia.
**2024** The Cid, in spite of his great power and standing, has made a public display of the most absolute submission
to Alfonso's will. The act of taking the grass in the teeth is a form of self-abasement before a lord or conqueror
widely recorded and ancient in origin.

Bishop Don Jerónimo, finest of priests,
Álvar Álvarez and Álvar Salvadórez,
Muño Gustioz, worthy knight,                                              1995
Galindo García, who came from Aragón;
these men made ready to go with the Battler,
and so too did all the others present.
Álvar Salvadórez and Galindo García of Aragón
were ordered by the Battler                                               2000
to protect Valencia with heart and soul,                                  2000b
and so too were all those under their command;
the gates of the citadel should not be opened by night or day,
for inside were his wife and his two daughters,
whom he loved with his heart and soul,
and other ladies who served them at their pleasure.                       2005
He had taken the precaution — good man that he was —
that not one of them was to leave the citadel
until the return of the man born in a favoured hour.
They left Valencia and spurred on their way,
taking with them so many swift and sturdy war - horses,                   2010
which My Cid had won — for they had not been freely given.
He went on his way to the audience which he had arranged with
                                    the King.
King Don Alfonso had arrived the day before.
When they saw that the good Battler was coming,
they went out to welcome him with great honour.                           2015
When the man born in a favoured hour saw this,
he ordered all his men to remain behind,
except those knights that he loved most dearly;
with some fifteen of them he dismounted,
as had been arranged by the man born in a favoured hour.                  2020
He went down on his hands and knees
and took the grass of the field in his teeth,
with tears flowing from his eyes, so great was his joy;
for this is the way he knew to show his submission before Alfonso
                                    his lord.
In this manner he fell at the King's feet.                                2025
King Alfonso was saddened by this:
"Arise, O Cid the Battler!
Kiss my hands, not my feet!

si esto non feches      non avredes mi amor.'
Hinojos fitos      sedie el Campeador:                    2030
'¡Merçed vos pido      a vos mio natural señor!
Assi estando      dedes me vuestra amor,
que lo oyan      quantos aqui son.'                       2032b
Dixo el rey:      '¡Esto fere d'alma e de coraçon!
Aqui vos perdono      e dovos mi amor,
[y] en todo mio reino      parte desde oy.'               2035
Fablo mio Çid      e dixo [esta razon]:
'¡Merçed! Yo lo reçibo,      Alfonsso mio señor;          2036b
¡gradescolo a Dios del çielo      e despues a vos
e a estas mesnadas      que estan aderredor!'
Hinojos fitos      las manos le beso,
levos en pie      y en la bocal saludo.                   2040
Todos los demas      desto avien sabor;
peso a Albar Diaz      e a Garçi Ordoñez.
Fablo mio Çid      e dixo esta razon:
'¡Esto gradesco      al Criador                           2043b
quando he la graçia      de don Alfonsso mio señor;
valer me a Dios      de dia e de noch!                    2045
Fuessedes mi huesped      si vos plogiesse, señor.'
Dixo el rey:      'Non es aguisado oy;
vos agora legastes      e nos viniemos anoch;
mio huesped seredes,      Çid Campeador,
e cras feremos      lo que plogiere a vos.'               2050
Beso le la mano,      mio Çid lo otorgo.
Essora sele omillan      los iffantes de Carrion:
'Omillamos nos, Çid:      ¡en buen ora nasquiestes vos!
En quanto podemos      andamos en vuestro pro.'
Respuso mio Çid:      '¡Assi lo mande el Criador!'        2055
Mio Çid Ruy Diaz      que en ora buena na[çi]o
en aquel dia      del rey so huesped fue;
non se puede fartar del,      tantol querie de coraçon,
catandol sedie la barba      que tan ainal creçi[o].
Maravillan se de mio Çid      quantos que i son.          2060
Es dia es passado      y entrada es la noch.
Otro dia mañana      claro salie el sol:
el Campeador      a los sos lo mando
que adobassen cozina      pora quantos que i son;
de tal guisa los paga      mio Çid el Campeador           2065
todos eran alegres      e acuerdan en una razon:

---

**2042** The name of Álvar Díaz appears in documents from 1068 to 1111; he was lord of Oca, and is known to have accompanied Alfonso on campaign. He was, in fact, married to Teresa, sister of García Ordóñez, and through the marriage of their granddaughter his line was to be linked to the Vani-Gómez family.

Otherwise, you shall not gain my love."
The Battler remained on his knees:                              2030
"I beg a favour of you, as my natural lord!
As I kneel before you, I ask that you grant me your love;
may all those present be my witnesses."                         2032b
The King replied: "This I will do with my heart and soul!
Here and now I pardon you and grant you my love,
and from today I give you a place in my kingdom."               2035
My Cid spoke, and said this:
"I thank you!  I accept it, Alfonso my lord.                     2036b
I give thanks to God in heaven and then to you
and to these vassals who surround us."
Still kneeling, he kissed Alfonso's hands,
rose to his feet and kissed him on the mouth.                   2040
All the others were pleased at this,
but Álvar Díaz and García Ordóñez were saddened.
My Cid spoke, and said this:
"I give thanks to the Creator                                   2043b
since I have the favour of Don Alfonso, my lord;
God will protect me both by day and by night.                   2045
Be now my guest, if you are willing."
The King replied: "Today, that is not proper;
you have just arrived and we came last night;
you will be my guest, O Cid the Battler,
and tomorrow we shall do what you wish."                        2050
My Cid, kissing his hand, agreed.
Now the Infantes of Carrión bowed before him:
"We offer our humble respects to you born in a favoured hour!
All that we can, we do for you."
My Cid replied: "So may the Creator decree it!"                 2055
My Cid Ruy Díaz, born in a favoured hour,
on that day was the guest of the King.
Alfonso could not tire of his company, so deeply did he love him.
He sat gazing at his beard, which had grown so greatly.
All those present marvelled at My Cid.                          2060
Day had passed and night had fallen.
The next morning the sun rose brightly in the sky;
the Battler ordered his men
to prepare food for all those present.
My Cid the Battler treated them so well                         2065
that all were happy and agreed on one thing:

passado avie .iii. años    no comieran mejor.
Al otro dia mañana    assi commo salio el sol
el obispo don Jheronimo    la missa canto;
al salir de la missa    todos juntados son,       2070
non lo tardo el rey,    la razón conpeço:
'¡Oid me, las escuellas,    cuendes e ifançones!
Cometer quiero un ruego    a mio Çid el Campeador;
¡asi lo mande Christus    que sea a so pro!
Vuestras fijas vos pido,    don Elvira e doña Sol,    2075
que las dedes por mugieres    a los ifantes de Carrion.
Semejam el casamiento    ondrado e con grant pro;
ellos vos las piden    e mando vos lo yo.
Della e della part    quantos que aqui son
los mios e los vuestros    que sean rogadores;    2080
¡dandos las, mio Çid,    si vos vala el Criador!'
'Non abria fijas de casar'    —respuso el Campeador—
'ca non han grant heda(n)d    e de dias pequeñas son.
De grandes nuevas son    los ifantes de Carrion,
perteneçen pora mis fijas    e aun pora mejores.    2085
Hyo las engendre amas    e criastes las vos;
entre yo y ellas    en vuestra merçed somos nos,
afellas en vuestra mano    don Elvira e doña Sol:
dad las a qui quisieredes vos    ca yo pagado so.'
'Graçias' —dixo el rey— 'A vos e a tod esta cort.'    2090
Luego se levantaron    los iffantes de Carrion,
ban besar las manos    al que en ora buena naçio;
camearon las espadas    ant'el rey don Alfonsso.
Fablo el rey don Alfonsso    commo tan buen señor:
'Grado e graçias, Çid, commo tan bueno,    e primero al
                                          Criador,
quem dades vuestras fijas    pora los ifantes de Carrion.   2096
D'aqui las prendo por mis manos    don Elvira e doña Sol
e dolas por veladas    a los ifantes de Carrion.
Hyo las caso a vuestras fijas    con vuestro amor;

---

**2079-80** The King asks that all those present should play the part of *rogador*: the person responsible for requesting the lady's hand in marriage on behalf of the suitor.

**2083** The Cid's comment here contradicts his remark in l.1650 that the girls are already of an age to be wed (which would seem convincing in view of the time that has passed since the Cid's departure into exile). The Cid hesitates here, giving tactful expression to his doubts about the suitability of the alliance.

**2086** Though it was the custom for the children of noblemen to be brought up in the household of the king, it is highly unlikely that this would have been the case with the Cid's daughters, still very young when their father was exiled and not likely to be accorded such favour subsequently.

**2088** The Cid symbolically places his daughters 'in the King's hands' (see also l.2097). The terminology used here reflects the form of the wedding ceremony itself; see note to l.2234.

**2093** The exchange of arms commonly took place as a sign of friendship or alliance.

**2097 ff.** This symbolical *traditio* ('handing over') is performed by Alfonso in the absence of the brides-to-be. At the ceremony in Valencia, Álvar Fáñez is to act as the King's representative.

164

that in the past three years they had not eaten better.
The next morning, as soon as the sun rose,
Bishop Don Jerónimo sang mass;
when they left the mass, they all assembled;                                    2070
the King, without delay, began to speak:
"Hear me, my courtiers, counts and lords!
I wish to make a request of My Cid the Battler;
may Christ ensure that it brings him advantage!
I ask you to give your daughters, Doña Elvira and Doña Sol,        2075
as wives to the Infantes of Carrión.
I consider the marriage to be honourable and to bring great prestige;
the Infantes ask it of you and I command it.
In both parties, let all those present,
both my men and yours, join me in the request.                                2080
Give them to us, My Cid, so may the Creator protect you!"
"I would not have my daughters marry," replied the Battler,
"for they are still girls, young in years.
The Infantes of Carrión are of high rank,
fitted for my daughters or even for those of higher standing.        2085
I fathered the two of them and you brought them up.
Both they and I will do as you desire;
I now place Doña Elvira and Doña Sol in your hands;
give them to whomseover you will, for with that I am pleased."
"I thank you," said the King, "you and all this court."                      2090
Then the Infantes of Carrión arose
and went to kiss the hands of the man born in a favoured hour.
They exchanged swords in the presence of King Alfonso.
King Don Alfonso, so good a lord, spoke:
"I am deeply grateful to you, my good Cid — and above all to
                                        the Creator —                                             2095
that you are giving me your daughters for the Infantes of Carrión.
Now I take into my hands Doña Elvira and Doña Sol
and give them in marriage to the Infantes of Carrión.
I marry your daughters, with your blessing;

2103-04 The reason for this gift is not clear. Whilst, as Menéndez Pidal points out, the feudal lord was expected to make some contribution to his vassals' wedding expenses, it is perhaps significant that Alfonso should make it clear that the money can be used for any other purpose. M.N.Pavlović and R.M.Walker suggest that this gift could relate to the sum which, according to some contemporary law codes, the husband or his father should contribute for the bride's trousseau; or alternatively that Alfonso's remarks contain a veiled reference to the custom of setting aside a sum of money to be handed over to the wife when the husband was satisfied that she had been married a virgin. This would provide further evidence of the legitimacy of the marriages. See 'Money, Marriage and the Law in the *Poema de Mio Cid*', pp.203-04.

¡al Criador plega    que ayades ende sabor!    2100
Afellos en vuestras manos    los ifantes de Carrion;
ellos vayan con vusco    ca d'aquen me torno yo.
Trezientos marcos de plata    en ayuda les do yo
que metan en sus bodas    o do quisieredes vos.
Pues fueren en vuestro poder    en Valençia la mayor    2105
los yernos e las fijas    todos vuestros fijos son;
lo que vos plogiere    dellos fet, Campeador.'
Mio Çid gelos reçibe,    las manos le beso:
'¡Mucho vos lo gradesco    commo a rey e a señor!
Vos casades mis fijas    ca non gelas do yo.'    2110
Las palabras son puestas    que otro dia mañana quando salie
el sol
ques tornasse cada uno    don salidos son.
Aquis metio en nuevas    mio Çid el Campeador:
tanta gruessa mula    e tanto palafre de sazon
conpeço mio Çid a dar    a quien quiere prender so don,    2115
tantas buenas vestiduras    que d'alfaya son;
cada uno lo que pide    nadi nol dize de no.
Mio Çid de los cavallos    .lx. dio en don;
todos son pagados de las vistas    quantos que i son.
Partir se quieren    que entrada era la noch.    2120
El rey a los ifantes    a las manos les tomo,
metiolos en poder    de mio Çid el Campeador:
'Evad aqui vuestros fijos    quando vuestros yernos son,
de oy mas    sabed que fer dellos, Campeador.'
'Gradescolo, rey,    e prendo vuestro don;    2125
¡Dios que esta en çielo    de[vos] dent buen galardon!'
Sobr'el so cavallo Bavieca    mio Çid salto d[io]:
'Aqui lo digo    ante mio señor el rey Alfonsso:
qui quiere ir comigo a las bodas    o reçebir mi don
d'aquend vaya comigo;    cuedo quel avra pro.    2130

105 Yo vos pido merçed    a vos, rey natural:
pues que casades mis fijas    asi commo a vos plaz
dad manero a qui las de    quando vos las tomades;
non gelas dare yo con mi mano    nin dend non se alabaran.'
Respondio el rey:    'Afe aqui Albar Fañez:    2135

2110 The Cid's statement could not be clearer. This scene and that in which he tells his wife and daughters of what has been arranged are shot through with details emphasizing that Alfonso, and not his vassal, bears the responsibility for the misjudged alliance, not just morally but also legally.
2121 The gesture by which the King places the Infantes in the Cid's hands, both figuratively and literally, resembles that by which they in turn are given authority over their wives (see ll.2097-98).

166

may the Creator will that from this you gain joy!  2100
Now take the Infantes of Carrión into your hands;
let them go with you, for I shall turn back.
Three hundred silver marks I give them, to help
with the expenses of the wedding or whatever you think most fitting.
When they are under your protection in the great city of Valencia,
both sons - in - law and daughters will be as your own children.
Do with them as you wish, Battler."
My Cid received them from Alfonso and kissed his hands:
"I am very grateful to you, as my king and lord.
You are marrying my daughters, not I."  2100
It was arranged that the next morning at sunrise
each should return whence he had come.
Then My Cid the Battler won further fame:
so many sturdy mules and palfreys in prime condition
he began to give to any who would accept his gift;  2115
so many fine garments, great of value.
No man was denied what he asked.
My Cid gave away sixty of the horses;
all those present at the audience were well satisfied.
It was time to take their leave, for night had fallen.  2120
The King took the Infantes by the hands,
and placed them under the authority of My Cid the Battler:
"These men before you are your sons — since they are your
                    sons - in - law —
and from today you must know how to behave towards them."
"I thank you, my king, and I accept your gift;  2125
may God in heaven reward you for it!"
My Cid mounted his horse Babieca:
"Here and now I say, in the presence of my lord, King Alfonso:
Let any man who wishes to go with me to the wedding or receive
                    my gift
leave with me now; I think that he will gain advantage by it.  2130

I ask a favour of you, my natural king:
since you are giving my daughters in marriage, for such is your will,
send a representative into whose care I may give them since you
                    take them from me:
I shall not give them away with my own hand — the Infantes shall
                    not claim that!"
The King replied: "Here is Álvar Fáñez.  2135

167

prendellas con vuestras manos     e daldas a los ifantes
assi commo yo las prendo d'aquent     commo si fosse delant;
sed padrino dell[a]s     a tod el velar.
Quando vos juntaredes comigo     quem digades la verdat.'
Dixo Albar Fañez:     Señor, afe que me plaz.'     2140


106  Tod esto es puesto     sabed, en grant recabdo.
'¡Hya rey don Alfonsso     señor tan ondrado!
Destas vistas que oviemos     de mi tomedes algo:
trayo vos .xx. palafres,     estos bien adobados,
e .xxx. cavallos coredores,     estos bien enssellados;     2145
tomad aquesto,     e beso vuestras manos.'
Dixo el rey don Alfonsso:     '¡Mucho me avedes enbargado!
Reçibo este don     que me avedes mandado;
¡plega al Criador     con todos los sos santos
este plazer quem feches     que bien sea galardonado!     2150
Mio Çid Ruy Diaz:     mucho me avedes ondrado,
de vos bien so servido     e tengon por pagado;
¡aun bivo seyendo     de mi ayades algo!
A Dios vos acomiendo,     destas vistas me parto.


¡Afe Dios del çielo:     que lo ponga en buen logar!'     2155


107  Hyas espidio mio Çid     de so señor Alfonsso;
non quiere quel escura,     quitol dessi luego.
Veriedes cavalleros     que bien andantes son
besar las manos,     espedir se del rey Alfonsso:
'Merçed vos sea     e fazed nos este perdon:     2160
hiremos en poder de mio Çid     a Valençia la mayor;
seremos a las bodas     de los ifantes de Carrion
he de las fijas de mio Çid,     de don Elvira e doña Sol.'
Esto plogo al rey     e a todos los solto;
la conpaña del Çid creçe     e la del rey mengo,     2165
grandes son las yentes     que van con el Canpeador;
adeliñan pora Valençia     la que en buen punto gano,
e a don Fernando e a don Diego     aguardar los mando
a Pero Vermuez     e Muño Gustioz
—en casa de mio Çid     non a dos mejores—     2170
que sopiessen sos mañas     de los ifantes de Carrion.


**2142** The speaker is the Cid.
**2155** The poet uses a form of dramatic irony here, for the narrative has contained clear hints that Alfonso's hopes will not be fulfilled.

Take the girls into your hands and give them to the Infantes,
as I take them from their father, as though both were present now.
You are to be their sponsor throughout the wedding ceremony;
and when you come to me again, tell me the truth of what has
                                        happened."
Álvar Fáñez replied: "My lord, by my faith I undertake to do so."

All this, I tell you, was arranged with great care.
"King Don Alfonso, most honoured lord,
take this gift with you from our audience:
I have brought you twenty palfreys — these well equipped —
and thirty chargers — these well saddled;                        2145
I kiss your hands and beg you to accept them."
King Don Alfonso said: "You overwhelm me!
I accept this gift which you have offered;
may it please the Creator and all his saints
that the joy you have brought me may be well rewarded!           2150
My Cid Ruy Díaz, greatly have you honoured me.
I am well served by you, and I am well satisfied;
so long as I live, may you receive reward from me!
I commend you to God, and now I leave this audience.

I pray to God in heaven that all may turn out well!"            2155

Then My Cid took his leave of his lord, Alfonso;
he did not want to escort him, but bade him farewell there and then.
You could see knights, men favoured with fortune,
kiss the King's hands to take their leave of him:
"Be generous to us, and grant us this favour:                   2160
we shall go to serve My Cid, to the great city of Valencia;
we shall be at the wedding of the Infantes of Carrión
and of the daughters of My Cid, Doña Elvira and Doña Sol."
The King was pleased at this and consented to their departure.
My Cid's company grew larger, and that of the King smaller;     2165
great were the numbers of men accompanying the Battler.
They made straight for Valencia, which he had won in a favoured hour.
My Cid commanded that Don Fernando and Don Diego
be attended by Pedro Bermúdez and Muño Gustioz
— there were not two better men in My Cid's court —             2170
and that these men should become familiar with the ways of the
                                        Infantes of Carrión.

E va i Asur Gonçalez     que era bulidor,
que es largo de lengua     mas en lo al non es tan pro.
Grant ondra les dan     a los ifantes de Carrion.
Afelos en Valençia     la que mio Çid gaño;                    2175
quando a ella assomaron     los gozos son mayores.
Dixo mio Çid a don Pero     e a Muño Gustioz:
'Dad les un reyal     (e) a los ifantes de Carrion;
vos con ellos sed     que assi vos lo mando yo.
Quando viniere la mañana     que apuntare el sol                2180
veran a sus esposas,     a don Elvira e·a doña Sol.'

108  Todos essa noch     fueron a sus posadas;
     mio Çid el Campeador     al alcaçar entrava,
     reçibiolo doña Ximena     e sus fijas amas:
     '¿Venides, Campeador?     ¡En buen ora çinxiestes
                                              espada!           2185
     ¡Muchos dias vos veamos     con los ojos de las caras!'
     '¡Grado al Criador,     vengo, mugier ondrada!
     Hyernos vos adugo     de que avremos ondrança;
     ¡gradid melo, mis fijas,     ca bien vos he casadas!'
     Besaron le las manos     la mugier e las fijas amas,        2190
     e todas las dueñas     que las sirven [sin falla]:

109  '¡Grado al Criador     e a vos, Çid, barba velida!
     Todo lo que vos feches     es de buena guisa;
     ¡non seran menguadas     en todos vuestros dias!'
     'Quando vos nos casaredes     bien seremos ricas.'          2195

110  '¡Mugier doña Ximena,     grado al Cria(a)dor!
     A vos digo, mis fijas     don Elvira e doña Sol:
     deste vu[e]stro casamiento     creçremos en onor,
     mas bien sabet verdad     que non lo levante yo;
     pedidas vos ha e rogadas     el mio señor Alfonsso          2200
     atan firme mientre     e de todo coraçon
     que yo nulla cosa     nol sope dezir de no.
     Metivos en sus manos     fijas, amas a dos;
     bien melo creades     que el vos casa, ca non yo.'

111  Penssaron de adobar     essora el palaçio;                  2205
     por el suelo e suso     tan bien encortinado,

2172-73 Asur (or Ansur) González, who appears in the *Poema* as the Infantes' elder brother, is a figure whose historical existence is not documented. Perhaps his character is introduced to form a direct contrast with that of the silent but forceful Pedro Bermúdez (mentioned in l.2169).
2180 Such repetition, the second clause expressing in different words the sense of the first, could be associated with the device known by the grammarians as *expolitio*. There is, however, no need to see in the poet's practice here the conscious use of a technique learned from the theorists: for such a line of two balanced hemistichs forms a convenient and natural unit for composition.

170

With them was Asur González, a rowdy character,
with much to say but little else to commend him.
The Infantes of Carrión were shown great honour.
Here they are in Valencia, won by My Cid.                                    2175
When they made their appearance there, great was the joy.
My Cid said to Don Pedro and to Muño Gustioz:
"Provide lodging for the Infantes of Carrión,
and keep them company; that is my command.
When morning comes and when the sun rises,                                   2180
they shall see their wives, Doña Elvira and Doña Sol."

They all went to their lodging for the night;
My Cid the Battler entered the citadel,
and was welcomed by Doña Jimena and his two daughters:
"You are come, Battler!  In a favoured hour you girded your sword!
May our eyes be able to gaze on you for many days!"
"My honoured wife, I am come!  Thanks be to the Creator!
I bring you sons - in - law through whom we shall gain honour.
Be grateful to me, my daughters, for I have married you well!"
His wife and his two daughters kissed his hands,                             2190
and so too did all the ladies who served them faithfully.

[Doña Jimena spoke:] "Thanks be to the Creator, and to you, O Cid
                              with your fine beard!
All that you are doing is good;
they will not know want, in all your days!"
[The girls spoke:] "Since you have brought about our marriages, we
                              shall indeed be wealthy."                      2195

"Doña Jimena, my wife, let us give thanks to the Creator!
I say this to you, my daughters, Doña Elvira and Doña Sol:
by these marriages our honour will grow,
but you must know that they were not brought about by me;
my lord, Alfonso, sought and asked for you,                                  2200
so earnestly and so much from the heart,
that I could in no way oppose his command.
I placed you both in his hands, my daughters.
You should realize that he, and not I, offers you in marriage."

Now they began to make the palace ready:                                     2205
the floor was carpeted, there were hangings overhead;

171

tanta porpola e tanto xamed    e tanto paño preçiado:
¡sabor abriedes de ser    e de comer en el palaçio!
Todos sus cavalleros    a priessa son juntados,
por los iffantes de Carrion    essora enbiaron,                    2210
cavalgan los iffantes,    adelant adeliñavan al palaçio
con buenas vestiduras    e fuerte mientre adobados;
de pie e a sabor    ¡Dios, que quedos ent[r]aron!
Reçibio los mio Çid    con todos sus vasallos,
a el e (e) a ssu mugier    delant sele omillaron              2215
e ivan posar    en un preçioso escaño.
Todos los de mio Çid    tan bien son acordados,
estan parando mientes    al que en buen ora nasco;
el Campeador    en pie es levantado:
'Pues que a fazer lo avemos    ¿por que lo imos tardando?  2220
¡Venit aca, Albar Fañez,    el que yo quiero e amo!
Affe amas mis fijas,    metolas en vuestra mano;
sabedes que al rey    assi gelo he mandado,
no lo quiero falir por nada    de quanto ay parado;
a los ifantes de Carrion    dad las con vuestra mano        2225
e prendan bendiçiones    e vayamos recabdando.'
Estoz dixo Minaya:    '¡Esto fare yo de grado!'
Levantan se derechas    e metiogelas en mano;
a los ifantes de Carrion    Minaya va fablando:
'Afevos delant Minaya;    amos sodes hermanos.            2230
Por mano del rey Alfonsso    —que a mi lo ovo mandado—
dovos estas dueñas    —amas son fijas dalgo—
que las tomassedes por mugieres    a ondra e a recabdo.'
Amos las reçiben    d'amor e de grado,
a mio Çid e a su mugier    van besar la mano.                2235
Quando ovieron aquesto fecho    salieron del palaçio
pora Santa Maria    a priessa adelinnando;
el obispo don Jheronimo    vistios tan privado,
a la puerta de la eclegia    sediellos sperando,
dioles bendictiones,    la missa a cantado.                  2240
Al salir de la ecclegia    cavalgaron tan privado,
a la glera de Valençia    fuera dieron salto;
¡Dios, que bien tovieron armas    el Çid e sus vassalos!
Tres cavallos cameo    el que en buen ora nasco.
Mio Çid de lo que veye    mucho era pagado,              2245
los ifantes de Carrion    bien an cavalgado.

---

**2234** Álvar Fáñez has continued to hold the brides by the hand, as a sign of the authority which he (as Alfonso's representative) has at this point assumed over them, and now he places their hands in those of their husbands.
**2240** The marriage has taken place in three stages: the *traditio* performed by Alfonso, the ceremony of the *traditu in manu* (see note to l.2234), and then a blessing of the union in the cathedral. This process is described in the law codes of the period. It was the Church's desire that the actual transference should be made by the priest.

172

so much purple, so much fine silk and so much rich cloth;
you would have gained much pleasure from sitting and eating in
the palace!
Speedily all My Cid's knights were assembled,
and then they sent for the Infantes of Carrión. 2210
The Infantes mounted their horses and made for the palace,
finely robed and fully armed.
On foot and in fitting style, Lord God, what an entry they made!
My Cid received them in the company of all his vassals;
the Infantes bowed to My Cid and his wife 2215
and went to sit on a rich couch.
All My Cid's men, so prudent,
gazed on the man born in a favoured hour.
The Battler rose to his feet:
"Since this is to be done, why do we delay? 2220
Come here, Álvar Fáñez, whom I love most dearly!
Here are my two daughters; I place them in your hands.
You know that this is what I promised the King I would do,
and I will not fail to carry out all that was agreed.
Give them to the Infantes of Carrión with your own hand; 2225
let them receive the blessing, and let us bring the ceremony to a close."
Minaya replied thus: "This I shall willingly do!"
The girls stood up and the Cid gave them into his hand.
Minaya addressed the Infantes of Carrión:
"Here I stand, Minaya, before you two brothers. 2230
With the hand of King Alfonso, who entrusted me with this authority,
I give to you these ladies — they are both of noble birth —
that you may take them as wives, to your honour and advantage."
They both received them with love and pleasure,
and went to kiss the hands of My Cid and his wife. 2235
When they had done this, they left the palace,
making rapidly for Santa María.
Bishop Don Jerónimo robed himself quickly
and was waiting for them at the church door;
he gave them his blessing and sang mass. 2240
On leaving the church, they mounted rapidly
and rode out to the sandy sea - shore of Valencia.
Lord God, how well the Cid and his vassals handled their arms!
Three times the man born in a favoured hour changed his horse.
My Cid was well pleased at what he saw, 2245
for the Infantes of Carrión rode well.

Tornan se con las dueñas,      a Valençia an entrado,
ricas fueron las bodas      en el alcaçar ondrado;
e al otro dia fizo mio Çid      fincar .vii. tablados,
antes que entrassen a yantar      todos los quebrantaron.   2250
Quinze dias conplidos      en las bodas duraron,
hya çerca de los .xv. dias      yas van los fijos dalgo.
Mio Çid don Rodrigo      el que en buen ora nasco
entre palafres e mulas      e corredores cavallos
en bestias sines al      .c. son mandados,   2255
mantos e pelliçones      e otros vestidos largos;
non fueron en cuenta      los averes monedados.
Los vassallos de mio Çid      assi son acordados
cada uno por si      sos dones avien dados.
Qui aver quiere prender      bien era abastado,   2260
ricos tornan a Castiella      los que a las bodas legaron.
Hyas ivan partiendo      aquestos ospedados,
espidiendos de Ruy Diaz      el que en buen ora nasco
e a todas las dueñas      e a los fijos dalgo;
por pagados se parten      de mio Çid e de sus vassallos,   2265
grant bien dizen dellos      ca sera aguisado.
Mucho eran alegres      Diego e Ferrando,
estos fueron fijos      del conde don Gonçalo.
Venidos son a Castiella      aquestos ospedados,
el Çid e sos hyernos      en Valençia son rastados;   2270
hi moran los ifantes      bien çerca de dos años,
los amores que les fazen      mucho eran sobejanos;
alegre era el Çid      e todos sus vassallos.
¡Plega a Santa Maria      e al Padre santo
ques page des casamiento mio Çid      o el que lo ovo algo.   2275
Las coplas deste cantar      aquis van acabando:
¡El Criador vos valla      con todos los sos santos!

2266 Following the display of generosity on the part of the Çid and his vassals, it is to be expected that the fame of their wealth and magnanimity will be carried far afield. For the importance of their behaviour here, see Introduction, V (b).

174

They returned with the ladies and rode back into Valencia,
and rich was the wedding celebration in the fine citadel.
The next day My Cid had seven mock castles set up,
and the men broke all of them down before going in to eat.     2250
The wedding celebration lasted a full fifteen days,
and towards the end of the fifteen days the noblemen began to leave.
My Cid Don Rodrigo, the man born in a favoured hour,
made gifts of palfreys and mules and chargers;
he gave away a hundred of these animals alone,               2255
together with cloaks and furs and a great many other garments;
the money was beyond reckoning.
My Cid's vassals had agreed,
each one of them, to make further gifts.
Anyone who wanted to take possessions was given plenty,      2260
and those who had come to the wedding returned to Castile
                                     wealthy men.
Now the guests were going on their way,
taking their leave of Ruy Díaz, the man born in a favoured hour,
of the ladies and of the noblemen.
Well satisfied, they left My Cid and his vassals,            2265
speaking highly of them, as was proper.
Full of joy were Diego and Fernando,
the sons of Count Don Gonzalo.
The guests arrived in Castile,
and My Cid and his sons - in - law remained in Valencia.       2270
There the Infantes stayed for almost two years,
and great indeed was the love lavished upon them.
Joyful were the Cid and all his vassals.
May it please Saint Mary and the holy Father
that My Cid, and the man who valued him so highly, should gain
                             joy from this wedding!     2275
Now the verses of this song are coming to an end;
may the Creator, with all his saints, protect you!

# CANTAR III

112  En Valençia seye mio Çid        con todos sus vassallos,

con el amos sus yernos        los ifantes de Carrion.
Yazies en un escaño,        durmie el Campeador;                     2280
mala sobrevienta        sabed que les cuntio:
salios de la red        e desatos el leon.
En grant miedo se vieron        por medio de la cort;
enbraçan los mantos        los del Campeador
e çercan el escaño        e fincan sobre so señor.                     2285
Ferran Gonçalez non vio alli dos alçasse,        nin camara abierta
nin torre,
metios so'l escaño        tanto ovo el pavor;
Diego Gonçalez        por la puerta salio
diziendo de la boca:        '¡Non vere Carrion!'
Tras una viga lagar        metios con grant pavor,                     2290
el manto y el brial        todo suzio lo saco.
En esto desperto        el que en buen ora naçio,
vio çercado el escaño        de sus buenos varones:
'¿Ques esto, mesnadas,        o que queredes vos?'
'¡Hya señor ondrado        rebata nos dio el leon!'                     2295
Mio Çid finco el cobdo,        en pie se levanto,
el manto trae al cuello        e adeliño pora[l] leon;
el leon quando lo vio        assi envergonço
ante mio Çid la cabeça premio        y el rostro finco;
mio Çid don Rodrigo        al cuello lo tomo                     2300

2289 Compare the Infantes' reaction when faced with battle against Búcar's troops. Repeatedly, the Infantes are shown to hanker after the security of Carrión, an attachment to a home which they see not only as a place of safety but also as a symbol of their illustrious birth.

2290 In a city reconquered from the Moslems, a wine press may well have been a recent introduction, though the area was sufficiently westernized for the Moslems to have drunk wine in large quantities. It is rather surprising, however, that the press should occupy so central a position in the palace.

2278 The manuscript indicates the start of the third *cantar* merely by the use of a large capital letter.

2282 It was not uncommon for a medieval potentate to keep a menagerie, partly as a symbol of wealth. The lion was commonly associated with kingship, but was also often used in medieval art to represent the figure of Christ. For a detailed analysis of this important episode, see D. Hook, 'Some Observations upon the Episode of the Cid's Lion', *Modern Language Review*, 71 (1976), 553-64.

2284-85 The poet contrasts the purposeful action taken by the Cid's vassals with the cowardice of the Infantes, who here give public proof of their true weakness of character. They should look upon the Cid as their father (see l.2106), and their first duty here is to ensure his safety.

The vassals wear their cloaks tightly wound around their arms to give them protection; in contrast with this the poet draws our attention to the disorder in which Diego González withdraws his cloak from his hiding place, and, on the other hand, he comments on the normal, heroic position in which the Cid wears his cloak as he confidently approaches the lion. Hook ('Some Observations', p.563) comments that 'the state of the cloaks, as well as the actions of the characters, thus seems to indicate the relative moral worth of the participants in this episode.'

# CANTAR III

My Cid was in Valencia, with all his vassals,

and with him his two sons‐in‐law, the Infantes of Carrión.

*contrast notably*

Lying on a couch, the Battler slept;                               2280
the Infantes, I tell you, had a terrible shock:
the lion broke free and escaped from his cage.
They were stricken with fear in the middle of the hall.
Rolling their cloaks on their arms, the Battler's men
surrounded the couch, to protect their lord.                       2285
Fernando González saw nowhere to flee, no open chamber or tower,
and he hid under the couch, so great was his terror.
Diego González ran out through the door,
crying: "Never again shall I see Carrión!"
Behind the beam of a wine press he hid in his terror;              2290
when he emerged his cloak and tunic were all covered in dirt.
At this point the man born in a favoured hour awoke
and saw the couch surrounded by his good men:
"What is this, my vassals?   What do you want?"
"Honoured lord, the lion filled us with terror!"                   2295
My Cid sat up, leaning on his elbow, and then rose to his feet;
with his cloak fastened on his shoulders, he went towards the lion.
When it saw him, the lion felt such shame
that before My Cid it lowered its head and looked to the ground.
My Cid Don Rodrigo took it by the neck,                            2300

---

**2291** The stain on Diego's clothes can be seen as symbolizing the stain on his honour and the obvious faults in his character. Perhaps this detail can be associated with that of the stains of blood on the clothes of the Cid's daughters, mentioned in l.2744. Certainly, Diego González's claim during the court scene (l.3354) that he and his brother are 'counts of the purest (literally "cleanest") descent' is immediately rebutted by Martín Anto‐línez's allusion to the dirtying of Diego's clothes,which were never again worn (l.3366). Deyermond and Hook examine these parallels in greater detail in 'Doors and Cloaks'.

**2294** Hook ('Some Observations', p.561) points out that the Cid, on waking to see his vassals gathered around him, might have had serious doubts about their intentions: a source, perhaps, not only of dramatic tension but also of humour.

**2300-01** The lion has humbled itself before a 'king' of men. It does not look at the Cid for shame – compare the reaction of the Infantes during the court scene (l.3126). It has been pointed out that in the description of the way in which the Cid has acted calmly and confidently to subdue the lion there are a series of parallels with the depiction in Matthew 8.23-27 of Christ rising from his sleep amidst the terror of his apostles to calm the storm, an action which provokes the wonder of all those present. C.Bandera Gómez, for whom the form of the wine press suggests that it may represent the cross, argues that in this episode we are meant to see the Cid as a Christ-figure – see *El Poema de Mio Cid: poesía, historia, mito* (Madrid, 1969), pp.82-114. Hook ('Some Observations') gives further consideration to the possible religious symbolism of the scene.

e lieva lo adestrando,    en la red le metio.
A maravilla lo han    quantos que i son
e tornaron se al (a)palaçio    pora la cort.
Mio Çid por sos yernos    demando e no los fallo,
mager los estan lamando    ninguno non responde.    2305
Quando los fallaron    assi vinieron sin color;
¡non viestes tal guego    commo iva por la cort!
Mandolo vedar    mio Çid el Campeador.
Muchos tovieron por enbaidos    los ifantes de Carrion;
fiera cosa les pesa    desto que les cuntio.    2310

113 Ellos en esto estando    don avien grant pesar,
fuerças de Marruecos    Valençia vienen çercar;
çinquaenta mill tiendas    fincadas ha de las cabdales,
aqueste era el rey Bucar,    sil oyestes contar.

114 Alegravas el Çid    e todos sus varones    2315
que les creçe la ganançia    ¡grado al Criador!
Mas, sabed, de cuer les pesa    a los ifantes de Carrion
ca veyen tantas tiendas de moros    de que non avien sabor.
Amos hermanos    apart salidos son:
'Catamos la ganançia    e la perdida no;    2320
ya en esta batalla    a entrar abremos nos,
¡esto es aguisado    por non ver Carrion,
bibdas remandran    fijas del Campeador!'
Oyo la poridad    aquel Muño Gustioz,
vino con estas nuevas    a mio Çid Ruy Diaz el Campeador:
'¡Evades que pavor han vuestros yernos:    tan osados son, 2326
por entrar en batalla    desean Carrion!
Hid los conortar,    ¡si vos vala el Criador!
Que sean en paz    e non ayan i raçion,
¡nos con vusco la vençremos    e valer nos ha el Criador!'    2330
Mio Çid don Rodrigo    sonrrisando salio:
'¡Dios vos salve, yernos,    ifantes de Carrion!

**2308** Though the Cid is well aware that the mockery of the Infantes is justified, he must forbid it, for the protection of his family honour and for good military discipline and also in accordance with the obligation imposed upon him by King Alfonso (see ll.2121-24).

**2309** Such public loss of face is of great significance, given the importance in medieval Spanish society of a man's reputation among his fellows – see Introduction, V (d). The Infantes know that word of their cowardice will be carried far and wide (contrast the Cid's repeated assurances after the battle that good reports of their conduct will go to Carrión). This episode is thus to trigger the action of the remainder of the poem, for it is in large part the Infantes' shame and resentment at knowing themselves to be generally held in ridicule that will lead them to assert themselves in the most base and spiteful fashion. The term *enbayr* is found in at least one twelfth-century legal code dealing with offences against an individual's honour, in a passage which makes it clear that the correct course of action for the Infantes is to seek redress through a formal challenge (Lacarra, pp.84-86). At Toledo,

and, leading it along on his right hand side, put it in the cage.
All those present marvelled at this,
and they made their way back to the palace and to the hall.
My Cid asked for his sons - in - law, but they were not to be found;
although people were calling them, they gave no answer.          2305
When they were found, they came along — the colour had gone
                                        from their cheeks.
Never did you see such mockery as spread through the court!
My Cid the Battler forbade it to continue.
The Infantes of Carrión considered themselves greatly insulted;
they were deeply hurt by what had happened to them.          2310

While they were still greatly upset,
forces from Morocco came to lay siege to Valencia;
they pitched fifty thousand large tents.
This was the Emir Búcar; perhaps you have heard tell of him.

The Cid was delighted, and so were all his men,          2315
for their wealth was growing — thanks be to the Creator!
But, I tell you, the Infantes of Carrión were downhearted,
for seeing so many Moorish tents pleased them not at all.
The two brothers went off together:
"We are looking for gains; we do not wish for losses;          2320
now we shall have to enter this battle;
this may well mean we shall never see Carrión again.
The Battler's daughters will be left widows."
The notable Muño Gustioz overheard the secret discussion,
and came with a report of it to My Cid Ruy Díaz the Battler:          2325
"Look at the fear of your sons - in - law; they are so bold
at the thought of going into battle that they long for Carrión!
Go and give them encouragement, may the Creator protect you!
Let them be at ease and not take part in the battle.
We shall win it with you and the Creator will give us his aid!"          2330
My Cid Don Rodrigo went out with a smile on his face:
"May God watch over you, my sons - in - law, Infantes of Carrión!

when the Cid's vassals issue their challenges to the Infantes, they make much of the way that the latter have
brought dishonour upon themselves by their behaviour during the encounter with the lion (ll.3330-34 and
ll.3363-66).
**2314** It is most likely that the allusion here is to Sir Ben Abu Beker, an Almoravid general and Yusuf's son-in-law,
though this individual is not known to have attacked Valencia or to have had any dealings with the city.

¡En braços tenedes mis fijas    tan blancas commo el sol!
Hyo desseo lides        e vos a Carrion;
en Valençia folgad      a todo vuestro sabor                    2335
ca d'aquelos moros      yo so sabidor:
arrancar melos trevo    con la merçed del Criador.'

115
'¡Aun vea el ora        que vos meresca dos tanto!'
En una conpaña         tornados son amos;
assi lo otorga don Pero     cuemo se alaba Ferrando.            2340
Plogo a mio Çid        e a todos sos vassallos:
'¡Aun si Dios quisiere      y el Padre que esta en alto
amos los mios yernos    buenos seran en campo!'
Esto van diziendo       e las yentes se alegando,
en la ueste de los moros    los atamores sonando;             2345
a marav[i]lla lo avien    muchos dessos christianos
ca nunqua lo vieran,     ca nuevos son legados.
Mas se maravillan      entre Diego e Ferando,
por la su voluntad      non serien alli legados.
Oid lo que fablo        el que en buen ora nasco:             2350
'¡Ala. Pero Vermuez,    el mio sobrino caro!
Curies me a Diego      e curies me a don Fernando
mios yernos amos a dos,     las cosas que mucho amo,
ca los moros —con Dios—     non fincaran en canpo.'

116 'Hyo vos digo, Çid,    por toda caridad,                   2355
que oy los ifantes      a mi por amo non abran;
¡curielos qui quier,    ca dellos poco m'incal!
Hyo con los mios       ferir quiero delant,
vos con los vuestros    firme mientre a la çaga tengades;
si cueta fuere         bien me podredes huviar.'              2360
Aqui lego     Minaya Albar Fañez:
'¡Oid, ya Çid     Canpeador leal!                             2361b

**2333** Literally, 'you have my daughters in your arms'. Menéndez Pidal points out that in some twelfth-century charters a knight was excused from going to war during the first year of his marriage, though in this case the Infantes have been married for longer than this (see l.2271). When the poet mentions the sun ('el sol') he, perhaps unintentionally, recalls the name of the daughter Sol.

**2337** At this point there is a lacuna in the manuscript. A folio has been removed, but it need not be assumed that a full fifty lines of text are missing (see Smith, 'On Editing the *Poema de mio Cid*', pp.12-13). Menéndez Pidal gives the following passage from the *Chronicle of Twenty Kings of Castile* (see note to ll.1-2) which supplies the missing account of the early events of the battle:

As they were saying this, Emir Búcar sent word to the Cid that he should depart from Valencia in peace, otherwise he would make him pay for all that he had done. The Cid said to the messenger: 'Go and tell Búcar, that traitor's son, that within three days I will give him what he is demanding.' The next day, the Cid commanded all his men to be armed, and went out to do battle with the Moors. Then the Infantes of Carrión asked him for the right to strike the first blows; and after the Cid had drawn up his lines of battle, Don Fernando, one of the Infantes, rode forward to strike a Moor called Aladraf. When the Moor saw him he rode towards him too, and the Infante, in terror

You are married to my daughters, as white as the sun.
I long for battle, you for Carrión.
Rest in Valencia at your pleasure,                                    2335
for I know those Moors well.
I am brave enough to defeat them, with the Creator's blessing!"

. . . . . . . . . . . . . . . . . . . . .
. . . . . . . . . . . . . . . . . . . .

"May the time come when I repay this twice over."
They both rode back together;
Don Pedro confirmed Fernando's boastful claims.                      2340
My Cid and all his vassals were pleased:
"With the grace of God, the Father on high,
both my sons - in - law will come to fight well in battle."
While all this was being said, the two forces drew close;
from the Moorish army came the pounding of the drums;               2345
these filled many of the Christians with wonder,
for, having recently arrived, they had never encountered them before.
All the greater was the wonder of Diego and Fernando;
they would never have been there of their own desire.
Hear the words of the man born in a favoured hour:                   2350
"Listen, Pedro Bermúdez, my dear nephew!
Look after Diego for me, and look after Don Fernando,
my two sons - in - law, whom I greatly love;
the Moors, if God helps us, will be driven from the field."

"I ask you, O Cid, in all charity to grant that                      2355
I must no longer be responsible for the Infantes.
Let anybody who is willing watch over them, for I could not care
                                          less about them.
I, with my men, wish to attack at the front;
you, with yours, safely guard the rear.
If there is danger, you will be able to give me aid."                2360
At this point, Minaya Álvar Fáñez arrived:
"Hear me, Cid, O loyal Battler.                                      2361

*of him, pulled at his reins and fled, for he dared not even stand his ground. Pedro Bermúdez, who was riding near*
*him, on seeing this, went to strike the Moor, fought with him, and killed him. Then he took the Moor's horse, rode*
*after the Infante as he fled, and said to him: 'Don Fernando, take this horse and tell everyone that you slew the Moor*
*who rode it; and I shall bear witness for you.' The Infante said to him: 'Don Pedro Bermúdez, I am most grateful to*
*you for what you say.'*

Esta batalla     el Criador la fera,
e vos tan dinno     que con el avedes part.
Mandad no' los ferir     de qual part vos semejar;
el debdo que a cada uno     a conplir sera.                    2365
¡Verlo hemos con Dios     e con la vuestra auze!'
Dixo mio Çid:     'Ayamos mas de vagar.'
Afevos el obispo don Jheronimo     muy bien armado,
paravas delant al Campeador     siempre con la buen auze:
'Oy vos dix la missa     de Santa Trinidade,                   2370
por esso sali de mi tierra     e vin vos buscar
por sabor que avia     de algun moro matar.
Mi orden e mis manos     querria las ondrar
e a estas feridas     yo quiero ir delant;
pendon trayo a corças     e armas de señal,                    2375
si plogiesse a Dios     querria las ensayar,
mio coraçon     que pudiesse folgar
e vos, mio Çid,     de mi mas vos pagar.
Si este amor non feches     yo de vos me quiero quitar.'
Essora dixo mio Çid:     'Lo que vos queredes plaz me.    2380
Afe los moros a ojo,     id los ensayar;
¡nos d'aquent veremos     commo lidia el abbat!'

117 El obispo don Jheronimo     priso a espolonada
e iva los ferir     a cabo del albergada:
por la su ventura     e Dios quel amava                        2385
a los primeros colpes     dos moros matava de la lança;
el astil a quebrado     e metio mano al espada,
ensayavas el obispo,     ¡Dios, que bien lidiava!
Dos mato con lança     e .v. con el espada;
los moros son muchos,     derredor le çercavan,                2390
davan le grandes colpes     mas nol falssan las armas.
El que en buen ora nasco     los ojos le fincava,
enbraço el escudo     e abaxo el asta,
aguijo a Bavieca     el cavallo que bien anda,
hiva los ferir     de coraçon e de alma;                       2395

2367 The poet emphasizes the Cid's quiet confidence. In this scene, the hero is approached in turn by Pedro Bermúdez, acting with characteristic impetuousness, by Minaya, enthusiastic for the fray, and by Bishop Jerónimo, asking for the second time for the right to strike the first blows of a battle (see also ll.1706-09). The unbridled excitement of these three men is contrasted with the calmness and, indeed, the wry humour with which the Cid responds.

2373 Bishop Jerónimo belongs to the Order of Cluny. The influence of this French order in the Peninsula was extended during the reign of Alfonso VI and it played an important role in the reform of Church life and education. A number of Cluniac monks were given bishoprics; outstanding among them was Bernard, first archbishop of Toledo (and previously abbot of Sahagún), who sent Jerónimo to Valencia.

2375 The roe-deer presumably also constitutes part of the emblem on the arms. In this period, such a coat of arms would have belonged just to an individual and would not have been passed down within his family.

2382 Jerónimo was at no stage an abbot; the term is applied to him by the Cid loosely and probably humorously.

2398 This might seem a fairly simple and rapid way to put an end to a major battle! The structure of the battle

The Creator will win this battle for us,
with you, so worthy that you enjoy his favour.
Order us to attack from any point you will.
Each one must perform his duty.                                    2365
We shall settle this with the aid of God and of your good fortune!"
My Cid said: "Let us take things more calmly."
Now came Bishop Don Jerónimo, very heavily armed;
he stopped before the Battler, always a man of good fortune:
"Today I said for you the Mass of the Holy Trinity;              2370
for this I left my land and came in search of you,
out of the desire that I had to kill a few Moors.
I wish to bring honour to my order and to myself;
I want to go ahead to lead the attack.
I bring a pennant, emblazoned with a roe deer, and arms carrying
                                        my emblem;                  2375
if God were willing, I would like to put them to the test,
so that my own heart may rejoice and you, My Cid, may be all
                                        the more pleased with me.
If you do not give me this token of your love, I shall no longer
                                        remain with you."
Then My Cid spoke: "I am pleased by your request.                  2380
There are the Moors; go and do battle with them.
Now we shall see how the abbot fights!"

Bishop Don Jerónimo spurred on,
and met the Moors in battle near their camp.
As he enjoyed good fortune and the favour of God,                 2385
with his first blows he killed two Moors with his lance;
he broke the shaft and laid his hand upon his sword;
the Bishop attacked; Lord God, how well he fought!
He killed two with his lance and five with his sword;
there were many Moors and they gathered around him,               2390
striking him heavy blows, but without piercing his armour.
The man born in a favoured hour, setting his eyes upon him,
steadied his shield on his arm and lowered his lance;
he spurred - on Babieca, his fine charger,
and he rode to attack with all his heart and soul.                2395

description is similar to that customarily adopted in medieval epic: there is no attempt to give an overall view of
the development of the battle or of the tactics employed, but rather the narrative concentrates on a number of
hand-to-hand combats and on the progress of certain individuals. What is perhaps most striking here is the
relative brevity of this account, for in many medieval poems the stylized descriptions of the fighting are much
more extensive and repetitive.

en las azes primeras     el Campeador entrava,
abatio a .vii.     e a .iiii. matava.
Plogo a Dios     aquesta fue el arrancada.
Mio Çid con los suyos     cae en alcança:
veriedes quebrar tantas cuerdas     e arrancar se las estacas    2400
e acostar se los tendales,     con huebras eran tantas.
Los de mio Çid a los de Bucar     de las tiendas los sacàn.

118 Sacan los de las tiendas,     caen los en alcaz;
     tanto braço con loriga     veriedes caer apart,
     tantas cabeças con yelmos     que por el campo caen,     2405
     cavallos sin dueños     salir a todas partes;
     .vii. migeros conplidos     duro el segudar.
     Mio Çid al rey Bucar     cayol en alcaz:
     '¡Aca torna, Bucar!     Venist d'alent mar,
     verte as con el Çid     el de la barba grant,     2410
     ¡saludar nos hemos amos     e tajaremos amista[d]!'
     Respuso Bucar al Çid:     '¡Cofonda Dios tal amistad!
     El espada tienes desnuda en la mano     e veot aguijar,
     así commo semeja     en mi la quieres ensayar;
     mas si el cavallo non estropieça     o comigo non caye     2415
     ¡non te juntaras comigo     fata dentro en la mar!'
     Aqui respuso mio Çid:     '¡Esto non sera verdad!'
     Buen cavallo tiene Bucar     e grandes saltos faz
     mas Bavieca el de mio Çid     alcançando lo va.
     Alcançolo el Çid a Bucar     a tres braças del mar,     2420
     arriba alço Colada,     un grant golpe dadol ha,
     las carbonclas del yelmo     tollidas gela[s] ha,
     cortol el yelmo     e —librado todo lo hal—
     fata la çintura     el espada legado ha.
     Mato a Bucar     al rey de alen mar     2425
     e gano a Tizon     que mill marcos d'oro val.
     Vençio la batalla     maravillosa e grant.

     Aquis ondro mio Çid     e quantos con el son.

119 Con estas gananças     yas ivan tornando;
     sabet, todos de firme     robavan el campo.     2430
     A las tiendas     eran legados
     do estava     el que en buen ora nasco.

---

**2408** The pursuit of Búcar is the subject of a famous ballad, derived from the account in the *Poema* but differing markedly from it in tone – so much so that the poet tells us how, during the chase, the Cid's horse shouts out in anger! In the ballad, Búcar is ferried away to safety. See Roger Wright, *Spanish Ballads* (Warminster, 1987), pp.81-83 and 209-12.

**2424** There are precise parallels in French epic literature for the description of this blow (see Smith, *The Making* ..., p.193).

The Battler rode in among the foremost ranks;
he struck down seven men and killed four.
It pleased God that from this should spring the victory.
My Cid with his men charged in pursuit.
You could see so many ropes cut and so many stakes torn up,    2400
tent - poles, so richly decorated, laid flat.
My Cid's troops drove Búcar's men out from their tents.

They drove them from their tents and began the pursuit;
you could see so many arms hewn off with their armour,
so many helmeted heads falling to the ground,    2405
and riderless horses galloping off in all directions.
the pursuit lasted a full seven miles.
My Cid set off in pursuit of the Emir Búcar:
"Come back here, Búcar!  You came from over the sea;
you must face up to the Cid, the man with the flowing beard.    2410
The two of us must kiss each other and strike up a friendship!"
Búcar replied to the Cid: "God confound such a friendship!
You have your sword unsheathed in your hand and I can see you
                                    spurring - on your horse.
It seems to me as if you want to test out the sword on me;
but, if my horse does not stumble or fall with me,    2415
you will not reach me till we are in the sea."
Then My Cid replied: "That will not be so!"
Búcar had a good horse, and it galloped on swiftly,
but My Cid's Babieca gradually caught up with it.
My Cid reached Búcar, three arm's lengths from the sea,    2420
and, raising Colada aloft, dealt him a mighty blow;
he cut through the gems of the helmet;
passing through the helmet and cutting everything else away,
the sword sliced through him down to the waist.
He killed Búcar, the emir from beyond the sea,    2425
and won the sword Tizón, worth a thousand gold marks.
He won the battle, which had been awesome and great.

There My Cid won honour, and so too did all those with him.

Now they returned with their booty.
All of them, I tell you, plundered the field.    2430
They had reached the tents
where the man born in a favoured hour was to be found.

Mio Çid Ruy Diaz    el Campeador contado
con dos espadas    que el preçiava algo
por la matança    vinia tan privado,    2435
la cara fronzida    e almofar soltado,
cofia sobre los pelos    fronzida della yaquanto.
Algo vie mio Çid    de lo que era pagado:
alço sos ojos,    est[a]va adelant catando
e vio venir    a Diego e a Fernando    2440
—amos son fijos    del conde don Gonçalo—.
Alegros mio Çid,    fermoso sonrrisando:
'¿Venides, mios yernos?    ¡Mios fijos sodes amos!
Se que de lidiar    bien sodes pagados;
a Carrion de vos    iran buenos mandados    2445
commo al rey Bucar    avemos arrancado.
¡Commo yo fio por Dios    y en todos los sos santos
desta arrancada    nos iremos pagados!'
Minaya Albar Fañez    essora es legado,
el escudo trae al cuello    e todo espad[ad]o;    2450
de los colpes de las lanças    non avie recabdo,
aquelos que gelos dieran    non gelo avien logrado.
Por el cobdo ayuso    la sangre destellando,
de .xx. arriba    ha moros matado.
De todas partes    sos vassalos van legando:    2455
'¡Grado a Dios    e al Padre que esta en alto
e a vos, Çid,    que en buen ora fuestes nado!
Matastes a Bucar    e arrancamos el canpo;
todos estos bienes    de vos son e de vuestros vassallos.
E vuestros yernos    aqui son ensayados,    2460
fartos de lidiar    con moros en el campo.'
Dixo mio Çid:    'Yo desto so pagado;
quando agora son buenos    adelant seran preçiados.'

Por bien lo dixo el Çid    mas ellos lo tovieron a mal.

119ᵇ Todas las ganançias    a Valençia son legadas;    2465
alegre es mio Çid    con todas sus conpañas
que a la raçion caye    seis çientos marcos de plata.

119ᶜ Los yernos de mio Çid    quando este aver tomaron
desta arrancada,    que lo tenien en so salvo,

2426 *Tizón* means 'fire-brand'. This sword is said to have passed into the possession of the kings of Aragón. See also note to l.1010.
2443 Compare the King's words in l.2123.

My Cid Ruy Díaz, the illustrious Battler,
with two swords which he greatly prized,
rode swiftly through the slaughter,                                    2435
with his face revealed and his cowl of chain mail removed;
his cap was rolled back some way over his hair.
My Cid could see something which pleased him:
he looked up and gazed before him,
and he saw the arrival of Diego and Fernando —                        2440
the two of them sons of Count Don Gonzalo.
My Cid was joyful, and gave a broad smile:
"It is you, my sons - in - law!  You are as sons to me!
I know that you have taken pleasure in the battle;
good reports will go to Carrión of you,                               2445
telling how we have defeated the Emir Búcar.
As I trust in God and all his saints,
we shall gain pleasure from this victory."
Then Minaya Álvar Fáñez arrived,
at his neck bearing the shield, marked by sword blows;                2450
the blows dealt with lances were beyond reckoning,
but those who had struck them had done so in vain.
Blood flowed down to his elbow —
he had killed upwards of twenty Moors.
My Cid's vassals were arriving from all directions:                   2455
"Thanks be to God, the Father on high,
and to you, O Cid, who were born in a favoured hour!
You have killed Búcar and we have won the battle;
all this wealth belongs to you and your vassals.
Your sons - in - law have proved themselves here,                     2460
and are tired now with fighting against Moors on the field of battle."
My Cid said: "With this I am pleased.
They are now fine men — in future they will be even more highly
                              esteemed."


My Cid meant it well, but they took it badly.


All the booty has now been taken into Valencia;                       2465
joyful is My Cid, and all his retainers too,
for to each man's share there fall six hundred silver marks.


My Cid's sons - in - law, when they had taken their part of the booty
from this victory, and when they had it in their safekeeping,

cuidaron que en sus dias     nunqua serien minguados.     2470
Fueron en Valençia     muy bien arreados,
conduchos a sazones,     buenas pieles e buenos mantos.
Mucho(s) son alegres     mio Çid e sus vassallos.

120  Grant fue el dia     [por] la cort del Campeador
despues que esta batalla vençieron     e al rey Bucar mato.     2475
Alço la mano,     a la barba se tomo:
'¡Grado a Christus     que del mundo es señor
quando veo     lo que avia sabor,
que lidiaron comigo en campo     mios yernos amos a dos!
Mandados buenos     iran dellos a Carrion     2480
commo son ondrados     e aver [n]os [an] grant pro.

121  Sobejanas son las ganançias     que todos an ganadas.

Lo uno es nuestro,     lo otro han en salvo.'
Mando mio Çid     el que en buen ora nasco
desta batalla     que han arrancado     2485
que todos prisiessen     so derecho contado
e la su quinta     non fuesse olbidado;
assi lo fazen todos     ca eran acordados.
Cayeron le en quinta     al Çid seix çientos cavallos
e otras azemillas     e camelos largos;     2490
tantos son de muchos     que non serien contados.

122  Todas estas ganançias     fizo el Canpeador:
'¡Grado ha Dios     que del mundo es señor!
Antes fu minguado,     agora rico so,
que he aver e tierra     e oro e onor,     2495
e son mios yernos     ifantes de Carrion;
arranco las lides     commo plaze al Criador,
moros e christianos     de mi han grant pavor;
ala dentro en Marruecos     o las mezquitas son
que abram de mi salto     quiçab alguna noch     2500
ellos lo temen,     ca non lo piensso yo;
no los ire buscar,     en Valençia sere yo;
ellos me daran parias     con ayuda del Criador
que paguen a mi     o a qui yo ovier sabor.'

---

2483 The sense seems to be that part of the booty is in the possession of the *quiñoneros*, the officials responsible
for its just distribution. Michael interprets the meaning as 'part of it belongs to me and my vassals, part of it is in
the Infantes' possession', and points to the mention in l.2509 of the Infantes' large share and to Fernando's
comment in l.2531.

thought that in all their days they would never be in need.                    2470
In Valencia they had been richly provided for;
they ate excellent meals, and wore fine furs and fine cloaks.
Full of joy were My Cid and his vassals.

It was a great day in the court of the Battler,
since they had won this battle and My Cid had killed the Emir Búcar.
My Cid raised his hand, and held his beard:
"Thanks be to Christ, who is Lord of the world,
for now I see what I have desired,
that my two sons - in - law have fought at my side on the field of
                                        battle.
Good reports of them will go to Carrión,                    2480
telling of how they have won honour, and we shall gain great
                                        advantage by it.

Rich is the booty won by all.

Part of the booty is already ours, part is in safekeeping."
My Cid, the man born in a favoured hour, commanded
that from this victory they had won                    2485
each should take exactly his due share,
and that his own fifth part should not be forgotten;
this they all did, for they were prudent men.
To My Cid in his fifth share there fell six hundred horses,
and also pack animals and many camels;                    2490
there were so many that they could not be counted.

The Battler took all this booty:
"Thanks be to God, who is Lord of the world!
Before, I was in need, now I am rich.
For I have possessions and lands and gold and fame,                    2495
and my sons - in - law are the Infantes of Carrión.
I win battles as the Creator wills,
and both Moors and Christians are in great terror of me.
In Morocco, where the mosques are to be found,
lest they suffer an attack by me one night                    2500
they live in fear, though I do not intend to make one.
I shall not go out in search of them, but shall remain in Valencia;
with the Creator's aid, I shall receive tribute from them,
paid to me or to whomseover I wish."

Grandes son los gozos     en Valençia [la mayor]     2505
de todas sus conpañas     [de] mio Çid el Canpeador;
grandes son los gozos     de sus yernos amos a dos,
d'aquesta arrancada     que lidiaron de coraçon
valia de çinco mill marcos     ganaron amos a dos,
muchos tienen por ricos     los ifantes de Carrion.     2510
Ellos con los otros     vinieron a la cort;
aqui esta con mio Çid     el obispo don Jheronimo,
el bueno de Albar Fañez     cavallero lidiador,
e otros muchos     que crio el Campeador.
Quando entraron     los ifantes de Carrion     2515
reçibiolos Minaya     por mio Çid el Campeador:
'¡Aca venid, cuñados,     que mas valemos por vos!'
Assi commo legaron     pagos el Campeador:
'Evades aqui, yernos,     la mi mugier de pro
e amas la[s] mis fijas     don Elvira e doña Sol;     2520
bien vos abraçen     e sirvan vos de coraçon.
¡Grado a Santa Maria     madre del nuestro señor Dios!     2524
Destos [v]uestros casamientos     vos abredes honor;     2525
buenos mandados iran     a tierras de Carrion.'

123 A estas palabras     fablo Feran Gonçalez:

'¡Grado al Criador     e a vos, Çid ondrado!
Tantos avemos de averes     que no son contados;
por vos avemos ondra     e avemos lidiado,     2530
vençiemos moros en campo     e matamos     2522
a aquel rey Bucar,     traidor provado.     2523
Pensad de lo otro,     que lo nuestro tenemos lo en salvo.'
Vassallos de mio Çid     seyen se sonrrisando
quien lidiara mejor     o quien fuera en alcanço;
mas non fallavan i     a Diego ni a Ferrando.
Por aquestos guegos     que ivan levantando     2535
e las noches e los dias     tan mal los escarmentando
tan mal se conssejaron     estos iffantes amos;
amos salieron apart     —vera mientre son hermanos—
desto que ellos fablaron     nos parte non ayamos:

---

2508 The poet's description of the Infantes' enthusiasm for the fight is, of course, heavily ironical.
2517 Álvar Fáñez, with a totally undeserved generosity, tells the Infantes that through their actions the Cid and his vassals will literally 'be worth more'. The notion that honourable or dishonourable conduct adds to or detracts from the 'worth' of an individual and those associated with him will be mentioned repeatedly in the final stages of the poem, and it is the *menos valer* ('loss of worth') of the Infantes which the Cid is to attack in the accusation levelled at them at Toledo (l.3268).
2522-23 Smith has here (as have some other editors) moved these lines to fit the new assonance in *a-o*. They do, however, make equally good sense in the position (in *tirada* 122) which they occupy in the manuscript.
2539 ff. The device used here by the poet was defined by the grammarians as *occultatio*: he states that he will not tell us what plans the Infantes make, and then proceeds to do so.

190

There is much joy in the great city of Valencia,                          2505
felt by all the retainers of My Cid the Battler.
Great is the joy of his two sons - in - law;
for, from this victorious battle which they had fought with all their
                                    heart,
both of them had won booty worth five thousand marks.
The Infantes of Carrión thought themselves very wealthy men.          2510
With the others they came to the court;
there, with My Cid, was Bishop Don Jerónimo,
good Álvar Fáñez, a warrior knight,
and many others brought up in the household of the Battler.
When the Infantes of Carrión entered,                                 2515
Minaya welcomed them on behalf of My Cid the Battler;
"Come here, my brothers - in - law; you have increased our prestige."
At their arrival, the Battler was well pleased:
"Here, my sons - in - law, is my worthy wife,
and here are my two daughters, Doña Elvira and Doña Sol;              2520
they are to embrace you warmly and serve you faithfully.
Thanks be to Saint Mary, the Mother of our Lord God!                  2524
From your marriages you will gain honour,
and good reports will go to the lands of Carrión."

To these words Fernando González replied:

"Thanks be to the Creator, and to you, honoured Cid!
We have so many possessions that they are beyond reckoning;
through you we have gained honour, and we have fought,                2530
defeated Moors on the field of battle and killed                      2522
the renowned Emir Búcar, a proven traitor.                            2523
Think of other matters, for we have our share safely stored away."
At this My Cid's vassals smiled;
some had been the best of the fighters and others had gone in pursuit,
but they had not found Diego or Fernando among them.
As a result of the mockery which now began among the men,            2535
by night and day teaching the Infantes so cruel a lesson,
the two Infantes devised so .wicked a plan.
The two of them went off to one side — truly they were brothers —
and in what they discussed, let us have no part.

'Vayamos pora Carrion,     aqui mucho detardamos;     2540
los averes que tenemos     grandes son e sobejanos,

mientra que visquieremos     despender no lo podremos.

124 Pidamos nuestras mugieres     al Çid Campeador,
digamos que las levaremos     a tierras de Carrion,
enseñar las hemos     do las heredades son;     2545
sacar las hemos de Valençia,     de poder del Campeador,
despues en la carrera     feremos nuestro sabor
ante que nos retrayan     lo que cuntio del leon.
¡Nos de natura somos     de condes de Carrion!
Averes levaremos grandes     que valen grant valor;     2550
¡escarniremos     las fijas del Canpeador!'
'D'aquestos averes     sienpre seremos ricos omnes,
podremos casar con fijas     de reyes o de enperadores
¡ca de natura somos     de condes de Carrion!
Assi las escarniremos     a las fijas del Campeador     2555
antes que nos retrayan     lo que fue del leon.'
Con aqueste conssejo     amos tornados son.
Fablo Feran Gonçalez     e fizo callar la cort:
'¡Si vos vala el Criador,     Çid Campeador!
Que plega a doña Ximena     e primero a vos     2560
e a Minaya Albar Fañez     e a quantos aqui son:
dad nos nuestras mugieres     que avemos a bendiçiones,
levar las hemos     a nuestras tierras de Carrion,
meter las hemos     en las villas
que les diemos     por arras e por onores;     2565
veran vuestras fijas     lo que avemos nos,
los fijos que ovieremos     en que avran partiçion.'
Dixo el Campeador:     'Darvos he mis fijas e algo de lo mio.'
El Çid que nos curiava     de assi ser afontado:
'Vos les diestes villas por arras     en tierras de Carrion;     2570

---

**2557** The use here of the term *conssejo* (see also l.2537) is significant, for it is used in some medieval Spanish law codes to mean 'evil intent' or 'premeditated action' (see Pavlović and Walker, 'Roman Forensic Procedure in the *Cort* Scene in the *Poema de Mio Cid*', p.102). The Infantes' action is coldly calculated, and, when they are accused in the law court, there is no question of taking into account the extenuating factor of 'anger', which must involve immediate execution of vengeance (Lacarra, p.89). Moreover, the verb *escarnir* (to humiliate, l.2555) is used in contemporary law codes to designate a kind of action causing dishonour. The poet is at pains to underline that the Infantes are about to commit an act for which it is appropriate that they be punished by a court of law.
**2565** The *arras* constitute the payment made as part of the marriage settlement by the husband or his family to his wife, to provide security in the case of widowhood or (provided that she has not caused the breakdown of the marriage) divorce. This contribution corresponds to the *donatio* which figures in the legal system of the late Roman Empire, and in Roman law it is clear that if the wife is the innocent party she is to retain the *arras* after divorce. It appears from l.2565 and l.2570 that the *arras* (in this case, estates) have already been made over to the

192

"Let us set off for Carrión; we delay too long here;          2540
the wealth we possess is great and magnificent;

in all our days we cannot spend it all.

Let us ask My Cid the Battler to allow our wives to accompany us.
Let us say we are going to take them to the lands of Carrión
and to show them where their estates are.                     2545
We shall take them away from Valencia, out of the power of the
                                            Battler,
and then on the journey we shall do all we wish with them,
before the business of the lion can be thrown in our face;
for we are of the line of the counts of Carrión.
We shall take with us vast riches, possessions great of value;    2550
and we shall humiliate the Battler's daughters!
With this wealth we shall for ever be rich men,
and we shall be able to marry the daughters of kings or emperors,
for we are of the line of counts of Carrión!
So, we shall humiliate the Battler's daughters,                  2555
before the affair of the lion can be thrown in our face."
Having made this plan, the two of them returned.
Fernando González spoke and silenced the court:
"May the Creator protect you, O Cid the Battler!
May what I ask please Doña Jimena, and you before all,           2560
and Minaya Álvar Fáñez and all those here present!
Give us our wives, our marriage to whom has been blessed;
we are going to take them to our lands in Carrión,
and put them in possession of the properties
which we have given them as wedding gifts and as an inheritance.
Your daughters shall see what we possess,
and what it is that our children will share."
The Battler said: "I shall give you my daughters and some of my
                                            wealth."
The Cid, who did not suspect that he was to be dishonoured, said:
"You have given them as wedding presents properties in the lands
                              of Carrión;                          2570

girls, perhaps in writing or perhaps just through an oral promise. For an examination of the importance of this
institution in law and in the *Poema*, see Pavlović and Walker, 'Money, Marriage and the Law', pp.200-03.
**2567** The question of future provision for children is likewise treated in medieval legal documents connected with
marriage settlements. Hook ('On Certain Correspondences', p.44) cites a passage on this subject from Jimena's
own *carta de arras*.

hyo quiero les dar axuvar       .iii. mill marcos de [valor],
darvos e mulas e palafres       muy gruessos de sazon,
cavallos pora en diestro       fuertes e corredores
e muchas vestiduras       de paños e de çiclatones;
dar vos he dos espadas,       a Colada e a Tizon,                    2575
bien lo sabedes vos       que las gane a guisa de varon.
Mios fijos sodes amos       quando mis fijas vos do;
alla me levades       las telas del coraçon.
¡Que lo sepan en Gallizia       y en Castiella y en Leon
con que riqueza enbio       mios yernos amos a dos!              2580
A mis fijas sirvades,       que vuestras mugieres son;
si bien las servides       yo vos rendre buen galardon.'
Atorgado lo han esto       los iffantes de Carrion.
Aqui reçiben       las fijas del Campeador,
conpieçan a reçebir       lo que el Çid mando.                      2585
Quando son pagados       a todo so sabor
hya mandavan cargar       iffantes de Carrion.
Grandes son las nuevas       por Valençia la mayor,
todos prenden armas       e cavalgan a vigor
por que escurren sus fijas del Campeador       a tierras de
                                                      Carrion.
Hya quieren cavalgar,       en espidimiento son.                   2591
Amas hermanas       don Elvira e doña Sol
fincaron los inojos       ant'el Çid Campeador:
'¡Merçed vos pedimos, padre!       ¡Si vos vala el Criador!
Vos nos engendrastes,       nuestra madre nos pario;             2595
delant sodes amos,       señora e señor.
Agora nos enviades       a tierras de Carrion,
debdo nos es a cunplir       lo que mandaredes vos.
Assi vos pedimos merçed       nos amas a dos
que ayades vuestros menssajes       en tierras de Carrion.'   2600
Abraçolas mio Çid       e saludolas amas a dos.

125 El fizo aquesto,       la madre lo doblava:
'¡Andad, fijas,       d'aqui el Criador vos vala!
De mi e de vuestro padre       bien avedes nuestra graçia.
Hid a Carrion       do sodes heredadas;                              2605

**2571** The *axuvar* was very similar in nature to the Roman *dos*, a marriage settlement which was made by a father
on his daughter and usually handed over to the husband at the time of, or just before, the marriage (see Pavlović
and Walker, 'Money, Marriage and the Law', pp.197-200). This custom did not exist in Germanic legal tradition,
which did not expect the wife to bring a substantial financial contribution to the marriage; and there is no
evidence that it was common in Castile at the time of the composition of the *Poema*; this text seems to be unique
in using the term *axuvar* to denote such a settlement. Pavlović and Walker suggest that here, as in his presentation
of other legal matters, the poet reflects 'the transitional period of Castilian law, in which the old Germanic
custom-law was battling to survive against the romanizing zeal of Alfonso VIII' (p.209). l.2571 seems to indicate
that the *axuvar* consisted only of cash: the Cid's other gifts do not constitute part of the dowry, and they are not

I wish this day to give them the sum of three thousand marks as
                              a dowry.
I give you mules and palfreys, sturdy and in prime condition,
and chargers, strong and swift,
and many garments, of cloth and fine silk.
I shall give you two swords, Colada and Tizón;                    2575
you know well that I won them in manly combat.
You are both my sons, since I give you my daughters;
you take away my heart strings.
Let it be known in Galicia and in Castile and in León
with what wealth I am sending away my two sons - in - law.         2580
Look after my daughters, for they are your wives;
if you look after them well, I shall give you good reward."
This, the Infantes of Carrión promised.
Then they received the Battler's daughters,
and they began to receive the gifts My Cid commanded they be given.
When they were satisfied in every respect,
the Infantes of Carrión commanded their possessions to be loaded
                              for the journey.
Great is the excitement throughout the great city of Valencia;
all the men take up arms and mount swiftly;
for the Battler's daughters are departing for the lands of Carrión. 2590
Now they are about to ride, and are taking their leave.
The two sisters, Doña Elvira and Doña Sol,
kneel down before the Cid the Battler:
"We ask a favour of you, father!  May the Creator protect you!
You fathered us, our mother bore us;                              2595
here you are before us, lady and lord.
Now you are sending us to the lands of Carrión,
and it is our duty to fulfil your command.
Thus we both beg of you
that you send your own envoys to the lands of Carrión."          2600
My Cid embraced them and kissed them both.

He did this and their mother did likewise:
"Go, my daughters!  Henceforth may the Creator protect you!
You have the blessing of myself and of your father.
Go to Carrión, where your estates are.                           2605

reclaimed at the court together with the three thousand marks. To this sum of money, however, Roman law
makes it clear that, after the breakdown of the marriage, the Cid has every right.

assi commo yo tengo    bien vos he casadas.'
Al padre e a la madre    las manos les besavan;
amos las bendixieron    e dieron les su graçia.
Mio Çid e los otros    de cavalgar penssavan
a grandes guarnimientos,    a cavallos e armas.    2610
Hya salien los ifantes    de Valençia la clara
esp[id]iendo de las dueñas    e de todas sus compañas;
por la huerta de Valençia    teniendo salien armas,
alegre va mio Çid    con todas sus compañas.
Violo en los avueros    el que en buen ora çinxo espada  2615
que estos casamientos    non serien sin alguna tacha;
nos puede repentir,    que casadas las ha amas.

126  '¿O heres, mio sobrino,    tu, Felez Muñoz?
Primo eres de mis fijas amas    d'alma e de coraçon.
Mandot que vayas con ellas    fata dentro en Carrion,    2620
veras las heredades    que a mis fijas dadas son;
con aquestas nuevas    vernas al Campeador.'
Dixo Felez Muñoz:    'Plazme d'alma e de coraçon.'
Minaya Albar Fañez    ante mio Çid se paro:
'Tornemos nos, Çid    a Valençia la mayor,    2625
que si a Dios ploguiere    e al Padre Criador
hir las hemos ver    a tierras de Carrion.'
'A Dios vos hacomendamos    don Elvira e doña Sol:
atales cosas fed    que en plazer caya a nos.'
Respondien los yernos:    '¡Assi lo mande Dios!'    2630
Grandes fueron los duelos    a la departiçion;
el padre con las fijas    loran de coraçon
assi fazian    los cavalleros del Campeador.
'¡Oyas, sobrino,    tu, Felez Muñoz!
Por Molina iredes,    i yazredes una noch,    2635
saludad a mio amigo    el moro Avengalvon;
reçiba a mios yernos    commo el pudier mejor.
Dil que enbio mis fijas    a tierras de Carrion.
De lo que ovieren huebos    sirvan las a so sabor,
desi escurra las fasta Medina    por la mi amor;    2640
de quanto el fiziere    yol dar[e] por ello buen galardon.'
Cuemo la uña de la carne    ellos partidos son.

---

**2620-22** To a certain extent, the estates are used as a pretext to provide the girls with the reassuring presence of Félez Muñoz; but the Cid is also clearly keen to find out the true value of the *arras* which have been given to his daughters.

**2642** Similes are rare in the *Poema*, and this one – suggesting the cruel pain of the moment – is particularly memorable. It is here used for the second time, the first (1.375) being at the moment of the Cid's parting from his family on going into exile. The second occasion recalls the first, and a journey leading to honour and success is contrasted with one which is to threaten great dishonour – for discussion of the poet's technique here, see Introduction, VII (c).

I firmly believe that I have married you well."
In thanks they kissed the hands of their father and their mother,
both of whom gave them every blessing.
My Cid and the others rode off,
dressed magnificently, with fine horses and arms.                    2610
The Infantes left the famed city of Valencia,
taking their leave of the ladies and all their companions.
Through the plantations of Valencia the men rode out, giving a
                              display of their skills.
Joyful was My Cid, and all his vassals too.
But the man who girded his sword in a favoured hour saw from
                              the omens                    2615
that these marriages would not be without some stain;
he could not repent now, for he had married them both.

"Where are you, my nephew, Félez Muñoz?
You are the cousin of my daughters, whom I love with heart and soul.
I command you to accompany them as far as Carrión,                    2620
and see the estates which have been given to my daughters as an
                              inheritance.
With a report of this you shall come to the Battler."
Félez Muñoz said: "In my heart and soul I am pleased to do this."
Minaya Álvar Fáñez stopped before My Cid:
"Let us return, O Cid, to the great city of Valencia,                    2625
for if God, the Father and Creator, is willing,
we shall go and see them in the lands of Carrión."
[The Cid said:] "We commend you to God, Doña Elvira and Doña Sol;
may all you do be such as to give us pleasure."
The sons - in - law replied: "May God be willing that it is so!"     2630
Great was the sorrow at their parting;
the father and daughters wept from the heart,
and so too did the knights of the Battler.
"Hear me, my nephew, Félez Muñoz!
You shall pass through Molina and spend one night there,              2635
and give my greetings to my friend, the Moor Abengalbón;
let him give to my sons - in - law the finest possible welcome.
Tell him that I am sending my daughters to the lands of Carrión;
let them be given all they need and attended to in all matters,
and from there let him escort them to Medinaceli, as a token of
                              his love for me.                    2640
For all he does, I shall give him a good reward."
Like the nail from the flesh, they parted.

Hyas torno pora Valençia     el que en buen ora nasçio.
Pienssan se de ir     los ifantes de Carrion;
por Santa Maria d'Alvarrazin     fazian la posada,          2645
aguijan quanto pueden     ifantes de Carrion;
felos en Molina     con el moro Avengalvon.
El moro quando lo sopo     plogol de coraçon,
saliolos reçebir     con grandes avorozes;
¡Dios, que bien los sirvio     a todo so sabor!              2650
Otro dia mañana     con ellos cavalgo,
con dozientos cavalleros     escurrir los mando;
hivan troçir los montes     los que dizen de Luzon.
A las fijas del Çid     el moro sus donas dio,
buenos seños cavallos     a los ifantes de Carrion.        2655
Troçieron Arbuxuelo     e legaron a Salon,
o dizen el Anssarera     ellos posados son.
Tod esto les fizo el moro     por el amor del Çid Campeador.
Ellos veyen la riqueza     que el moro saco,
entramos hermanos     conssejaron traçion:                 2660
'Hya pues que a dexar avemos     fijas del Campeador
si pudiessemos matar     el moro Avengalvon
quanta riquiza tiene     aver la iemos nos.

Tan en salvo lo abremos     commo lo de Carrion,
nunqua avrie derecho     de nos el Çid Campeador.'         2665
Quando esta falssedad     dizien los de Carrion
un moro latinado     bien gelo entendio;
non tiene poridad,     dixolo [a] Avengalvon:
'Acayaz, curiate destos,     ca eres mio señor;
tu muert oi conssejar     a los ifantes de Carrion.'       2670

127  El moro Avengalvon     mucho era buen barragan,
con dozientos que tiene     iva cavalgar.
Armas iva teniendo,     paros ante los ifantes;
de lo que el moro dixo     a los ifantes non plaze:
'Dezid me: ¿que vos fiz     ifantes de Carrion?            2675
¡Hyo sirviendo vos sin art     e vos conssejastes pora mi muert!
Si no lo dexas     por mio Çid el de Bivar
tal cosa vos faria     que por el mundo sonas
e luego levaria sus fijas     al Campeador leal;
¡vos nunqua en Carrion     entrariedes jamas!              2680

---

**2657** El Ansarera has not been identified; it was probably situated on the north bank of the Jalón, near Medinaceli.

198

Then the man born in a favoured hour returned to Valencia.
The Infantes of Carrión begin their journey,
and halt at Santa María de Albarracín. 2645
The Infantes of Carrión spur on their way as fast as they can;
here they are in Molina with the Moor Abengalbón.
When the Moor knew of this, he was deeply pleased,
and went out to welcome them with great rejoicing.
Lord God, how well he attended to their every desire! 2650
The next morning he rode out with them,
and ordered them to be escorted by two hundred knights.
They made their way over the heights of Luzón.
The Moor made his gifts to the Cid's daughters,
and gave fine horses to each of the Infantes of Carrión. 2655
They passed along the Arbujuelo and reached the Jalón,
resting at a place known as El Ansarera.
All this was done by the Moor out of love for the Cid the Battler.
Seeing the wealth that the Moor displayed,
together the two brothers plotted treachery: 2660
"Now, since we are going to abandon the Battler's daughters,
if we could kill the Moor Abengalbón,
we would take all his wealth.
It would be as securely ours as our possessions in Carrión,
and My Cid the Battler would have no claim on us." 2665
As the men of Carrión spoke these treacherous words,
a Spanish - speaking Moor took in all they said;
rather than keeping the matter secret, he told Abengalbón:
"Governor, I tell you as my lord, beware of those men;
I heard the Infantes of Carrión plotting your death." 2670

The Moor Abengalbón was a man of great valour,
and he rode out with two hundred of his knights.
With a display of arms, he stopped in front of the Infantes.
What the Moor said gave them no pleasure:
"Tell me what I have done to you, Infantes of Carrión. 2675
Though I served you without malice, you plotted my death.
Were I not to hold back on account of My Cid of Vivar,
I would do such a thing to you that news of it would echo throughout
                                the world,
and then I would take back to the loyal Battler his daughters.
You would never re - enter Carrión! 2680

199

128   Aquim parto de vos      commo de malos e de traidores.
      Hire con vuestra graçia,      don Elvira e doña Sol;
      ¡poco preçio las nuevas      de los de Carrion!
      Dios lo quiera e lo mande,      que de tod el mundo es señor,
      d'aqueste casamiento      que[s] grade el Campeador.'      2685
      Esto les ha dicho      y el moro se torno;
      teniendo ivan armas      al troçir de Salon,
      cuemmo de buen seso      a Molina se torno.
      Ya movieron del Anssarera      los ifantes de Carrion;
      acojen se a andar      de dia e de noch,      2690
      a ssiniestro dexan Ati[en]za      una peña muy fuert,
      la sierra de Miedes      passaron la estoz,
      por los Montes Claros      aguijan a espolon,
      a ssiniestro dexan a Griza      que Alamos poblo
      —alli son caños      do a Elpha ençerro—      2695
      a diestro dexan a Sant Estevan,      mas cae aluen;
      entrados son los ifantes      al robredo de Corpes,
      los montes son altos,      las ramas pujan con las nues,
      e las bestias fieras      que andan aderredor.
      Falaron un vergel      con una linpia fuent,      2700
      mandan fincar la tienda      ifantes de Carrion;
      con quantos que ellos traen      i yazen essa noch.
      Con sus mugieres en braços      demuestran les amor:
      ¡mal gelo cunplieron      quando salie el sol!

---

**2681** The accusation of treachery is later to be formally levelled at the Infantes in the court. For the connotations of *traidor*, see note to 1.3343.

**2693** Michael ('Geographical Problems in the *Poema de Mio Cid*: II. The Corpes Route', pp.83-84) points out that the itinerary described in this passage is a highly improbable one, for the mountains still known as the Montes Claros lie a good way to the south-west and to cross them would involve a very great detour. This is yet another indication that there are flaws in the poet's geographical knowledge.

**2694** Probably this is an allusion either to the village of Riaza or to some spot on the river Riaza. Álamos is possibly a person, but the poet could have in mind a grove of poplars (= *álamos*) along the river (see Michael, 'Geographical Problems: II', p.84).

**2695** Elpha could be a girl's name, but could also plausibly represent an allusion to a local legend about an elf (Michael, 'Geographical Problems: II', pp.84-85). The detail possibly bears no relation at all to the region in question, and could well be fictitious. The air of fantasy which the poet is seeking to create at this point prepares the way for the sinister and, perhaps, supernatural overtones of the description of Corpes.

**2697** There has been much debate about the situation of the oakwood of Corpes. For a summary of the arguments put forward by a number of scholars, see Michael, 'Geographical Problems: II', pp.85-87. Michael considers that Menéndez Pidal may well have been right in identifying the oakwood with a spot called El Páramo, near Castillejo del Robledo (see map), where large roots of trees have been uncovered. The site is a plausible one, but it must be borne in mind that the poet, in his creation of this powerful scene, need not necessarily have had any real place in mind.

**2698** There is a close parallel here and in a number of details of this scene with the depiction in the *Chanson de Florence de Rome*, a French epic poem dating from the early thirteenth century, of a similar violent assault taking place in a terrifying forest; the two passages are analyzed by R.M.Walker in 'A Possible Source for the "Afrenta de Corpes" Episode in the *Poema de Mio Cid*', *Modern Language Review*, 72 (1977), pp.335-47. A number of other studies examine the origins and nature of the Corpes episode: for example, in 'The *Afrenta de Corpes* and

Here and now I take my leave of you as evil and treacherous men.
With your blessing I shall go, Doña Elvira and Doña Sol.
I care little for the reputation of those of Carrión.
May God, Lord of the whole world, will and command
that this marriage may bring the Battler joy!"                                    2685
Having said this, the Moor turned back;
with a display of arms as he crossed the Jalón,
the prudent man returned to Molina.
Now the Infantes of Carrión move on from El Ansarera.
They ride on their way both by day and by night,                                 2690
to their left passing Atienza, an imposing crag;
then they crossed the mountains of Miedes,
spurring on over the Montes Claros.
to their left, they leave behind Griza, founded by Álamos —
in that place there are caves where Elpha was imprisoned —                        2695
and to their right, in the distance, they leave behind San Esteban.
The Infantes enter the oak - wood of Corpes;
the forests are high and the branches rise up into the clouds,
and wild beasts prowl all around.
They find a grassy spot, with a clear spring.                                     2700
The Infantes of Carrión command the tent to be pitched;
they spend the night there with all their company,
taking their wives into their arms and making love to them.
But how ill they kept their vows when the sun rose!

Other Stories'(see note to ll.1141-42) Deyermond and Hook, questioning the validity of Walker's study, point to
the resemblance of aspects of this scene to the story of Philomela, Procne and Tereus in Ovid's *Metamorphoses*;
they emphasize the complexity of the links of this episode with European tradition, and conclude that it is
unsound to argue with confidence that similarities between the *Poema* and works such as the *Chanson de Florence
de Rome* are the result of direct influence. Other studies make clear the richness of the Corpes episode: for
example, J.K. Walsh examines the influence of hagiographic tradition in literature and the visual arts in
'Religious Motifs in Early Spanish Epic', *Revista Hispánica Moderna*, 36 (1970-71), 165-72; and D.J. Gifford
considers parallels both with the Roman festival of the Lupercalia and with fertility rituals which have survived
until quite recent times - 'European Folk-Tradition and the "Afrenta de Corpes" in *Mio Cid Studies*, edited by
A.D.Deyermond (London, 1977), pp.49-62.
    For a treatment of the Corpes episode in a later ballad, see Wright, *Spanish Ballads*, pp.83-84 and 212-214.
**2700** This scene is often cited as an example of a *locus amoenus*, the description of a place of great natural beauty
which is a common topic in European literature. It contains the conventional elements (trees, grassy spot, spring)
but it is not developed as fully as the literary theorists would recommend; a more extensive example,
representative of their teachings, is present in the *Libro de Alexandre* (stanzas 935-40). Certainly, however, there
is a striking contrast between the tender love scene that we might expect to find depicted against such a setting and
the brutal and cowardly act which the poet is about to describe.
**2703** The Infantes' assault on their wives is to have strong sexual overtones. Walker ('A Possible Source', p.342)
compares the sadistic and perverted nature of the young men's subsequent behaviour with that of the villain of
*Florence*.

Mandaron cargar las azemilas    con grandes averes;    2705
cogida han la tienda    do albergaron de noch,
adelant eran idos    los de criazon.
Assi lo mandaron    los ifantes de Carrion
que non i fincas ninguno,    mugier nin varon,
si non amas sus mugieres    doña Elvira e doña Sol;    2710
deportar se quieren con ellas    a todo su sabor.
Todos eran idos,    ellos .iiii. solos son.
Tanto mal comidieron    los ifantes de Carrion:
'Bien lo creades    don Elvira e doña Sol:
aqui seredes escarnidas    en estos fieros montes;    2715
oy nos partiremos    e dexadas seredes de nos,
non abredes part    en tierras de Carrion.
Hiran aquestos mandados    al Çid Campeador;
¡nos vengaremos aquesta    por la del leon!'
Alli les tuellen    los mantos e los pelliçones,    2720
paran las en cuerpos    y en camisas y en çiclatones.
Espuelas tienen calçadas    los malos traidores,
en mano prenden las çinchas    fuertes e duradores.
Quando esto vieron las dueñas    fablava doña Sol:
'¡Por Dios vos rogamos    don Diego e don Ferando!    2725
Dos espadas tenedes    fuertes e tajadores
—al una dizen Colada    e al otra Tizon—
¡cortandos las cabeças,    martires seremos nos!
Moros e christianos    departiran desta razon,
que por lo que nos mereçemos    no lo prendemos nos;    2730
¡atan malos enssienplos    non fagades sobre nos!
Si nos fueremos majadas    abiltaredes a vos,
retraer vos lo an    en vistas o en cortes.'
Lo que ruegan las dueñas    non les ha ningun pro.
Essora les conpieçan a dar    los ifantes de Carrion,    2735
con las çinchas corredizas    majan las tan sin sabor,
con las espuelas agudas    don ellas an mal sabor
ronpien las camisas e las carnes    a ellas amas a dos;
linpia salie la sangre    sobre los çiclatones.
Ya lo sienten ellas    en los sos coraçones.    2740
¡Qual ventura serie esta    si ploguiesse al Criador
que assomasse essora    el Çid Campeador!
Tanto las majaron    que sin cosimente son,
sangrientas en las camisas    e todos los çiclatones.

---

2722 Spurs are specifically mentioned in the *Fuero de Cuenca* (see also notes to l.2762 and l.3257) as an instrument whose use aggravates the seriousness of the dishonour caused by physical assault.
2744 See note to l.2291.

They ordered the pack animals to be laden with their great riches.
The tent in which they spent the night was gathered up,
and their retainers had gone on ahead.
The Infantes of Carrión commanded
that no man or woman should remain behind,
except their wives, Doña Elvira and Doña Sol;                    2710
they wanted to enjoy themselves with them at their pleasure.
All others had gone; just the four of them were left.
So evil were the thoughts of the Infantes of Carrión:
"You can well believe, Doña Elvira and Doña Sol,
that you will be thoroughly humiliated in this wild forest.        2715
Today we shall part, and you will be abandoned by us;
you will have no share in the lands of Carrión.
News of this will go to the Cid the Battler;
this will be our revenge for being humiliated with the lion!"
Now they tear off their cloaks and furs,                          2720
and strip them to their silken undergarments.
The wicked traitors are wearing spurs,
and in their hands they take the saddle - girths, harsh and tough.
When the ladies see this, Doña Sol speaks out:
"In God's name, we beg of you, Don Diego and Don Fernando!
You have two swords, strong and sharp —
one is known as Colada and the other as Tizón;
cut off our heads and we shall be martyrs!
Both Moors and Christians shall say of this
that we have not done anything to deserve this treatment.         2730
Do not make such wretched examples of us!
If we are beaten, you will bring dishonour on yourselves,
and you will be accountable for it at an assembly or at a royal court."
The ladies' plea is in vain.
Now the Infantes of Carrión begin to beat them.                   2735
With the saddle - girths they strike them cruelly,
and with their sharp spurs they cut into them to cause them great pain,
tearing through the undergarments of each of them and into their flesh.
Brightly their blood flows out onto the silk.
They feel such pain in their hearts!                              2740
What a blessing it would be if it were to please the Creator
that at this moment the Cid the Battler should appear!
They beat them until they are numb,
with their silken undergarments all covered in blood.

Canssados son de ferir     ellos amos a dos        2745
ensayandos amos     qual dara mejores colpes.
Hya non pueden fablar     don Elvira e doña Sol,
por muertas las dexaron     en el robredo de Corpes.

129 Levaron les los mantos     e las pieles armiñas
     mas dexan las maridas     en briales y en camisas      2750
     e a las aves del monte     e a las bestias de la fiera guisa.
     Por muertas la[s] dexaron     sabed, que non por bivas.

130 ¡Qual ventura serie     si assomas essora el Çid Campeador!
     Los ifantes de Carrion     en el robredo de Corpes
     por muertas las dexaron,        2755
     que el una al otra     nol torna recabdo.
     Por los montes do ivan     ellos ivan se alabando:
     'De nuestros casamientos     agora somos vengados;
     non las deviemos     tomar por varraganas
     si non fuessemos     rogados,        2760
     pues nuestras parejas     non eran pora en braços.
     ¡La desondra del leon     assis ira vengando!'

131 Alabandos ivan     los ifantes de Carrion.
     Mas yo vos dire     d'aquel Felez Muñoz,
     sobrino era     del Çid Campeador:      2765
     mandaron le ir adelante     mas de su grado non fue.
     En la carrera do iva     doliol el coraçon;
     de todos los otros     aparte se salio,
     en un monte espesso     Felez Muñoz se metio
     fasta que viesse venir     sus primas amas a dos      2770
     o que an fecho     los ifantes de Carrion.
     Violos venir     e oyo una razon,
     ellos nol vien     ni dend sabien raçion;
     sabet bien que si ellos le viessen     non escapara de muert.
     Vansse los ifantes,     aguijan a espolon.      2775
     Por el rastro     tornos Felez Muñoz,
     fallo sus primas     amorteçidas amas a dos;
     lamando '¡Primas, primas!'     luego descavalgo,
     arrendo el cavallo,     a ellas adeliño:
     '¡Ya primas, las mis primas     don Elvira e doña Sol!      2780

---

**2762** Some law codes of the twelfth century do in fact uphold the right of the aggrieved individual to exact a private and bloody vengeance for dishonour suffered, and thus could be argued to sanction the action which the Infantes are going to take (see Lacarra, p.99). The Infantes are not, however, acting in accordance with the legislation, based on Roman law and codified, for example, in the *Fuero de Cuenca* , which pointed to the formal judicial challenge as the solution to such a problem of honour (see note to l.3257). More obviously, their action is patently reprehensible in moral and human terms: instead of seeking to vindicate their honour by an open display of courage, they choose the most cowardly and shameful way of asserting themselves. We now feel only contempt and anger towards them.

Both men have grown tired with beating them,                          2745
each striving to strike the harsher blows.
Doña Elvira and Doña Sol can no longer speak.
They left them for dead in the oak - wood of Corpes.

They carried off the cloaks and the ermine robes,
leaving their wives with just their tunics and undergarments,         2750
exposed to the birds of the forest and the fierce beasts.
They left them for dead, I tell you; they did not think them alive.

What a blessing it would be if the Cid the Battler were to appear now!
The Infantes of Carrión, in the oak - wood of Corpes,

left them for dead;                                                   2755
for neither was able to give any aid to the other.
As they rode through the forest, the Infantes boasted to each other:
"Now we have our revenge for our marriages.
We ought not to have accepted them even as concubines,
had we not been formally requested to do so.                         2760
They were not our equals in status, to be our wives.
In this way the dishonour brought on us by the lion will be avenged."

The Infantes of Carrión went off, proud of what they had done.
But I shall tell you of Félez Muñoz, well known to us;
he is nephew of the Cid the Battler.                                 2765
He had been commanded to go on ahead, but had done so unwillingly.
As he went along, he felt troubled in his heart;
he left all the others;
Félez Muñoz hid in a thick part of the forest,
until he should see both is cousins arrive,                          2770
or know what the Infantes of Carrión had done.
He saw them come, and heard them speak;
they did not see him or know anything of his presence.
I tell you for certain that had they seen him he would not have
                                        escaped death.
The Infantes left, spurring on their horses.                         2775
Along their trail Félez Muñoz returned
and found his cousins both lying as if dead.
Crying out, "Cousins! Cousins!" he quickly dismounted,
and, tying up his horse by the reins, he went over to them:
"O cousins! My cousins, Doña Elvira and Doña Sol!                    2780

205

¡Mal se ensayaron     los ifantes de Carrion!
¡A Dios plega e a Santa Maria     que dent prendan ellos mal
                                    galardon!'
Valas tornando     a ellas amas a dos;
tanto son de traspuestas     que non pueden dezir nada.
Partieron se le las tellas     de dentro del coraçon,          2785
lamando '¡Primas, primas     don Elvira e doñ[a] Sol!
¡Despertedes, primas     por amor del Criador!
Mientra es el dia,     ante que entre la noch,
¡los ganados fieros     non nos coman en aqueste mont!'
Van recordando     don Elvira e doña Sol,                      2790
abrieron los ojos     e vieron a Felez Muñoz.
'¡Esforçad vos, primas,     por amor del Criador!
De que non me fallaren     los ifantes de Carrion
a grant priessa     sere buscado yo;
si Dios non nos vale     aqui morremos nos.'                   2795
Tan a grant duelo     fablava doña Sol:
'¡Si vos lo meresca, mio primo,     nuestro padre el Campeador!
¡Dandos del agua,     si vos vala el Criador!'
Con un sonbrero     que tiene Felez Muñoz
—nuevo era e fresco,     que de Valençial saco—               2800
cogio del agua en el     e a sus primas dio;
mucho son lazradas     e amas las farto.
Tanto las rogo     fata que las assento;
valas conortando     e metiendo coraçon
fata que esfuerçan,     e amas las tomo                        2805
e privado     en el cavallo las cavalgo;
con el so manto     a amas las cubrio,
el cavallo priso por la rienda     e luego dent las part[io].
Todos tres señeros     por los robredos de Corpes
entre noch e dia     salieron de los montes;                  2810
a las aguas de Duero     ellos arribados son,
a la torre de don Urraca     elle las dexo.
A sant Estevan     vino Felez Muñoz,
fallo a Diego Tellez     el que de Albar Fañez fue;
quando el lo oyo     pesol de coraçon,                         2815
priso bestias     e vestidos de pro,
hiva reçebir     a don Elvira e a doña Sol;
en Sant Estevan     dentro las metio,

---

**2812** The site of this tower can be identified from a twelfth-century document: it is not on the banks of the river, but five or six kilometres to the south. Michael ('Geographical Problems: II', p.87) points out that the route described here is an illogical one: it involves a descent of over six hundred feet, followed by an ascent of five hundred feet, though a much easier route exists.
**2814** Diego Téllez did have an historical existence. His name appears in a number of legal documents: he was governor of the town of Sepúlveda, with which Álvar Fáñez is known to have had dealings.

The Infantes of Carrión have given a bad account of themselves!
May it please God and Saint Mary that they be unkindly rewarded
for this!"
Gradually, he revives them both.
They are in such a state that they can say nothing.
His heart—strings are near to breaking,                              2785
and he cries out: "Cousins, cousins, Doña Elvira and Doña Sol!
Wake up, cousins, for the love of the Creator,
while it is still day and before night falls,
lest the fierce beasts devour us in this forest!"
Doña Elvira and Doña Sol regain consciousness.                        2790
They open their eyes and see Félez Muñoz.
"Take heart, cousins, for the love of the Creator!
As soon as the Infantes of Carrión find I have gone,
I shall be pursued with all haste.
If God does not protect us, here we shall die."                      2795
So sorrowfully spoke Doña Sol:
"May our father, the Batttler, reward you, my cousin!
Give us water, may the Creator protect you!"
Félez Muñoz, in his hat,
new, only recently made, that he had brought from Valencia,          2800
fetched water and gave it to his cousins.
They were in a wretched state, and to each he gave as much as
she could drink.
With many entreaties he encouraged them to sit up,
and gradually he comforted and heartened them,
until they recovered their strength; then he took them both         2805
and rapidly lifted them up onto his horse,
and covered them both with his cloak.
He took up the reins and rode off, taking the ladies away from
that place.
All three of them, alone, rode through the oak‑woods of Corpes,
as night fell, making their way from the forest.                     2810
They reached the waters of the Duero,
and he left them at the tower of Doña Urraca.
to San Esteban came Félez Muñoz.
He found Diego Téllez, Álvar Fáñez's vassal.
When he heard the news, he was deeply saddened.                      2815
He obtained horses and suitable clothing,
and went to meet Doña Elvira and Doña Sol.
He installed them in San Esteban,

quanto el mejor puede    alli las ondro.

Los de Sant Estevan    siempre mesurados son;    2820
quando sabien esto    pesoles de coraçon,
a llas fijas del Çid    dan les esfuerço;
alli sovieron ellas    fata que sanas son.
Allabandos seyan    los ifantes de Carrion.
De cuer peso esto    al buen rey don Alfonsso.    2825
Van aquestos mandados    a Valençia la mayor;
quando gelo dizen    a mio Çid el Campeador
una grand ora    pensso e comidio;
alço la su mano,    a la barba se tomo:
'¡Grado a Christus    que del mundo es señor    2830
quando tal ondra me an dada    los ifantes de Carrion!
¡Par aquesta barba    que nadi non messo
non la lograran    los ifantes de Carrion,
que a mis fijas    bien las casare yo!'
Peso a mio Çid    e a toda su cort    2835
e [a] Albar Fañez    d'alma e de coraçon.    2835b
Cavalgo Minaya    con Pero Vermuez
e Martin Antolinez    el burgales de pro
con .cc. cavalleros    quales mio Çid mando;
dixoles fuerte mientre    que andidiessen de dia e de noch,
aduxiessen a ssus fijas    a Valençia la mayor.    2840
Non lo detardan    el mandado de su señor,
a priessa cavalgan,    andan los dias e las noches;
vinieron a (sant Estevan de) Gormaz    un castiello tan fuert,
hi albergaron    por verdad una noch.
A Sant Estevan    el mandado lego    2845
que vinie Minaya    por sus primas amas a dos.
Varones de Sant Estevan    a guisa de muy pros
reçiben a Minaya    e a todos sus varones,
presentan a Minaya    essa noch grant enffurçion;
non gelo quiso tomar,    mas mucho gelo gradio:    2850
'Graçias, varones de Sant Estevan,    que sodes coñosçedores,
por aquesta ondra   que vos diestes    a esto que nos cuntio.
Mucho vos lo gradeçe    alla do esta, mio Çid el Campeador;
assi lo ffago yo    que aqui esto.
¡Affe Dios de los çielos:    que vos de dent buen galardon!'    2855

---

**2820** For an explanation of the warmth which the poet displays towards the people of San Esteban, see note to 1.394.

**2832** The plucking of the beard was one of the offences against a man's honour for which the harshest punishments were specified in the law codes, and a form of assault which they considered of equal seriousness to castration.

**2834** The poet emphasizes not the Cid's sorrow at the suffering of his daughters – though we have been made well aware of his love and care for them – but rather his concern at the lasting dishonour which the Infantes have sought to cause by their treatment of the girls and which he must take action to prevent.

208

and paid them all the honour that he could.
The people of San Esteban always show good sense; 2820
when they knew of this matter, they were deeply saddened.
They helped My Cid's daughters to recover their strength;
the girls remained there till they were well.
The Infantes of Carrión were priding themselves on what they had
done.
Good King Don Alfonso was greatly saddened. 2825
Reports of these events went to the great city of Valencia.
When My Cid the Battler was told,
for a full hour he thought and reflected;
he raised his hand and grasped his beard:
"Thanks be to Christ, Lord of the world, 2830
that the Infantes of Carrión should have paid me such honour!
By this beard which no man has plucked,
the Infantes of Carrión shall not succeed in this,
for I shall yet marry my daughters well!"
My Cid and all his court and Álvar Fáñez 2835
were all most deeply saddened. 2835b
Minaya mounted his horse; Pedro Bermúdez did likewise,
and Martín Antolínez, worthy citizen of Burgos,
with two hundred knights, as My Cid had commanded.
He told them clearly to travel by day and by night,
and to bring his daughters to the great city of Valencia. 2840
They did not delay in carrying out their lord's command,
but rode on quickly and travelled by day and by night;
they came to Gormaz, so strong a castle,
and there, it is true, they lodged for one night.
To San Esteban came word 2845
that Minaya was on his way to fetch his two cousins.
Men from San Esteban, very worthy people,
welcomed Minaya and all his men,
and set before Minaya that night a great tribute of provisions.
He would not take it, but showed them great gratitude: 2850
"Thank you, prudent men of San Esteban,
for this honour you have paid us in our misfortune.
My Cid the Battler, from afar, is grateful to you for this,
and so am I, here amongst you.
I call on heaven to reward you well for it!" 2855

---

**2843** It seems that here the scribe confuses the town of San Esteban de Gormaz with the castle of Gormaz, some fifteen kilometres away, where the escort from Valencia breaks its journey.

Todos gelo gradeçen    e sos pagados son;
adeliñan a posar    pora folgar essa noch.
Minaya va ver    sus primas do son,
en el fincan los ojos    don Elvira e doña Sol:
'¡Atanto vos lo gradimos    commo si viessemos al
                                          Criador!    2860
E vos a el lo gradid    quando bivas somos nos.

En los dias de vagar    toda nuestra rencura sabremos contar.'

132 Loravan de los ojos    las dueñas e Alvar Fañez
e Pero Vermuez    otro tanto las ha:
'Don Elvira e doña Sol:    cuidado non ayades    2865
quando vos sodes sanas e bivas    e sin otro mal.
Buen casamiento perdiestes,    mejor podredes ganar.
¡Aun veamos el dia    que vos podamos vengar!'
Hi yazen essa noche,    e tan grand gozo que fazen.
Otro dia mañana    pienssan de cavalgar;    2870
los de Sant Estevan    escurriendo los van
fata Rio d'Amor    dando les solaz,
d'allent se espidieron dellos,    pienssan se de tornar,
e Minaya con las dueñas    iva cabadelant.
Troçieron Alcoçeva,    a diestro de[xan] Gormaz,    2875
o dizen Bado de Rey    alla ivan p[a]sar,
a la casa de Berlanga    posada presa han.
Otro dia mañana    meten se a andar,
a qual dizen Medina    ivan albergar
e de Medina a Molina    en otro dia van.    2880
Al moro Avengalvon    de coraçon le plaz,
saliolos a reçebir    de buena voluntad;
por amor de mio Çid    rica çena les da.
Dent pora Valençia    adeliñechos van.
Al que en buen ora nasco    legava el menssaje;    2885
privado cavalga,    a reçebir los sale,
armas iva teniendo    e grant gozo que faze;
mio Çid a sus fijas    iva las abraçar,
besando las a amas    tornos de sonrrisar:
'¿Venides, mis fijas?    ¡Dios vos curie de mal!    2890
Hyo tome el casamiento    mas non ose dezir al.
¡Plega al Criador    que en çielo esta

They all thanked him, pleased with what he had said;
they went to their lodging to rest for the night.
Minaya went to see his cousins where they lay.
Doña Elvira and Doña Sol set their eyes upon him:
"We are as grateful to you as if we saw the Creator himself!     2860
And you must thank Him that we are alive.

In times of leisure we shall be able to tell of all our grief."

Tears flowed from the eyes of the ladies and of Álvar Fáñez,
and Pedro Bermúdez wept too:
"Doña Elvira and Doña Sol, do not be troubled,     2865
for you are alive and well, and suffer no further misfortune.
You have lost a good marriage, but you will be able to gain a
                              better one.
May we yet see the day when we can take vengeance on your behalf!"
They spent the night there and great was their rejoicing.
The next morning they rode off.     2870
The men of San Esteban provided them with an escort,
keeping them company as far as Río de Amor.
There they took their leave of them and set off back,
while Minaya and the ladies rode on their way.
They passed along the Alcoceba gorge, and left Gormaz behind on
                              their right hand side.     2875
At the place called Vadorrey they crossed the river,
and they rested in the village of Berlanga.
The next morning they set off again;
they stopped at Medinaceli,
and from Medinaceli to Molina they rode in one more day.     2880
The Moor Abengalbón rejoiced from the heart,
and went out to welcome them most warmly;
for love of My Cid he gave them a rich feast,
and they set off directly for Valencia.
Their messenger reached the man born in a favoured hour;     2885
he mounted quickly and rode out to welcome them
with a display of arms to show his great joy.
My Cid went to embrace his two daughters,
and, kissing them both, he smiled once more:
"You are come, my daughters! May God protect you from evil!
I accepted the marriage, and dared say no more.
May it please the Creator who is in heaven

211

que vos vea mejor casadas   d'aqui en adelant,
de mios yernos de Carrion   Dios me faga vengar!'
Besaron las manos   las fijas al padre.         2895
Teniendo ivan armas,   entraron se a la çibdad;
grand gozo fizo con ellas   doña Ximena su madre.
El que en buen ora nasco   non quiso tardar;
fablos con los sos   en su poridad,
al rey don Alfonsso de Castiella   pensso de enbiar:   2900

133   '¿O eres, Muño Gustioz,   mio vassallo de pro?
¡En buen ora te crie   a ti en la mi cort!
Lieves el mandado   a Castiella al rey Alfonsso;
por mi besa le la mano   d'alma e de coraçon
—cuemo yo so su vassallo   y el es mio señor—   2905
desta desondra que me an fecha   los ifantes de Carrion
quel pese al buen rey   d'alma e de coraçon.
El caso mis fijas,   ca non gelas di yo;
quando las han dexadas   a grant desonor
si desondra i cabe   alguna contra nos   2910
la poca e la grant   toda es de mio señor.
Mios averes se me an levado   que sobejanos son,
esso me puede pesar   con la otra desonor.
Aduga melos a vistas   o a juntas o a cortes
commo aya derecho   de ifantes de Carrion,   2915
ca tan grant es la rencura   dentro en mi coraçon.'
Muño Gustioz   privado cavalgo,
con el dos cavalleros   quel sirvan a so sabor
e con el escuderos   que son de criazon;
salien de Valençia   e andan quanto pueden,   2920
nos dan vagar   los dias e las noches.
Al rey   en San Fagunt lo fallo.
Rey es de Castiella   e rey es de Leon
e de las Asturias   bien a San Çalvador,
fasta dentro en Santi Yaguo   de todo es señor   2925
e llos condes gallizianos   a el tienen por señor.

---

**2894** The marriages are at an end, and no formal act of divorce is necessary. The Cid's words do not indicate that he seeks bloodshed as a form of satisfaction in itself; the vengeance of which he speaks is essential if he is to free himself and his family from the stain of dishonour.

**2912** This is the *axuvar* (see note to l.2571). In the light of Roman law, the Cid has the legal (as well as moral) right to the return of the three thousand marks, since the breakdown of the marriages clearly resulted from the action of the Infantes (see Pavlović and Walker, 'Money, Marriage and the Law', p.199).

**2916** The Cid thus sets in motion the process which is to restore his honour. His immediate action here is in keeping with the procedures established by Roman law; he is to accuse his former sons-in-law of bringing him *deshonor*, corresponding to the Roman concept of *iniuria* (see Pavlović and Walker, 'Roman Forensic Procedure', p.99). He stresses in ll.2910-11 that the dishonour properly belongs to the King and not to himself (see also ll.3149-50), for it was Alfonso who was responsible for the marriages. Nevertheless, he is to seek redress for the wrong which he also has suffered; that the Cid does indeed see himself as dishonoured is made clear, for

that I may see you better married in time to come
and that on my sons - in - law from Carrión God may grant me
                                    vengeance!"
The daughters kissed their father's hands in thanks.                    2895
To a display of arms, they entered the city.
Greatly did their mother, Doña Jimena, rejoice with them.
The man born in a favoured hour did not want to delay;
he spoke with his men in secrecy.
To King Don Alfonso of Castile he determined to send word.             2900


"Where are you, Muño Gustioz, my worthy vassal?
In a favoured hour I brought you up in my court!
Carry this message to Castile to King Alfonso;
on my behalf, from your heart and soul, kiss his hand —
as I am his vassal and he is my lord:                                   2905
at this dishonour done to me by the Infantes of Carrión
let the good King in heart and soul be saddened.
He married my daughters to the Infantes, not I.
Since they have abandoned them, in great dishonour,
if in this there is any affront to my honour,                          2910
whether small or great, it is entirely the concern of my lord.
They have carried off possessions of mine, which are very great,
and that can cause me sorrow, together with the other dishonour.
Let him bring them to a meeting with me, at an assembly or the
                                    royal court,
that I may have justice of the Infantes of Carrión,                    2915
for great is the sorrow in my heart."
Muño Gustioz mounted quickly,
and with him two knights, to serve him as he wished,
and with him squires, members of the Cid's household.
They left Valencia and rode as fast as they could,                     2920
and they allowed themselves no rest by day or by night.
He found the King in Sahagún.
He is King of Castile, and is King of León,
and of the Asturias, and of Oviedo too, the capital.
And as far as Santiago, he is lord of all,                             2925
and the counts of Galicia consider him their lord.

example, by his initial reaction to the news of the outrage and also by Muño Gustioz's message to the King
(1.2950).
**2924** In the Spanish text Oviedo is referred to by the name of its cathedral, San Salvador.

Assi commo descavalga     aquel Muño Gustioz
omillos a los santos     e rogo a[l] Criador;
adeliño pora'l palaçio     do estava la cort,
con el dos cavalleros     quel aguardan cum a sseñor.     2930
Assi commo entraron     por medio de la cort
violos el rey     e connosçio a Muño Gustioz;
levantos el rey,     tan bien los reçibio.
Delant el rey     los inojos finco,
besaba le los pies     aquel Muño Gustioz:     2935
'¡Merçed, rey Alfonsso:     de largos reinos a vos dizen señor!
Los pies e las manos     vos besa el Campeador;
ele es vuestro vassallo     e vos sodes so señor.
Casastes sus fijas     con ifantes de Carrion,
alto fue el casamien[t]o     ca lo quisiestes vos.     2940
Hya vos sabedes la ondra     que es cuntida a nos,
cuemo nos han abiltados     ifantes de Carrion;
mal majaron sus fijas     del Çid Campeador,
majadas e desnudas     a grande desonor
desenparadas las dexaron     en el robredo de Corpes     2945
a las bestias fieras     e a las aves del mont.
Afe las sus fijas     en Valençia do son.
Por esto vos besa las manos     commo vassallo a señor
que gelos levedes a vistas     o a juntas o a cortes.
Tienes por desondrado,     mas la vuestra es mayor,     2950
e que vos pese, rey,     commo sodes sabidor;
¡que aya mio Çid derecho     de ifantes de Carrion!'
El rey una grand ora     callo e comidio:
'Verdad te digo yo     que me pesa de coraçon,
e verdad dizes en esto     tu, Muño Gustioz,     2955
ca yo case sus fijas     con ifantes de Carrion.
Fiz lo por bien,     que ffuesse a su pro;
¡si quier el casamiento     fecho non fuesse oy!
Entre yo e mio Çid     pesa nos de coraçon.
Ayudar le [e] a derecho,     ¡sin salve el Criador!     2960
Lo que non cuidava fer     de toda esta sazon,
andaran mios porteros     por todo mio reino,
pregonaran mi cort     pora dentro en Tolledo;

---

**2951** For the term *sabidor*, see note to l.3070. It is revealing that Muño Gustioz should here emphasize the King's understanding of the law, which must determine the action which he takes.

**2963** The word *cort* has been used several times to designate a royal or noble court. The royal court or *curia ordinaria* constituted a judicial body which the king could call upon at any time, and which would commonly deal with criminal matters and cases brought by one nobleman against another. The *cortes* which Alfonso now summons corresponds to the *curia extraordinaria* or *plena*, whose function in principle was to discuss matters of general importance to the state. It is evidently exceptional that such an assembly should be summoned to deal with a private dispute, for such a matter would usually be handled by the *curia ordinaria*. As Alfonso himself makes clear (ll.3129-33), it is as a token of his love for the Cid that he takes this unusual action. For a detailed analysis of the function of the *cortes* in history and in the *Poema*, see Lacarra, pp.65-77.

214

As soon as Muño Gustioz, well known to us, dismounted,
he bowed down before the saints and prayed to the Creator;
he made for the royal apartments where the court was situated,
and with him went the two knights who obeyed him as their lord. 2930
As soon as they went in, and came amongst the court,
the King saw them and recognized Muño Gustioz;
the King stood up and welcomed them warmly.
Kneeling down before the King,
Muño Gustioz, well known to us, kissed his feet:                    2935
"A favour, King Alfonso, you who are called lord throughout many
                                            kingdoms,
the Battler kisses your feet and hands —
he is your vassal and you are his lord.
You married his daughters to the Infantes of Carrión.
It was a prestigious marriage, for such was your wish.              2940
You already know what great honour it has brought upon us;
how we have been insulted by the Infantes of Carrión.
Cruelly they beat the daughters of the Cid the Battler;
beaten and naked, in great dishonour,
they left them helpless in the oak - wood at Corpes,                2945
at the mercy of the wild beasts and the birds of the forest.
See how his daughters are now in Valencia.
For this reason he kisses your hands, as vassal to lord,
and requests that you take the Infantes to meet him at an assembly
                                   or at a royal court.
He considers himself dishonoured, but your dishonour is greater.   2950
May this fill you with sadness, since you are wise in the law!
Let My Cid have justice of the Infantes of Carrión!"
For a good hour the King reflected in silence:
"I tell you in truth that I am deeply saddened;
you speak the truth in this, Muño Gustioz,
for I married his daughters to the Infantes of Carrión.
I did it seeking good, that it might be to his advantage.
Today, I wish that I had not brought about the marriage!
Both I and My Cid are deeply saddened;
I shall help him to obtain justice, may the Creator save me!       2960
I did not imagine I should have to do this now:
my messengers shall travel throughout my kingdom
and proclaim that a court is to gather in Toledo,

que alla me vayan    cuendes e ifançones,
mandare commo i vayan    ifantes de Carrion    2965
e commo den derecho    a mio Çid el Campeador,

e que non aya rencura    podiendo yo vedallo.
134 Dizid le al Campeador    que en buen ora nasco
que destas .vii. semanas    adobes con sus vassallos;
vengam a Tolledo,    estol do de plazo.    2970
Por amor de mio Çid    esta cort yo fago.
Saludad melos a todos,    entr'ellos aya espaçio;
desto que les abino    aun bien seran ondrados.'
Espidios Muño Gustioz,    a mio Çid es tornado.
Assi commo lo dixo    suyo era el cuidado:    2975
non lo detiene por nada    Alfonsso el Castellano,
enbia sus cartas    pora Leon e a Santi Yaguo
a los portogaleses    e a galizianos
e a los de Carrion    e a varones castellanos
que cort fazie en Tolledo    aquel rey ondrado,    2980
a cabo de .vii. semanas    que i fuessen juntados;
qui non viniesse a la cort    non se toviesse por su vassallo.
Por todas sus tierras    assi lo ivan pensando,
que non faliessen    de lo que el rey avie mandado.

135 Hya les va pesando    a los ifantes de Carrion    2985
por que en Tolledo    el rey fazie cort;
miedo han que i verna    mio Çid el Campeador.
Prenden so conssejo    assi parientes commo son,
ruegan al rey    que los quite desta cort.
Dixo el rey:    '¡No lo fere, sin salve Dios!    2990
Ca i verna    mio Çid el Campeador,
dar le [e]des derecho    ca rencura ha de vos.
Qui lo fer non quisiesse    o no ira [a] mi cort,
quite mio reino    ca del non he sabor.'
Hya lo vieron que es a fer    los ifantes de Carrion;    2995

**2964** The King mentions just the counts and members of the lesser nobility. Normally the *cortes* would also be attended by dignitaries of the Church, and from 1188 the cities – in theory, at least – sent representatives (see Lacarra, p.66).

    The city of Toledo stands on a dominating site on a mountain spur, almost entirely circled by the river Tagus. It had first played an important role under the late Roman Empire; the Visigoths had made it their capital, and under Moslem rule it became the chief town of the 'Middle Frontier'. As the caliphate of Córdoba began to disintegrate, Toledo achieved independence under its Moslem king, but it was steadily brought under Christian influence. Alfonso VI, exploiting the conflicts among factions within the city, subjected it to increasing pressure, besieging it from 1081 and eventually forcing it to capitulate in May, 1085. The capture of Toledo was seen as a great triumph for Alfonso and for Christendom, and no other setting for the court scene could remind us so clearly of Alfonso's prestige and power.

**2969-70** Pavlović and Walker point out ('Roman Forensic Procedure', p.100), that, as the law stipulated that the plaintiff had to deliver his formal accusation two months from the serving of the summons, Alfonso is allowing almost the maximum amount of time to the Cid (who, indeed, delays a further five days).

216

and that counts and noblemen are to go to meet me there.
I shall command the Infantes of Carrión to attend          2965
and to give justice to My Cid the Battler,

that he may have no grievance, if I am able to prevent it.

Tell the Battler, who was born in a favoured hour,
that seven weeks from now he is to make ready with his vassals
and to come to me in Toledo; that is the period of time I give him.
For love of My Cid I summon this court.
Give my greetings to all his people, and let them be at ease,
for from this event they will yet emerge with honour."
Muño Gustioz took his leave and returned to My Cid.
As the King had spoken, so he was determined to act;          2975
Alfonso the Castilian did not delay at all;
he sent out his letters, to León and to Santiago,
to the Portuguese and the Galicians,
to those from Carrión and to the men of Castile,
announcing that a court was being summoned to Toledo by that
                                      honoured King,          2980
and that at the end of seven weeks they should be assembled there;
anyone who failed to attend his court should not consider himself
                                      his vassal.
Throughout his lands, men judged
that they should not fail to obey the King's command.

Now the Infantes of Carrión were saddened,          2985
because, in Toledo, the King was holding his court.
They were afraid that My Cid the Battler would be there.
They sought the advice of all their relatives,
and asked the King to exempt them from attendance at this court.
The King said: "I shall not, may God save me!          2990
For My Cid the Battler will be there,
and you are to give him justice as he has a grievance against you.
Anyone who is unwilling to obey or who fails to attend my court
is to leave my kingdom, for he will not enjoy my favour."
Now the Infantes of Carrión saw what was to be done.          2995

2976 Alfonso, in spite of his original role as king of León, has now, by his just treatment of his vassal, earned the epithet 'the Castilian'.
2978 In 1095 Portugal, the southern extension of Galicia, was given by Alfonso to his natural daughter Teresa as a dowry. It became an independent county, in suzerainty to Castile, and in 1143 was recognized as an independent kingdom.

prenden conssejo    parientes commo son;
el conde don Garçia    en estas nuevas fue
—enemigo de mio Çid    que mal siemprel busco—
aqueste conssejo    los ifantes de Carrion.

Legava el plazo,    querien ir a la cort:          3000
en los primeros    va el buen rey don Alfonsso,
el conde don Anrrich    y el conde don Remond
—aqueste fue padre    del buen enperador—
el conde don Fruella    y el conde don Beltran.
Fueron i de su reino    otros muchos sabidores    3005
de toda Castiella    todos los mejores:
el conde don Garçia    con ifantes de Carrion
e Asur Gonçalez    e Gonçalo Assurez
e Diego e Ferrando    i son amos a dos
e con ellos grand bando    que aduxieron a la cort;    3010
enbair le cuidan    a mio Çid el Campeador.
De todas partes    alli juntados son;
aun non era legado    el que en buen ora naçio,
por que se tarda    el rey non ha sabor.
Al quinto dia    venido es mio Çid el Campeador;    3015
[a] Alvar Fañez    adelantel enbio
que besasse las manos    al rey so señor,
bien lo sopiesse    que i serie essa noch.
Quando lo oyo el rey    plogol de coraçon;
con grandes yentes    el rey cavalgo    3020
e iva reçebir    al que en buen ora naçio.
Bien aguisado viene el Çid    con todos los sos,
buenas conpañas    que assi an tal señor.
Quando lo ovo a ojo    el buen rey don Alffonsso,
firios a tierra    mio Çid el Campeador,    3025
biltar se quiere    e ondrar a so señor.
Quando lo [vio] el rey    por nada non tardo:
'¡Par Sant Esidro    verdad non sera oy!
Cavalgad. Çid; si non,    non avria dend sabor;
saludar nos hemos    d'alma e de coraçon.    3030
De lo que a vos pesa    a mi duele el coraçon;
¡Dios lo mande que por vos    se ondre oy la cort!'

---

**2999** For the enmity between Garcia Ordóñez and the Cid, see note to l.1345. There is no direct connection between the Count's quarrel with the hero and that of the Infantes.

**3002** Enrique (Henri), Prince of Burgundy, married Alfonso's daughter, Teresa, and became Count of Portugal (see note to l.2978). Ramón (Raymond) was Enrique's cousin; he married Alfonso's legitimate daughter, Urraca, and received the county of Galicia.

**3003** Ramón's son became Alfonso VII of León (1126-57); he was crowned emperor in 1135, though his assumption of this title conceals the division and consequent weakening of Christian Spain which was steadily taking place.

**3004** Froila Díaz, Count of León, was Jimena's brother. The figure of Don Beltrán had no known counterpart in

218

They sought the advice of their relatives.
Count Don García took part in this discussion —
he was an enemy of My Cid and always endeavoured to do him harm —
and he gave advice to the Infantes of Carrión.
The time came, and they set off for the meeting place.        3000
Among the first was good King Alfonso,
Count Don Enrique too, and Count Don Ramón —
father of the good Emperor —
Count Don Fruela and Count Don Beltrán.
From his kingdom there went many other men, learned in the law,
and from Castile, all the best men.
Count Don García was there, with the Infantes of Carrión
and Asur González and Gonzalo Ansúrez.
Diego and Fernando were both present,
and with them a great band of men that they took to the court;   3010
they thought they would dishonour My Cid the Battler.
Men came together there from all directions.
The man born in a favoured hour had not yet arrived,
and at this delay the King was not pleased.
On the fifth day My Cid the Battler arrived.                  3015
He sent Álvar Fáñez on ahead
to kiss the hands of the King his lord,
that he might know for certain that he would be there that night.
When he heard this, the King was greatly pleased.
With a great assembly, the King mounted                       3020
and rode out to welcome the man born in a favoured hour.
Finely equipped came the Cid, with all his men,
a worthy company for such a lord.
When he came within sight of good King Don Alfonso,
My Cid the Battler dismounted.                                3025
He wanted to prostrate himself and honour his lord.
When the King saw this he did not delay:
"By Saint Isidore, this shall not happen today!
Mount, O Cid; if you do not, I shall be displeased;
we shall kiss each other warmly.                              3030
I am deeply grieved by your sorrow.
May God command that through you the court may today gain honour!"

the eleventh century, but an individual of that name became Count of Carrión in 1117.
**3008** Gonzalo Ansúrez is the father of the Infantes.
**3011** They hope by intimidation to prevent the Cid from making his accusations and his challenge, and thus to prevent him from wiping away the stain of dishonour.

'¡Amen!'    dixo mio Çid el Campeador.
Beso le la mano    e despues le saludo:
'¡Grado a Dios    quando vos veo, señor!    3035
Omillom a vos    e al conde don Remond
e al conde don Anrrich    e a quantos que i son;
¡Dios salve a nuestros amigos    e a vos mas, señor!
Mi mugier doña Ximena    —dueña es de pro—
besa vos las manos    e mis fijas amas a dos    3040
desto que nos abino    que vos pese, señor.'
Respondio el rey:    '¡Si fago, sin salve Dios!'

136  Pora Tolledo    el rey tornada da.
Essa noch mio Çid    Tajo non quiso passar:
'¡Merçed, ya rey;    si el Criador vos salve!    3045
Penssad, señor    de entrar a la çibdad,
e yo con los mios    posare a San Servan.
Las mis compañas    esta noche legaran;
terne vigilia    en aqueste santo logar.
Cras mañana    entrare a la çibdad    3050
e ire a la cort    enantes de yantar.'
Dixo el rey:    'Plazme de veluntad.'
El rey don Alfonsso    a Tolledo es entrado,
mio Çid Ruy Diaz    en San Servan posado.
Mando fazer candelas    e poner en el altar;    3055
sabor a de velar    en essa santidad
al Criador rogando    e fablando en poridad.
Entre Minaya    e los buenos que i ha
acordados fueron    quando vino la man.

137  Matines e prima    dixieron faza'l alba.    3060

Suelta fue la missa    antes que saliesse el sol
e ssu ofrenda han fecha    muy buena e [a sazon].
'Vos, Minaya Albar Fañez    el mio braço mejor
vos iredes comigo    y el obispo don Jheronimo
e Pero Vermuez    e aqueste Muño Gustioz    3065
e Martin Antolinez    el burgales de pro
e Albar Albarez    e Albar Salvadorez
e Martin Muñoz    que en buen punto naçio
e mio sobrino    Felez Muñoz;

3039 Possibly the Cid is here reminding Alfonso of Jimena's noble birth (see note to l.210).
3047 The castle of San Servando was rebuilt by Alfonso as a monastery. It stands to the east of Toledo and is
linked to the city by the Bridge of Alcántara which crosses the Tagus gorge. The castle now standing there was
built in the fourteenth century.

"Amen!" said My Cid the Battler.
He kissed his hand and then kissed him on the mouth:
"I thank God that I see you, my lord!                              3035
I give my humble respects to you and to Count Don Ramón,
and to Count Don Enrique and to all those present.
May God watch over our friends and you above all, my lord!
My wife, Doña Jimena, is a worthy lady;
she kisses your hands, and so too do my two daughters,           3040
asking you to feel sorrow at what has happened to us."
The King replied: "I do, may God save me!"

The King made ready to ride into Toledo.
That night My Cid would not cross the Tagus:
"I thank you, O King, may the Creator save you!                   3045
Go back, my lord, into the city,
and with my men I shall spend the night at San Servando.
My troops will arrive tonight.
I shall keep a vigil in this holy place.
In the morning I shall enter the city                            3050
and go to the court before I eat."
The King replied: "With this I am well pleased."
King Don Alfonso entered Toledo
and My Cid Ruy Díaz spent the night at San Servando.
He ordered candles to be lit and set on the altar;              3055
he desired to keep a vigil in that holy place,
praying to the Creator and speaking to Him alone.
Both Minaya and the good men with him
were ready when the morning came.

Matins, then Prime, were said as dawn approached.               3060

The Mass was finished before the sun rose,
and they had already made their offerings, excellent and worthy.
"You, Minaya Álvar Fáñez, my right arm,
you shall go with me, and so too shall Bishop Don Jerónimo
and Pedro Bermúdez and Muño Gustioz here,                       3065
and Martín Antolínez, worthy man of Burgos,
and Álvar Álvarez and Álvar Salvadórez,
and Martín Muñoz, born at a favoured time,
and my nephew Félez Muñoz.

221

comigo ira Malanda     que es bien sabidor      
e Galind Garçiez     el bueno d'Aragon;
con estos cunplansse çiento     de los buenos que i son.
Velmezes vestidos     por sufrir las guarnizones,
de suso las lorigas     tan blancas commo el sol,
sobre las lorigas     armiños e peliçones,       3075
e que non parescan las armas,     bien presos los cordones;
so los mantos las espadas     dulçes e tajadores;
d'aquesta guisa     quiero ir a la cort
por demandar mios derechos     e dezir mi razon;
si desobra buscaren     ifantes de Carrion       3080
¡do tales çiento tovier     bien sere sin pavor!'
Respondieron todos:     '¡Nos esso queremos, señor!'
Assi commo lo a dicho     todos adobados son.
Nos detiene por nada     el que en buen ora naçio:
calças de buen paño     en sus camas metio,       3085
sobr'ellas unos çapatos     que a grant huebra son;
vistio camisa de rançal     tan blanca commo el sol,
con oro e con plata     todas las presas son,
al puño bien estan,     ca el selo mando;
sobr'ella un brial     primo de çiclaton,       3090
obrado es con oro,     pareçen por o son;
sobr'esto una piel vermeja,     las bandas d'oro son,
siempre la viste     mio Çid el Campeador;
una cofia sobre los pelos     d'un escarin de pro,
con oro es obrada,     fecha por razon,       3095
que non le contalassen los pelos     al buen Çid Canpeador.
La barba avie luenga     e prisola con el cordon;
por tal lo faze esto     que recabdar quiere todo lo so.
De suso cubrio un manto     que es de grant valor,
en el abrien que ver     quantos que i son.       3100
Con aquestos çiento     que adobar mando
a priessa cavalga,     de San Servan salio;
assi iva mio Çid     adobado a lla cort.
A la puerta de fuera     descavalga a sabor,
cuerda mientra entra mio Çid     con todos los sos,       3105
el va en medio     e los çiento aderredor.
Quando lo vieron entrar     al que en buen ora naçio
levantos en pie     el buen rey don Alfonsso

**3098** Such a precaution is particularly necessary in view of the presence of García Ordóñez, no doubt mindful of the insult that he suffered at Cabra (see note to l.1345).

**3070** No individual by the name of Malanda is known in connection with the Cid, and this character seems most likely to be a fictitious creation. He is a *sabidor*, a legal expert, a representative of a profession which was becoming important by the end of the twelfth century, when the presence of such specialists was essential for the accurate application of the body of Roman law (see Lacarra, pp.99-101). The arrival of other *sabidores* is mentioned in l.3005, and the term is applied to the King himself in l.2951.

With me shall go Malanda, a man knowledgeable in the law,                3070
and Galindo García, good man of Aragón.
With us let there be a hundred of these good men,
wearing quilted tunics to take the weight of their armour,
and, covering them, cuirasses shining white like the sun,
and over the cuirasses, capes of fur and ermine                          3075
with the cords firmly fastened lest their armour be seen;
beneath their cloaks let them carry swords clean and sharp.
Thus I wish to go to the court
to demand my rights and state my case.
Should the Infantes of Carrión seek trouble,                             3080
where I have a hundred such men I shall be without fear."
They all replied: "That, lord, is our desire."
As soon as he had finished speaking they all made ready.
The man born in a favoured hour did not delay;
he put on breeches of fine cloth                                         3085
and over them shoes richly worked;
he dressed in a fine shirt, of cloth shining white like the sun,
with all the fastenings of silver and gold,
and carefully fitted at the cuff, as he had ordered.
Over it he wore a fine long tunic of brocade,                            3090
worked with gold which shone in many places,
and over this a scarlet cape with edging of gold
which My Cid was accustomed to wear.
He wore a cap of fine linen over his hair —
it was embroidered with gold and skilfully made —                       3095
lest they should pull at the hair of My Cid the good Battler.
His flowing beard was tied up with a ribbon,
for he wished to be sure against any harm.
Over it all he put on a cloak which was great of value.
All those present would gaze upon him.                                   3100
With the hundred men that he had commanded to make ready,
he swiftly mounted and rode out from San Servando.
Thus equipped, My Cid went to the court.
At the outer gate My Cid duly dismounted.
My Cid prudently entered with all his men;                               3105
he walked in the centre with the hundred around him.
When the man born in a favoured hour was seen to enter,
good King Don Alfonso rose to his feet

y el conde don Anrrich     y el conde don Remont
e desi adelant     sabet, todos los otros;     3110
a grant ondra lo reçiben     al que en buen ora naçio.
Nos quiso levantar     el Crespo de Grañon
nin todos los del bando     de ifantes de Carrion.
El rey dixo al Çid:     ·Venid aca ser, Campeador,
en aqueste escaño     quem diestes vos en don.     3115
¡Mager que [a] algunos pesa,     mejor sodes que nos!'
Essora dixo muchas merçedes     el que Valençia gaño:
'Sed en vuestro escaño     commo rey e señor;
aca posare     con todos aquestos mios.'
Lo que dixo el Çid     al rey plogo de coraçon.     3120
En un escaño torniño     essora mio Çid poso,
los çiento quel aguardan     posan aderredor.
Catando estan a mio Çid     quantos ha en la cort,
a la barba que avie luenga     e presa con el cordon;
¡en sos aguisamientos     bien semeja varon!     3125
Nol pueden catar de verguença     ifantes de Carrion.
Essora se levo en pie     el buen rey don Alfonsso:
'¡Oid, mesnadas;     si vos vala el Criador!
Hyo de que fu rey     non fiz mas de dos cortes,
la una fue en Burgos     e la otra en Carrion.     3130
Esta terçera     a Tolledo la vin fer oy
por el amor de mio Çid     el que en buen ora naçio
que reçiba derecho     de ifantes de Carrion.
Grande tuerto le han tenido,     sabemos lo todos nos.
Alcaldes sean desto     el conde don Anrrich y el conde don
                              Remond     3135
y estos otros condes     que del vando non sodes.
Todos meted i mientes,     ca sodes coñosçedores
por escoger el derecho,     ca tuerto non mando yo.
Della e della part     en paz seamos oy.
Juro por Sant Esidro,     el que bolviere mi cort     3140
quitar me a el reino,     perdera mi amor.
Con el que toviere derecho     yo dessa parte me so.
Agora demande     mio Çid el Campeador;
sabremos que responden     ifantes de Carrion.'
Mio Çid la mano beso al rey     y en pie se levanto:     3145
'Mucho vos lo gradesco     commo a rey e a señor

---

**3112** García Ordóñez appears in documents from 1098 as lord of Grañón. His nickname ('curly') is mentioned in some chronicles, but its use here indicates the scant respect which the poet has for him.

**3115** The poet has not previously mentioned this seat (or throne) which is recorded by later chronicles as having been seized from vanquished Moorish enemies.

**3134** That the Infantes have committed the outrage against the Cid's daughters is not questioned; indeed they do not themselves deny it. The case is to hinge on whether or not the disparity in status between the Infantes and their wives gave adequate cause for their action.

**3136** Alfonso is himself involved in the question of the Cid's dishonour, and therefore appoints impartial judges.

and so too did Count Don Enrique and Count Don Ramón,
and following them, I tell you, all the others.                      3110
With great honour, they welcomed the man born in a favoured hour.
Count García of Grañón, known for his curly hair, would not stand up,
nor would any of the party of the Infantes of Carrión.
The King said to the Cid: "Come and sit here, O Battler,
on this seat which you gave to me.                                   3115
Though this may upset some men, you are finer than us."
Then the man who had won Valencia thanked him greatly:
"Sit on your throne, as king and lord;
I shall remain here with all my men."
What the Cid said pleased the King deeply.                           3120
Then My Cid sat on a seat, finely turned on the lathe,
with the hundred who guarded him remaining round about.
Everybody in the court was gazing at My Cid,
at his flowing beard tied up in the ribbon.
All about his appearance betokened a fine man.                       3125
The Infantes of Carrión could not look on him for shame!
Then good King Don Alfonso rose to his feet:
"Listen, my vassals, may the Creator protect you!
Since I have been king, I have summoned only two courts:
one was in Burgos and the other in Carrión.                         3130
This third I have had meet today in Toledo
for love of My Cid, who was born in a favoured hour,
that he may receive justice of the Infantes of Carrión.
They have done him great wrong, we all know.
Let the judges of this be Count Don Enrique and Count Don Ramón,
and you other counts who are not of either party.
All give your attention to this — for you know how
to administer justice — I ask nothing that is wrong.
Let both sides be at peace today.
I swear by Saint Isidore that any man who causes trouble in my court
shall leave my kingdom and lose my favour.
I am on the side of the one who is in the right.
Now let My Cid the Battler put his case;
afterwards, we shall find out what answer the Infantes of Carrión
                                    will make."
My Cid thanked the King, and rose to his feet:                      3145
"I am very grateful to you. as my king and lord,

He does, however, remain the ultimate arbiter of points of law (see, for example, l.3214).
**3140-41** Alfonso again swears by Saint Isidore of León, here giving the clearest of evidence that he will act justly
to safeguard the interests of all his vassals, from any part of his kingdom.

por quanto esta cort    fiziestes por mi amor.
Esto les demando    a ifantes de Carrion:
por mis fijas quem dexaron    yo non he desonor,
ca vos las casastes, rey,    sabredes que fer oy;        3150
mas quando sacaron mis fijas    de Valençia la mayor
—hyo bien las queria    d'alma e de coraçon—
diles dos espadas    a Colada e a Tizon
—estas yo las gane    a guisa de varon—
ques ondrassen con ellas    e sirviessen a vos.        3155
Quando dexaron mis fijas    en el robredo de Corpes
comigo non quisieron aver nada    e perdieron mi amor;
¡den me mis espadas    quando mios yernos non son!'
Atorgan los alcaldes:    'Tod esto es razon.'
Dixo el conde don Garçia:    'A esto fablemos nos.'    3160
Essora salien aparte    iffantes de Carrion
con todos sus parientes    y el vando que i son,
a priessa lo ivan trayendo    e acuerdan la razon:
'Aun grand amor nos faze    el Çid Campeador
quando desondra de sus fijas    no nos demanda oy;    3165
bien nos abendremos    con el rey don Alfonsso.
Demos le sus espadas,    quando assi finca la boz,
e quando las toviere    partir se a la cort;
hya mas non avra derecho    de nos el Çid Canpeador.'
Con aquesta fabla    tornaron a la cort:    3170
'¡Merçed, ya rey don Alfonsso,    sodes nuestro señor!
No lo podemos negar,    ca dos espadas ños dio;
quando las demanda    e dellas ha sabor
dar gelas queremos    dellant estando vos.'
Sacaron las espadas    Colada e Tizon,    3175
pusieron las en mano    del rey so señor;
saca las espadas    e relumbra toda la cort,
las maçanas e los arriazes    todos d'oro son,
maravillan se dellas    todos los omnes buenos de la cort.

---

**3158** The Cid divides his case against the Infantes into three separate parts, seeking, in turn, the return of his swords, that of the dowry, and finally restitution for the dishonour done to him at Corpes. In terms of Roman law, he has an indisputable right to demand the return of the swords, since the Infantes have signally failed to use them to the end for which they were given and, in addition, since the Infantes have responded to his gift with marked ingratitude; see Pavlović and Walker ('Roman Forensic Procedure', p.97), who show how the form taken by the Cid's accusations and the structure of this part of the court scene correspond to procedure in the Roman legal system. Note how in each of the first two parts of the Cid's case the claim itself (corresponding to the *intentio*) is expressed in identical terms (l.3158 and l.3206), thus emphasizing the formal sructure of the proceedings. The exposition of the case would be quite a slow affair, with a lengthy break, for example, between the second and third parts, while the Infantes produce sufficient goods to pay the money owed.

**3169** The Infantes believe that, according to the law, since the Cid has not presented any demand other than for the return of the swords, he must now rest his case and they will be free to leave. Hence their shock and indignation when they find that he intends to pursue further his case against them. Significantly, however, as

for summoning this court out of love for me.
I make this claim against the Infantes of Carrión:
I have not been dishonoured because they abandoned my daughters,
for you married them, my king, and you will know what to do today;
but when from the great city of Valencia .they took my daughters,
whom I love tenderly, with my heart and soul,
I gave them two swords, Colada and Tizón,
which I had won in manly combat,
that with them they might win honour and serve you.          3155
When they abandoned my daughters in the oak—wood at Corpes,
they wanted to have nothing to do with me, and forfeited my love.
Let them give me back my swords, since they are no longer my
                              sons - in - law."
The judges agreed: "All this is just."

Count Don García said: "At this point, let us speak together."     3160
Then the Infantes of Carrión withdrew
with all their relatives and the party accompanying them.
Quickly they discussed the matter and came to an agreement:
"The Cid the Battler indeed shows us great favour
in not calling us to reckoning today for his daughters' dishonour; 3165
we shall indeed come to an agreement with King Alfonso.
Let us give him his swords since he rests his case at this,
and when he has them he must leave the court;
the Cid the Battler will no longer have a claim on us."
With these words they went back into the court:          3170
"We thank you, O King Don Alfonso, you who are our lord!
We cannot deny it — he gave us two swords;
since he asks and desires to have them,
we wish to return them to him in your presence."
They took out the swords, Colada and Tizón,          3175
and placed them in the hand of the King, their lord.
He drew the swords and dazzled the whole court:
the pommels and cross - guards were all of gold,
and all the noblemen of the court marvelled at them.

Pavlović and Walker point out (p.97), under Roman law the Cid is quite correct in dealing separately with each of
his claims against the Infantes.
3178 The attention of the whole court falls upon the swords, which will be the instruments of justice. There is a
strong suggestion here, in the Christian symbolism of the form of the swords – a shining cross of gold and silver –,
that the justice which is to be dispensed is divine as well as human.
3179 The term *omnes buenos* ('good men') was sometimes applied to the representatives sent to the *cortes* by the
towns, but it could also be used to denote members of the nobility (see Lacarra, pp.71-72). It is most likely that it
here refers to the 'counts and noblemen' of l.2964.

Reçibio las espadas,     las manos le beso,                    3180
tornos al escaño     don se levanto;
en las manos las tiene     e amas las cato,
nos le pueden camear     ca el Çid bien las connosçe.
Alegros le tod el cuerpo,     sonrrisos de coraçon,
alçava la mano,     a la barba se tomo:                          3185
'¡Par aquesta barba     que nadi non messo
assis iran vengando     don Elvira e doña Sol!'
A so sobrino [don Pero]     por nonbrel lamo,
tendio el braço,     la espada Tizon le dio:
'Prendet la, sobrino,     ca mejora en señor.'                  3190
A Martin Antolinez     el burgales de pro
tendio el braço,     el espada Coladal dio:
'Martin Antolinez     mio vassalo de pro
prended a Colada     —ganela de buen señor,
del conde d[on] Remont Verengel     de Barçilona la mayor—
por esso vos la do     que la bien curiedes vos.                3196
Se que si vos acaeçiere     con ella ganaredes grand prez e grand
valor.'
Beso le la mano,     el espada tomo e reçibio.
Luego se levanto     mio Çid el Campeador:
'¡Grado al Criador     e a vos, rey señor:                       3200
hya pagado so de mis espadas,     de Colada e de Tizon!
Otra rencura he     de ifantes de Carrion:
quando sacaron de Valençia     mis fijas amas a dos
en oro y en plata     tres mill marcos (de plata) les di [y]o.
Hyo faziendo esto,     ellos acabaron lo so;                    3205
den me mis averes,     quando mios yernos non son.'
¡Aqui veriedes quexar se     ifantes de Carrion!
Dize el conde don Remond:     'Dezid de ssi o de no.'
Essora responden     ifantes de Carrion:
'Por essol diemos sus espadas     al Çid Campeador,             3210
que al no nos demandasse,     que aqui finco la boz.'
'Si ploguiere al rey     assi dezimos nos:
a lo que demanda el Çid     quel recudades vos.'
Dixo el buen rey:     'Assi lo otorgo yo.'
Levant(ad)os en pie     el Çid Campeador:                       3215
'Destos averes     que vos di yo

---

**3202** The poet builds up the tension of the scene, showing how the Cid toys with the nervous Infantes. Diego and Fernando's sense of relief at believing that no more is to be asked of them is suddenly dispelled by the second demand.

**3212-13** It is not unreasonable that the Infantes should request time to raise so considerable a sum from their estates at Carrion. However, the judges refuse to grant them any respite: perhaps they are influenced in this by the belief that it could be difficult to enforce payment once the young men have returned to the safety of their lands and to the protection of their powerful family; perhaps, too, the freedom with which the spendthrift Infantes have been seen to borrow and part with their money in the past suggests that payment must be enforced before they plunge themselves even more deeply into debt.

My Cid took the swords, and kissed the King's hands, 3180
and went back to the seat from which he had risen.
He held them in his hands and looked at them both.
They could not have been changed, for the Cid knew them well.
He was filled with joy, and he smiled warmly.
He raised his hand and grasped his beard: 3185
"By this beard, which no man has plucked,
thus will Doña Elvira and Doña Sol be avenged."
He called by name his nephew Don Pedro,
held out his arm and gave him the sword Tizón:
"Take it, my nephew; it gains a better lord." 3190
To Martín Antolínez, worthy man of Burgos,
he held out his arm, and gave the sword Colada:
"Martín Antolínez, my worthy vassal,
take Colada — I won it from a noble lord,
Count Don Ramón Berenguer, from the great city of Barcelona — 3195
and I give it to you that you may take good care of it.
I know that if the opportunity arises you will win with it great
                                    fame and esteem."
Martín Antolínez kissed his hand and took the sword.
Then My Cid the Battler rose to his feet:
"Thanks be to the Creator, and to you, my lord king. 3200
I am well satisfied in the matter of my swords, Colada and Tizón.
I have another grievance against the Infantes of Carrión:
when they took my two daughters away from Valencia,
in gold and silver I gave them three thousand marks.
In spite of this, they carried out their plan; 3205
let them return my money, since they are no longer my sons - in - law."
At this, what complaints you would have seen from the Infantes
                                    of Carrión!
Count Don Ramón said: "Say yes, or no!"
Then the Infantes of Carrión replied:
"We returned the swords to the Cid the Battler 3210
that he should ask no more of us; there he rested his case."
"With the King's permission, we rule
that you are to comply with the Cid's demand."
The good King said: "I grant it."
The Cid the Battler rose to his feet: 3215
"The money which I gave you

si melos dades,    o dedes dello raçon.'        3216<sup>b</sup>
Essora salien aparte    ifantes de Carrion;
non acuerdan en consejo    ca los haveres grandes son,
espesos los han    ifantes de Carrion.
Tornan con el consejo    e fablavan a sso sabor:        3220
'Mucho nos afinca    el que Valençia gaño
quando de nuestros averes    assil prende sabor;
pagar le hemos de heredades    en tierras de Carrion.'
Dixieron los alcaldes    quando manfestados son:
'Si esso plogiere al Çid    non gelo vedamos nos;        3225
mas en nuestro juvizio    assi lo mandamos nos:
que aqui lo entergedes    dentro en la cort.'
A estas palabras    fablo el rey don Alfonsso:
'Nos bien la sabemos    aquesta razon
que derecho demanda    el Çid Campeador.        3230
Destos .iii. mill marcos    los .cc. tengo yo,
entramos melos dieron    los ifantes de Carrion.
Tornar gelos quiero    ca t[an] d[e]sfechos son,
enterguen a mio Çid    el que en buen ora naçio;
quando ellos los an a pechar    non gelos quiero yo.'    3235
Fablo Ferran Gonçalez:    'Averes monedados non tenemos
                                 nos.'
Luego respondio    el conde don Remond:
'El oro e la plata    espendiestes lo vos;
por juvizio lo damos    ant'el rey don Alfonsso:
pagen le en apreçiadura    e prendalo el Campeador.'    3240
Hya vieron que es a fer    los ifantes de Carrion.
Veriedes aduzir    tanto cavallo corredor,
tanta gruessa mula,    tanto palafre de sazon,
tanta buena espada    con toda guarnizon;
reçibiolo mio Çid    commo apreçiaron en la cort.    3245
Sobre los dozientos marcos    que tenie el rey Alfonsso
pagaron los ifantes    al que en buen ora na[çi]o;
enprestan les de lo ageno,    que non les cumple lo so.
Mal escapan jogados    sabed, desta razon.

138  Estas apreçiaduras    mio Çid presas las ha,    3250
     sos omnes las tienen    e dellas penssaran.

**3235** The handing over of this sum by the Infantes has not previously been mentioned. It seems likely that the two hundred marks represent fines imposed on the two Infantes for repudiating their wives: a fine of one hundred marks is specified in the *Fuero de Cuenca* (see note to l.3257) for such an offence. Under Roman law, immediate payment of the dowry could not be ordered if this were to leave the husband penniless, and the King here returns the two hundred marks in order to help avoid the Infantes' bankruptcy and thus make the payment possible. See Pavlović and Walker, 'Money, Marriage and the Law', pp.204-05; and J.García González, 'El matrimonio de las hijas del Cid', *Anuario de Historia del Derecho Espanol*, XXXI (1961), 55-68 (p.560).

**3242-44** The form of this passage recalls that of ll.1966-71 and ll.1987-89. The humiliation of the Infantes is thus contrasted with the splendour and dignity of Alfonso and of the Cid (see Deyermond, 'Structural and Stylistic Patterns', p.65).

must be returned to me, or you must give me satisfaction for it." 3216b
then the Infantes of Carrión withdrew from the court.
They did not come to an agreement, for it was a great sum of money,
and the Infantes of Carrión had spent it.
They went back into the council and spoke freely:                    3220
"The man who won Valencia is pressing us hard
as he is filled with desire for our possessions.
We shall pay him in property from our estates at Carrión."
Since they had recognized their debt, the judges said:
"If this pleases the Cid, we do not forbid it,                        3225
but, from our judgement of the matter, we decree
that you are to pay over the money here in the court."
At these words, King Don Alfonso spoke:
"We know well the truth of this:
that the Cid the Battler demands only his right.                      3230
Of these three thousand marks, I have two hundred.
They were given to me by the two Infantes of Carrión.
I wish to give them back to them since they are in such need.
Let them be handed over to My Cid, the man born in a favoured hour.
Since the Infantes must give them to him in payment, I do not
                                       want them."                     3235
Fernando González spoke: "We do not have money."
Then Count Don Ramón replied:
"You spent the gold and silver;
before King Don Alfonso, we judge that it must be repaid.
Let it be paid in kind; the Battler shall take it."                   3240
Then the Infantes of Carrión saw what was to be done.
You could see so many chargers being brought,
so many sturdy mules and palfreys in prime condition,
so many fine swords and suits of mail.
My Cid took what was judged fitting by the court.                     3245
Except for the two hundred marks in King Alfonso's possession,
the Infantes made full payment to the man born in a favoured hour.
They borrowed from others, for their own possessions were insufficient.
They came off badly, I tell you, from this judgement.

My Cid had taken possession of these goods;                           3250
his men guarded them and took good care of them.
But when he had dealt with this matter, another issue was raised:

Mas quando esto ovo acabado     penssaron luego d'al:
'¡Merçed, ya rey señor     por amor de caridad!
La rencura mayor     non se me puede olbidar.
Oid me toda la cort     e pesevos de mio mal:       3255
[a] los ifantes de Carrion     quem desondraron tan mal
a menos de riebtos     no los puedo dexar.

139 Dezid: ¿que vos mereçi,     ifantes

en juego o en vero     o en alguna razon?
Aqui lo mejorare     a juvizio de la cort.       3259b
¿A quem descubriestes     las telas del coraçon?       3260
A la salida de Valençia     mis fijas vos di yo
con muy grand ondra     e averes a nombre;
quando las non queriedes     —¡ya canes traidores!—
¿por que las sacavades     de Valençia sus honores?
¿A que las firiestes     a çinchas e a espolones?       3265
Solas las dexastes     en el robredo de Corpes
a las bestias fieras     e a las aves del mont:
¡por lo que les fiziestes     menos valedes vos!
Si non recudedes     vea lo esta cort.'

140 El conde don Garçia     en pie se levantava:       3270
'¡Merçed, ya rey     el mejor de toda España!
Vezos mio Çid     a llas cortes pregonadas;
dexola creçer     e luenga trae la barba,
los unos le han miedo     e los otros espanta.
Los de Carrion     son de natura tal       3275
non gelas devien querer     sus fijas por varraganas
¡o quien gelas diera     por parejas o por veladas!
Derecho fizieron     por que las han dexadas.
¡Quanto el dize     non gelo preçiamos nada!'
Essora el Campeador     prisos a la barba:       3280
'¡Grado a Dios     que çielo e tierra manda!

---

**3257** The *riebto* or *riepto* is the judicial challenge, introduced in the first half of the twelfth century by Alfonso VII as a means of controlling the disruptive private conflicts among the members of the nobility. It is described in detail, for example, in the *Fuero de Cuenca*, which specifies the judicial consequences of the different kinds of insult that an individual can suffer; this legal compilation (*fuero* = law-code or charter), produced in 1189-90 under Alfonso VIII, was heavily influenced by Roman law. The law dictated that a challenge issued by one nobleman to another had to be made before the king and in the presence of at least twelve noblemen: in this way a dispute, instead of being settled by private vengeance, was brought under the authority of the monarch. The *riepto* had not existed as an established institution in the time of the Cid. For a detailed study of its nature and of its importance in the *Poema*, see Lacarra, pp.77-96.

**3260** Compare 1.2578. The previous occasion on which the Cid described his daughters as his 'heart-strings' was when he entrusted them to the Infantes on their departure from Valencia. The repetition of this striking phase recalls the earlier scene and emphasizes the way in which the Infantes have failed in their responsibility to the Cid. See also 1.2785, where the same expression is used to convey the sorrow which the girls' suffering causes to Félez Muñoz.

'I beg a favour, my lord king, for the love of charity!
I cannot ignore the greatest part of my grievance.
Let all the court hear me, and feel sorrow at my misfortune!      3255
The Infantes of Carrión, who inflicted such dishonour upon me,
cannot be allowed by me to escape unchallenged.

Tell me: how did I deserve this of you, Infantes,

in jest, or in earnest, or in any respect?
Here, through the judgement of the court, I shall make amends.   3259b
Why did you lay bare the very strings of my heart?               3260
On your departure from Valencia, I gave you my daughters,
with great honour and with possessions in abundance.
Since you did not love them, you treacherous dogs,
why did you take them from their lands in Valencia?
For what reasons did you beat them with saddle - girths and spurs?
You left them alone in the oak - wood at Corpes,
prey to the wild beasts and the birds of the forest.
Through what you did you have lost honour!
If you do not give satisfaction, let this court bear witness!"

Count Don García rose to his feet:                              3270
"I beg a favour, O King, the noblest in all Spain!
My Cid has grown too accustomed to such solemn courts.
He has allowed his beard to grow, and wears it long.
Some are afraid of him, others he fills with terror.
Those of Carrión are of such descent                            3275
that they ought not to want his daughters even as concubines.
Who then gave them as partners in marriage?
They did right to abandon them.
On all that he says we set no value."
Then the Battler clutched his beard:                            3280
"Thanks be to God, who rules over heaven and earth.

---

**3268-69** The Cid does not deal in his accusation with the fact that the Infantes have repudiated his daughters, but with the calculated cruelty which they showed towards them, and with the dishonour which, he argues, they have brought upon themselves.

**3270 ff.** The Count now undertakes the defence of the Infantes, addressing himself directly to Alfonso and ignoring completely the Cid's accusation concerned with the Infantes' treatment of his daughters (l.3279). He shifts the emphasis, dealing with the fact that the Infantes abandoned their wives, and defending the young men on the grounds that they were greatly superior in status to the Cid's daughters and that their marriages in themselves were so unsuitable as to bring them dishonour. His pointed comment in l.3277 seems deliberately to be testing out the King's firmness of purpose.

Por esso es luenga     que a deliçio fue criada.
¿Que avedes vos, conde,     por retraer la mi barba?
Ca de quando nasco     a deliçio fue criada,
ca non me priso a ella     fijo de mugier nada,        3285
nimbla messo     fijo de moro nin de christiana
¡commo yo a vos, conde,     en el castiello de Cabra!
Quando pris a Cabra     e a vos por la barba
non i ovo rapaz     que non messo su pulgada;
¡la que yo messe     aun non es eguada!'        3290

141   Ferran Gonçalez     en pie se levanto,
a altas vozes     o(n)dredes que fablo:
'¡Dexassedes vos, Çid,     de aquesta razon!
De vuestros averes     de todos pagado(s) sodes;
non creçies varaja     entre nos e vos.        3295
¡De natura somos     de condes de Carrion!
Deviemos casar con fijas     de reyes o de enperadores
ca non perteneçien     fijas de ifançones.
Por que las dexamos     derecho fiziemos nos;
mas nos preçiamoš     sabet, que menos no.'        3300

142   Mio Çid Ruy Diaz     a Pero Vermuez cata:
'¡Fabla, Pero Mudo,     varon que tanto callas!
Hyo las he fijas     e tu primas cormanas;
a mi lo dizen,     a ti dan las orejadas.
Si yo respondier     tu non entraras en armas.'        3305

143   Pero Vermuez     conpeço de fablar;
detienes le la lengua,     non puede delibrar,
mas quando enpieça     sabed, nol da vagar:
'¡Direvos, Çid,     costumbres avedes tales!
¡Siempre en las cortes     Pero Mudo me lamades!        3310
Bien lo sabedes     que yo non puedo mas;
por lo que yo ovier a fer     por mi non mancara.
¡Mientes, Ferrando,     de quanto dicho has!
Por el Campeador     mucho valiestes mas.

**3288** It is, perhaps, surprising that the Cid should admit openly in court to this action, for it constitutes an offense for which the law specified heavy punishments. Possibly, as Pavlovic and Walker suggest, ('Roman Forensic Procedure', p.103), in this angry outburst he is falling into a trap laid by the Count. The point that the Cid seeks to make, however, is that García Ordóñez has never formally sought to gain redress and is therefore all the more dishonoured; the Cid tries to demonstrate that the Count is not worthy of attention or belief.
**3291** From this point on, the proceedings are to be of a different nature, as ordered and structured argument give way to increasingly abusive exchanges and the Cid's vassals proceed with the challenges.
**3296-98** The Infantes's justification of their action is based on a belief in their great natural superiority to the daughters of a lesser nobleman (*infanzón*) (see also note to l.3279). The events of the poem have already given the lie to their claims, however, and the greater worth of the Cid and his vassals is to be underlined by the judicial proceedings. The poet points to the need for nobility of blood to be accompanied both by personal merit and by a

It is long because it was tended carefully.
What reason have you, Count, to criticise my beard?
For since it started to grow it has been tended with great care.
No son of woman has ever caught me by it,                    3285
nor has any son of Moor or Christian ever plucked it,
as I did to you, Count, in the castle of Cabra.
When I took Cabra, and pulled you by the beard,
there was no young child who did not pluck his bit.
The piece which I plucked has not yet properly grown."       3290

Fernando González rose to his feet.
He spoke in a loud voice the words which you will hear:
"Say no more of this, Cid!
You have been satisfied with respect to all your possessions.
Let not the dispute between us continue!                     3295
We are of the line of the counts of Carrión!
We should have married daughters of kings or emperors,
for the daughters of lesser nobles were not suitable for us.
We were right to abandon them.
We consider ourselves the more honoured, I tell you, not less."  3300

My Cid Ruy Díaz looks at Pedro Bermúdez:
"Speak up, Pedro the Mute, man of silence!
The girls are my daughters and your first cousins.
These words are addressed to me, but your ears are being pulled.
If I answer first, you will not take up arms."               3305

Pedro Bermúdez begins to speak.
His tongue is tied, he cannot pronounce his first words,
but once he has begun, I tell you, he gives it no rest:
"I shall say this to you, Cid — you have such customs!
You always call me Pedro the Mute at the court!              3310
You know well that I cannot help it.
As for what I am to do, it will not remain undone through my neglect.
You lie, Fernando, in all you have said!
Through the Battler you gained greatly in prestige.

readiness to discharge to the full one's social and legal obligations.
**3305** It is those who issue the challenges who will fight the duels, and this the Cid intends to leave in the hands of his vassals.
**3313** This statement is in itself a reproach so profound and direct as to make a duel inevitable; it is mentioned in the *Fuero de Cuenca* as a conventional feature of a judicial challenge (see Lacarra, pp.81-82).

Las tus mañas    yo te las sabre contar:    3315
¿miembrat quando lidiamos    çerca Valençia la grand?
Pedist las feridas primeras    al Campeador leal,
vist un moro,    fustel ensayar,
antes fuxiste    que a'l te alegasses.    3318<sup>b</sup>
Si yo non uvias    el moro te jugara mal;
passe por ti,    con el moro me off de ajuntar,    3320
de los primeros colpes    of le de arrancar.
Did el cavallo,    toveldo en poridad,
fasta este dia    no lo descubri a nadi;
delant mio Çid e delante todos    oviste te de alabar
que mataras el moro    e que fizieras barnax;    3325
crovieron telo todos,    mas non saben la verdad.
¡Y eres fermoso,    mas mal varragan!
¡Lengua sin manos!    ¿cuemo osas fablar?


144 Di, Ferrando,    otorga esta razon:
¿non te viene en miente    en Valençia lo del leon,    3330
quando durmie mio Çid    y el leon se desato?
E tu, Ferrando,    ¿que fizist con el pavor?
¡Metistet tras el escaño    de mio Çid el Campeador!
¡Metistet, Ferrando,    por o menos vales oy!
Nos çercamos el escaño    por curiar nuestro señor    3335
fasta do desperto mio Çid ·    el que Valençia gaño,
levantos del escaño    e fues pora'l leon;
el leon premio la cabeça,    a mio Çid espero,
dexos le prender al cuelo    e a la red le metio.
Quando se torno    el buen Campeador    3340
a sos vassalos    violos aderredor,
demando por sus yernos:    ¡ninguno non fallo!
Riebtot el cuerpo    por malo e por traidor;
estot lidiare aqui    ant'el rey don Alfonsso
por fijas del Çid,    don Elvira e doña Sol.    3345
¡Por quanto las dexastes    menos valedes vos!
Ellas son mugieres    e vos sodes varones;
en todas guisas    mas valen que vos.
Quando fuere la lid    —si ploguiere al Criador—
tu lo otorgaras    a guisa de traidor;    3350
de quanto he dicho    verdadero sere yo.'
D'aquestos amos    aqui quedo la razon.


3343 The term *traidor* is one commonly associated with a judicial challenge, and is mentioned in the *Fuero de Cuenca*. It had come to be used quite generally to denote disloyalty to those to whom an individual was bound by ties of mutual obligation, and it incorporated the idea of deceit (see Lacarra, pp.81-82).

I can tell you of how cunning you have been.                     3315
Do you remember when we fought near the great city of Valencia?
You asked the loyal Battler for the right to strike the first blows;
you saw a Moor and went to engage him in battle,
but you fled before you reached him.                             3318b
Had I not helped you, the Moor would have had cruel sport;
I rode past you and joined battle with the Moor,               3320
and with the first blows I overcame him.
I gave you the horse, and kept the matter secret;
until today I had revealed this to nobody.
Before My Cid and before everybody you boasted
that you had killed the Moor and performed a great deed.       3325
They all believed you, but they do not know the truth.
You are handsome, but a coward!
A tongue without hands!   How dare you speak?

Tell me, Fernando, confess this:
don't you remember the episode of the lion in Valencia,        3330
when My Cid was asleep and the lion broke free?
And you, Fernando, what did you do in your fear?
You hid behind the couch of My Cid the Battler!
You hid, Fernando, and therefore you are less honoured today!
We surrounded the couch to protect our lord,                    3335
until My Cid, the man who won Valencia, awoke.
He rose from the couch and went towards the lion.
The lion lowered its head, and waited for My Cid,
and let him take it by the neck and put it in the cage.
When the good Battler returned,                                  3340
he saw his vassals all around,
and asked for his sons - in - law.   No one could find them!
I challenge you in person as an evil and treacherous man.
I shall fight this duel with you here, before King Alfonso,
on behalf of the Cid's daughters, Doña Elvira and Doña Sol.    3345
In abandoning them, you lost honour.
They are women and you are men;
in all respects they are more honoured than you.
When the fight takes place — if the Creator is willing —
you will make a traitor's confession.                           3350
In all that I say I shall be proved truthful."
Here rested the dispute between these two.

145 Diego Gonçalez     odredes lo que dixo:
'¡De natura somos     de los condes mas limpios!
¡Estos casamientos     non fuessen apareçidos     3355
por consagrar     con mio Çid don Rodrigo!
Por que dexamos sus fijas     aun no nos repentimos,
mientra que bivan     pueden aver sospiros;
lo que les fiziemos     ser les ha retraido,
¡esto lidiare     a tod el mas ardido:     3359b

que por que las dexamos     ondrados somos nos!'     3360

146 Martin Antolinez     en pie se levantava:

'¡Cala, alevoso,     boca sin verdad!
Lo del leon     non se te deve olbidar;
saliste por la puerta,     metistet al coral,
fusted meter     tras la viga lagar;     3365
mas non vesti[ste]d     el manto nin el brial.
Hyo llo lidiare,     non passara por al:
fijas del Çid     por que las vos dexastes
en todas guisas     sabed, que mas que vos valen.
¡Al partir de la lid     por tu boca lo diras     3370
que eres traidor     e mintist de quanto dicho has!'

Destos amos     la razon finco.

147 Asur Gonçalez     entrava por el palaçio
manto armiño     e un brial rastrando;
vermejo viene,     ca era almorzado;     3375
en lo que fablo     avie poco recabdo:

148 '¡Hya varones!     ¿Quien vio nunca tal mal?
¡Quien nos darie nuevas     de mio Çid el de Bivar!
¡Fuesse a Rio d'Orvina     los molinos picar
e prender maquilas     commo lo suele far!     3380
¿Quil darie     con los de Carrion a casar?'

149 Essora Muño Gustioz     en pie se levanto:
'¡Cala, alevoso,     malo e traidor!
Antes almuerzas     que vayas a oraçion,

**3362** The term *alevoso* that Martín Antolínez applies to the Infante (see also l.3383) is quite commonly mentioned in Castilian and Leonese legal texts of the latter part of the twelfth century and is roughly synonymous with *traidor* (see Lacarra, pp.81-83 and p.95).
**3374** Asur González's untidy and undignified appearance reflects his vulgarity and ignobility of character.
**3379** Asur González mocks the Cid's (relatively) humble origins. The Cid's village, Vivar, stands on the river Ubierna. His family could have owned a mill, though, as nobles, they would certainly not have worked it themselves.

You shall hear what Diego González said:
"By nature we are counts of the purest descent!
I wish that these marriages had never taken place,                3355
that we should be related by blood to My Cid Don Rodrigo!
We have not repented of abandoning his daughters.
As long as they live they can continue to sigh,
and they will be taunted with what we did to them.
Over this, I will fight against the boldest,                     3359b

for because we abandoned them we are honoured."                  3360

Martín Antolínez rose to his feet:

"Be silent, traitor, mouth without truth!
You must not forget the episode of the lion:
you fled through the door and hid in the yard,
and kept out of sight behind a beam of the wine - press;         3365
you never again put on that cloak and tunic.
I will fight with you over this; it shall not be otherwise:
the daughters of the Cid, because you abandoned them,
are in all respects, I tell you, more honoured than you.
When you leave the fight, with your own mouth you shall confess 3370
that you are a traitor and have lied in all you said."

Between these two the dispute rested.

Asur González entered the hall,
trailing an ermine cloak and a long tunic;
his face was bright red, for he had just eaten.                  3375
He was not careful in what he said:

"Now, my men!  Whoever heard such a sorry story?
Who would say we gained honour from being related to My Cid
                                          the man from Vivar?
He should go to the Ubierna river to dress the millstones
and to collect money for the grain as is his custom.             3380
Who could imagine him related by marriage to those of Carrión?"

At that point, Muño Gustioz rose to his feet:
"Be silent, liar, wicked traitor!
You eat before you go to mass!

a los que das paz    fartas los aderredor.    3385
Non dizes verdad    [a] amigo ni ha señor,
falsso a todos    e mas al Criador.
En tu amistad    non quiero aver raçion;
¡fazer telo [e] dezir    que tal eres qual digo yo!'
Dixo el rey Alfonsso:    'Calle ya esta razon.    3390
Los que an rebtado    lidiaran, ¡sin salve Dios!'
Assi commo acaban    esta razon
affe dos cavalleros    entraron por la cort:
al uno dizen Ojarra    e al otro Yeñego Simenez,
el uno es [del] ifante    de Navarra [rogador],    3395
y el otro    [del] ifante de Aragon;
besan las manos    al rey don Alfonsso,
piden sus fijas    a mio Çid el Campeador
por ser reinas    de Navarra e de Aragon
e que gelas diessen    a ondra e a bendiçion.    3400
A esto callaron    e ascucho toda la cort.
Levantos en pie    mio Çid el Campeador:
'¡Merçed, rey Alfonsso,    vos sodes mio señor!
¡Esto gradesco    yo al Criador
quando melas demandan    de Navarra e de Aragon!    3405
Vos las casastes antes,    ca yo non;
afe mis fijas    en vuestras manos son,
sin vuestro mandado    nada non fere yo.'
Levantos el rey,    fizo callar la cort:
'Ruego vos, Çid,    caboso Campeador,    3410
que plega a vos    e atorgar lo he yo
este casamiento    oy se otorge en esta cort,
ca creçe vos i ondra    e tierra e onor.'
Levantos mio Çid,    al rey las manos le beso:
'Quando a vos plaze    otorgo lo yo, señor.'    3415
Essora dixo el rey:    '¡Dios vos de den buen galardon!
A vos, Ojarra,    e a vos, Yeñego Ximenez,
este casamiento    otorgo vos le yo
de fijas de mio Çid    don Elvira e doña Sol
pora los ifantes    de Navarra e de Aragon,    3420
que vos las de    a ondra e a bendiçion.'

**3385** During the mass, the members of the congregation would kiss each other as the *Pax domini* was being said.
**3390-91** The trial has been degenerating into an exchange of abuse, and Alfonso now acts promptly to prevent matters from getting out of hand. It is these duels that the Cid has sought in the third and final part of his demand, for they are to repair the dishonour that he has suffered. The King's intervention makes it clear that the Cid has won his case.
**3394** The name of Íñigo Jiménez, an Aragonese nobleman, appears in documents of the early twelfth century. Nothing is known of the historical existence of Ojarra. Pavlović and Walker ('Roman Forensic Procedure', p.104) point out that the ambasadors' prompt entry at this juncture is particularly significant: since the future sons-in-law are of higher rank than the Infantes, the dishonour done to Alfonso is wiped out and his judgement of the Cid is vindicated. We are left in no doubt that the honour of the Cid and his family will be restored; the

240

When you give the kiss of peace you revolt those around you.　3385
You do not tell the truth to friend or to lord;
you are false to all men, and above all to the Creator.
I wish to have no share in your friendship.
I shall force you to confess that you are just as I say."
King Alfonso said: "Say no more of this!　3390
Those who have challenged will fight, so may God save me!"
Just as these words have been said,
behold two knights coming into the court:
one is called Ojarra, and the other Íñigo Jiménez;
the one is an emissary from the Prince of Navarre,　3395
and the other from the Prince of Aragón.
They kiss King Don Alfonso's hands,
and ask for the daughters of My Cid the Battler,
to be queens of Navarre and Aragón.
They ask that they be given to them in honour and with holy blessing.
At this there was silence and the whole court listened.
My Cid the Battler rose to his feet:
"I thank you, King Alfonso, you are my lord.
I am grateful to the Creator
that the lords of Navarre and Aragón ask me for my daughters.　3405
Previously, you gave them in marriage, not I;
here you have my daughters in your hands.
Without your command, I shall do nothing."
The King rose, and silenced the court:
"I ask you, O Cid, worthy Battler,　3410
to consent to this; I shall grant it.
Let permission for this marriage be given today in this court,
for by it you gain in honour, possessions and lands."
My Cid rose and kissed the King's hands:
"Since it pleases you, I give my consent, my lord."　3415
Then the King said: "May God reward you well for this!
To you, Ojarra, and you, Íñigo Jiménez,
I grant this marriage
of the daughters of My Cid, Doña Elvira and Doña Sol,
to the princes of Navarre and Aragón,　3420
that I may give them to you in honour and with holy blessing."

possibility that the Cid's representatives will lose in the judicial combat is not even considered.
**3399** The girls did not, in fact, become queens: historically, María (Sol) married Count Ramón Berenguer III of
Barcelona, nephew of the count depicted in the *Poema* as the Cid's adversary at Tévar; and Cristina (Elvira)
married Prince Ramiro of Navarre.

Los que an rebtado     lidiaran, ¡sin salve Dios!'
Assi commo acaban     esta razon
affe dos cavalleros     entraron por la cort:
al uno dizen Ojarra     e al otro Yeñego Simenez,
el uno es [del] ifante     de Navarra [rogador],        3395
y el otro     [del] ifante de Aragon;
besan las manos     al rey don Alfonsso,
piden sus fijas     a mio Çid el Campeador
por ser reinas     de Navarra e de Aragon
e que gelas diessen     a ondra e a bendiçion.        3400
A esto callaron     e ascucho toda la cort.
Levantos en pie     mio Çid el Campeador:
'¡Merçed, rey Alfonsso,     vos sodes mio señor!
¡Esto gradesco     yo al Criador
quando melas demandan     de Navarra e de Aragon!      3405
Vos las casastes antes,     ca yo non;
afe mis fijas     en vuestras manos son,
sin vuestro mandado     nada non fere yo.'
Levantos el rey,     fizo callar la cort:
'Ruego vos, Çid,     caboso Campeador,        3410
que plega a vos     e atorgar lo he yo
este casamiento     oy se otorge en esta cort,
ca creçe vos i ondra     e tierra e onor.'
Levantos mio Çid,     al rey las manos le beso:
'Quando a vos plaze     otorgo lo yo, señor.'       3415
Essora dixo el rey:     '¡Dios vos de den buen galardon!
aver las hedes a servir,     mal que vos pese a vos.
¡Grado a Dios del çielo     e [a] aquel rey don Alfonsso
asil creçe la ondra     a mio Çid el Campeador!
En todas guisas     tales sodes quales digo yo;
si ay qui responda     o dize de no        3455
¡hyo so Albar Fañez     pora tod el mejor!'
Gomez Pelayet     en pie se levanto:
'¿Que val, Minaya,     toda essa razon?
Ca en esta cort     afarto[s] ha pora vos
e qui al quisiesse     serie su ocasion.        3460
Si Dios quisiere     que desta bien salgamos nos
despues veredes     que dixiestes o que no.'

---

3429 Minaya's intervention at this stage is unnecessary and serves simply to provoke a further violent argument. The worthy Minaya is on a number of occasions in the *Poema* shown to be rather excitable, in this respect lacking the outstanding dignity and control of the Cid.

3457 The existence of a Count Gómez Peláyez is documented in the final years of the eleventh century and in the early part of the twelfth century.

Ojarra and Iñigo Jiménez rose
and kissed the hands of King Don Alfonso
and then those of My Cid the Battler.
They swore oaths and made promises                                   3425
that it would be done as they had said, or better.
Many members of all parties of the court were pleased by this,
but not the Infantes of Carrión.
Minaya Álvar Fáñez rose to his feet:
"I ask a favour of you, as my king and lord,                         3430
and wish that this does not cause sorrow to the Cid the Battler.
You have all had your opportunity to speak in this court;
I would like to say to you something of my own."
The King said: "I am most willing.
Say, Minaya, what you wish."                                         3435
"Members of the court, I ask you all to hear me,
for I have a great grievance against the Infantes of Carrión.
I gave them my cousins as King Alfonso had commanded,
and they took them in honour and with holy blessing.
My Cid the Battler gave them great wealth.                           3440
They abandoned them in spite of us.
I challenge them in person, as evil men and traitors.
By nature you belong to the Vani - Gómez family,
from which came counts of fame and of great worth;
but we know well the cunning ways they have today.                   3445
I give thanks to the Creator
that my cousins Doña Elvira and Doña Sol are sought
by the princes of Navarre and Aragón.
Before, you had them as your wives to hold in your arms,
but now you will kiss their hands in hommage and call them your ladies;
you will have to serve them, even though it causes you distress.
Thanks be to God in Heaven and to the illustrious King Don Alfonso,
that the honour of My Cid the Battler so increases!
In every respect you are just as I say;
if there is anybody who contradicts me or denies this,               3455
I stand here Álvar Fáñez, a match for any man."
Gómez Peláyez rose to his feet:
"What is the worth, Minaya, of all these words?
For in this court there are many men who are a match for you,
and if anybody claimed otherwise, it would be his misfortune.        3460
If God wills that we emerge safely from this,
then you will have to reconsider your words."

Dixo el rey:    'Fine esta razon;
non diga ninguno    della mas una entençion.
Cras sea la lid    quando saliere el sol                    3465
destos .iii. por tres    que rebtaron en la cort.'
Luego fablaron    ifantes de Carrion:
'Dandos, rey, plazo    ca cras ser non puede.
Armas e cavallos    tienen los del Canpeador,
nos antes abremos a ir    a tierras de Carrion.'            3470
Fablo el rey    contra'l Campeador:
'Sea esta lid    o mandaredes vos.'
En essora dixo mio Çid:    'No lo fare, señor;
mas quiero a Valençia    que tierras de Carrion.'
En essora dixo el rey:    'Aosadas, Campeador.           3475
Dad me vuestros cavalleros    con todas vuestras guarnizones,
vayan comigo.    yo sere el curiador;
hyo vos lo sobrelievo    commo [a] buen vassallo faze (a) señor
que non prendan fuerça    de conde nin de ifançon.
Aqui les pongo plazo    de dentro en mi cort:             3480
a cabo de tres semanas    en begas de Carrion
que fagan esta lid    delant estando yo.
Quien non viniere al plazo    pierda la razon,
desi sea vençido    y escape por traidor.'
Prisieron el juizio    ifantes de Carrion.                 3485
Mio Çid al rey    las manos le beso
e dixo:    'Plazme, señor.                                 3486b
Estos mis tres cavalleros    en vuestra mano son,
d'aqui vos los acomiendo    como a rey e a señor.
Ellos son adobados    pora cumpllir todo lo so.
¡Ondrados melos enbiad a Valençia    por amor del
                                        Criador!'         3490
Essora respuso el rey:    '¡Assi lo mande Dios!'
Alli se tollio el capielo    el Çid Campeador,
la cofia de rançal    que blanca era commo el sol,
e soltava la barba    e sacola del cordon.
Nos fartan de catarle    quantos ha en la cort.           3495
Adeliño al conde don Anrich    e al conde don Remond:
abraçolos tan bien    e ruega los de coraçon
que prendan de sus averes    quanto ovieren sabor.
A essos e a los otros    que de buena parte son

3464 Here Alfonso uses a technical term of Roman law: the *intentio* is a statement of a plaintiff's claim.
3474 The Cid, by returning to Valencia, shows complete faith both in his vassals – who have made the challenges and so are to defend his honour in the combat – and also in his lord, Alfonso, who has taken upon himself the responsibility to ensure that justice is done. It is not clear why the King nominates Carrión as the scene of the duels: probably, however, the poet wishes to show that, even at Carrión, Alfonso is able to act with fairness and authority; and the fact that the Infantes suffer their defeat at Carrión, on which they have always looked both as the source of their pride and wealth and as a haven of security, renders their experience all the more bitter and humiliating.

244

The King said: "Let there be an end to this argument!
Let no man make any further allegation!
Tomorrow when the sun rises, the combat shall take place          3465
between those who have made the challenges in the court, three
                              against three."
Then the Infantes of Carrión spoke:
"Grant us a delay, O King, for the combat cannot take place tomorrow.
The Battler's men have our arms and horses;
first we shall have to go to the lands of Carrión."               3470
The King spoke to the Battler:
"Let this combat take place where you wish."
Then My Cid replied: "I shall not decide, my lord;
I would rather go to Valencia than to the lands of Carrión."
Then the King said: "Of course, Battler.                          3475
Give me your knights, with all their arms;
let them go with me; I shall be their protector.
I guarantee to you, as a lord to his good vassal,
that they shall suffer no violence from count or nobleman.
Here in my court I appoint a time:                                3480
three weeks from now, in the fields of Carrión,
this combat shall take place in my presence.
Any man that fails to come at the due time shall lose his case,
and thus he shall be declared defeated and be held a traitor."
The Infantes of Carrión took the judgement.                       3485
My Cid kissed the King's hands
and said: "I am satisfied, my lord.                               3486b
These three knights of mine are in your hands;
henceforth I commend them to you as my king and lord.
They are equipped to do their duty to the full.
Send them in honour to me in Valencia, for love of the Creator." 3490
At that, the King replied: "May God so decree it!"
Then the Cid the Battler took off his cap,
the cap of fine cloth that was as white as the sun,
and he loosed his beard and freed it from the ribbon.
The whole court could not but gaze at him.                        3495
He approached Count Don Enrique and Count Don Ramón.
He embraced them warmly and with all his heart entreated them
to take from his possessions all that they desired.
Both themselves and all others on the side of right

a todos los rogava     assi commo han sabor;      3500
tales i a que prenden,     tales i a que non.
Los .cc. marcos     al rey los solto;
de lo al tanto priso     quanto ovo sabor.
'¡Merçed vos pido, rey     por amor del Criador!
Quando todas estas nuevas     assi puestas son     3505
beso vuestras manos     con vuestra graçia, señor;
e ir me quiero pora Valençia,     con afan la gane yo.'

       .    .    .    .
        .    .    .    .

El rey alço la mano,     la cara se santigo:
'¡Hyo lo juro     par Sant Esidro el de Leon
que en todas nuestras tierras     non ha tan buen varon!'  3510
Mio Çid en el cavallo     adelant se lego,
fue besar la mano     a so señor Alfonsso:
'Mandastes me mover     a Bavieca el corredor,
en moros ni en christianos     otro tal non ha oy:
hy[o] vos le do en don:     mandedes le tomar, señor.'     3515
Essora dixo el rey:     'Desto non he sabor;
si a vos le tollies     el cavallo no havrie tan buen señor.
Mas atal cavallo cum est     pora tal commo vos,
pora arrancar moros del canpo     e ser segudador;
¡quien vos lo toller quisiere     nol vala el Criador     3520
ca por vos e por el cavallo     ondrados somo[s] nos!'
Essora se espidieron     e luegos partio la cort.
El Campeador a los que han lidiar     tan bien los castigo:
'Hya Martin Antolinez     e vos, Pero Vermuez,
e Muño Gustioz:     firmes sed en campo a guisa de varones;
¡buenos mandados me vayan     a Valençia de vos!'     3526
Dixo Martin Antolinez:     '¿Por que lo dezides, señor?
Preso avemos el debdo     e a passar es por nos;
¡podedes oir de muertos,     ca de vençidos no!'
Alegre fue d'aquesto     el que en buen ora naçio;     3530
espidios de todos los     que sos amigos son,
Mio Çid pora Valençia     y el rey pora Carrion.
Mas tres semanas de plazo     todas complidas son:
felos al plazo     los del Campeador.

---

**3507** At this point a folio has been removed, though, as in the case of the lacuna following l.2337, we cannot be certain how many lines are in fact missing. Later chronicles include here an account of how the Cid, at the King's invitation, gives a demonstration of Babieca's qualities, and l.3513 seems to confirm that the missing section dealt largely with this episode.

he begged to take what they wished.                                    3500
Some there were who took the chance, others who did not.
The Cid freed the King of the obligation to pay the two hundred marks,
and of the rest he took what he desired.
"I ask a favour of you, my king, for love of the Creator!
Since these matters have thus all been settled,                        3505
with your permission, my lord, I will kiss your hands to take my leave.
I wish to go to Valencia, which I fought hard to win."

. . . . . . . . . . . . . . . . . . . . . . . . . . .
. . . . . . . . . . . . . . . . . . . . . . . . . . .

The King raised his hand, and made the sign of the cross on his
                              forehead:
"I swear by Saint Isidore of León
that in all our lands there is no other man so good!"                  3510
My Cid rode forward
and went to kiss the hand of his lord, Alfonso:
"You commanded me to show the speed of the charger Babieca;
among Moors and Christians there is no other such horse today.
I present him to you; order him to be received, my lord."              3515
Then the King said: "I do not wish for this.
If he were taken from you, the horse would not have so good a lord.
Such a horse as this is for a man like you —
to defeat Moors on the field of battle and go in their pursuit.
Let the Creator not protect any man who would take him from you,
for through you and through the horse we are honoured."
At that point, they took their leave and then the court departed.
The Battler gave careful instructions to those who were to fight:
"Now, Martín Antolínez, and you, Pedro Bermúdez
and Muño Gustioz: stand firm like men on the field of combat. 3525
Let good reports of you come to me in Valencia!"
Martín Antolínez said: "Why do you say that, my lord?
We have taken on this obligation, and it is up to us to fulfil it;
you may hear that we have died, but not that we have been
                              defeated."
The man born in a favoured hour was filled with joy at this.          3530
He took his leave of all those who were his friends.
My Cid set off for Valencia and the King for Carrión.
Now the permitted three weeks have passed.
Here are the Battler's men at the time appointed,

cunplir quieren el debdo     que les mando so señor.     3535
Ellos son en p[o]der     del rey don Alfonsso el de Leon.
Dos dias atendieron     a ifantes de Carrion;
mucho vienen bien adobados     de cavallos e de guarnizones,
e todos sus parientes     con ellos son;
que si los pudiessen apartar     a los del Campeador     3540
que los matassen en campo     por desondra de so señor.
El cometer fue malo,     que lo al nos enpeço,
ca grand miedo ovieron     a Alfonsso el de Leon.
De noche belaron las armas     e rogaron al Criador.
Troçida es la noche,     ya quiebran los albores:     3545
muchos se juntaron     de buenos ricos omnes
por ver esta lid     ca avien ende sabor;
de mas sobre todos     i es el rey don Alfonsso
por querer el derecho     e non consentir el tuerto.
Hyas metien en armas     los del buen Campeador;     3550
todos tres se acuerdan     ca son de un señor.
En otro logar se arman     los ifantes de Carrion;
sedielos castigando     el conde Garçi Ordoñez.
Andidieron en pleito,     dixieron lo al rey Alfonsso
que non fuessen en la batalla     las espadas tajadores Colada e
                                    Tizon,     3555
que non lidiassen con ellas     los del Campeador;
mucho eran repentidos los ifantes     por quanto dadas son.
Dixieron gelo al rey,     mas non gelo conloyo:
'Non sacastes ninguna     quando oviemos la cort.
Si buenas las tenedes     pro abran a vos;     3560
otrosi faran     a los del Canpeador.
¡Levad e salid al campo,     ifantes de Carrion!
Huebos vos es que lidiedes     a guisa de varones,
que nada non mancara     por los del Campeador.
Si del campo bien salides     grand ondra avredes vos,     3565
e ssi fuere[de]s vençidos     non rebtedes a nos
ca todos lo saben     que lo buscastes vos.'
Hya se van repintiendo     ifantes de Carrion,
de lo que avien fecho     mucho repisos son;
no lo querrien aver fecho     por quanto ha en Carrion.     3570
Todos tres son armados     los del Campeador.
Hiva los ver     el rey don Alfonsso,
dixieron     los del Campeador:

---

**3546** For the meaning of the term *ricos omnes*, see note to l.1980.
**3556** The Infantes see the swords as symbols of their guilt and as a clear sign that they will lose the combat. See Introduction, VII (c), and note to l.3178, above.

desiring to fulfil the obligation imposed upon them by their lord. 3535
They are in the hands of King Don Alfonso of León.
Two days they have waited for the Infantes of Carrión.
The infantes arrive well - equipped with horses and armour.
All their relatives are with them;
and if they could lure the Battler's men away                          3540
they would kill them in the country to dishonour their lord.
Their intention was wicked, but it went no further,
for they were in great fear of Alfonso of León.
That night they kept a vigil over their arms and prayed to the Creator.
Night had ended, and dawn was breaking;                            3545
many good nobles had gathered together
in their desire to see this combat.
And over them all presided King Don Alfonso,
to see that justice was done and to prevent any wrong.
Now the good Battler's men armed themselves;                       3550
all three were of one mind, having the same lord.
In another place, the Infantes of Carrión were putting on their armour,
and Count García Ordóñez was giving them instructions.
They discussed a grievance, which they put to King Alfonso,
saying that the keen - edged swords, Colada and Tizón, should play
                                   no part in the combat,          3555
and that they should not be used by the Battler's men.
The Infantes deeply regretted handing them over.
They said this to the King, but he did not support them:
"When we held the court, you asked for no sword to be excluded.
If you have good swords, they will be of value to you,             3560
and likewise two other swords will serve the Battler's men.
Stand and enter the field of combat, Infantes of Carrión.
You must fight in manly combat,
for those who represent the Battler will not fail in their duties.
If you leave the field victorious you will have won great honour,  3565
but if you are defeated you are not to blame us,
for all men know that you brought this on yourselves."
Now the Infantes of Carrión felt regret,
and bitterly repented of what they had done.
They would not have done it for all the wealth in Carrión.         3570
All three of the Battler's men were now armed,
and King Don Alfonso went to see them.
The Battler's men said to him:

'Besamos vos las manos      commo a rey e a señor
que fiel seades oy      dellos e de nos;          3575
¡a derecho vos valed,      a ningun tuerto no!
Aqui tienen su vando      los ifantes de Carrion,
non sabemos      ques comidran ellos o que non.
En vuestra mano      nos metio nuestro señor:
¡tenendos a derecho,      por amor del Criador!'      3580
Essora dixo el rey:      '¡D'alma e de coraçon!'
Aduzen les los cavallos      buenos e corredores,
santiguaron las sielas      e cavalgan a vigor,
los escudos a los cuellos      que bien blocados son;
e'mano prenden las astas      de los fierros tajadores,      3585
estas tres lanças      traen seños pendones;
e derredor dellos      muchos buenos varones.
Hya salieron al campo      do eran los mojones.
Todos tres son acordados      los del Campeador
que cada uno dellos      bien fos ferir el so.      3590
Fevos de la otra part      los ifantes de Carrion
muy bien aconpañados,      ca muchos parientes son.
El rey dioles fieles - por dezir el derecho e al non,
que non varagen con ellos      de si o de non.
Do sedien en el campo      fablo el rey don Alfonsso:      3595
'¡Oid que vos digo,      ifantes de Carrion!
Esta lid en Toledo la fizierades      mas non quisiestes vos.
Estos tres cavalleros      de mio Çid el Campeador
hyo los adux a salvo      a tierras de Carrion;
aved vuestro derecho,      tuerto non querades vos,      3600
ca qui tuerto quisiere fazer      mal gelo vedare yo,
en todo mio reino      non avra buena sabor.'
Hya les va pesando      a los ifantes de Carrion.
Los fieles y el rey      enseñaron los mojones;
libravan se del campo      todos aderredor.      3605
Bien gelo demostraron      a todos .vi. commo son
que por i serie vençido      qui saliesse del mojon.
Todas las yentes      esconbraron aderredor
mas de .vi. astas de lanças      que non legassen al mojon.
Sorteavan les el campo,      ya les partien el sol;      3610
salien los fieles de medio,      ellos cara por cara son.
Desi vinien los de mio Çid      a los ifantes de Carrion

---

**3603** Compare l.2985. For the technique employed here by the poet to bring out the appropriateness of the suffering now being inflicted on the Infantes, see Introduction, VII (c).

**3607** The function of the boundary markers is among the details of the procedure for judicial combats given in the *Fuero de Cuenca* (see Lacarra, p.84).

"We humbly beseech you as our king and lord
to be today the judge of both parties;                              3575
see justice done, and prevent wrong!
The Infantes of Carrión have their supporters here
and we do not know what they will plan to do.
Our lord placed us in your hands.
Uphold us in our just cause, for love of the Creator!"             3580
At that, the King replied: "With all my heart and soul."
Their horses, fine and fast, were brought to them;
they made the sign of the cross over the saddles and swiftly mounted.
At their necks they carry their shields, finely bossed;
in their hands they take the lances with their sharp iron tips;     3585
each of these lances carries a pennant.
Around them are many good men.
Now they have passed the boundary marks and entered the field
                                        of combat.
All three of the Battler's men are of one mind
that each of them is to strike to wound his adversary.             3590
There, on the other side, are the Infantes of Carrión,
with a great company of men, for many of their relatives are present.
The King has appointed judges for them, to determine merely what
                                        is just,
lest they argue over what has happened.
As they waited on the field, King Don Alfonso spoke:              3595
"Hear what I tell you, Infantes of Carrión!
You should have fought this fight in Toledo, but you would not.
These three knights of My Cid the Battler
I have brought under safe conduct to the lands of Carrión.
Win right for yourselves; you should not seek injustice,          3600
for I shall firmly prevent any man who tries to do so
and ensure that he does not find peace anywhere in my kingdom."
Now the Infantes were deeply saddened.
The judges and the King pointed out the boundary marks.
They all moved beyond the boundary of the field of combat.        3605
It was made clear to all six men
that any who went beyond the markers would be considered defeated.
They all left clear a space around,
more than the distance of six lance - shafts from the markers.
Lots were drawn for ends and account taken of the position of the sun.
The judges left the centre; the knights remained face to face.
Then the Cid's men moved to attack the Infantes of Carrión

251

e llos ifantes de Carrion     a los del Campeador.
Cada uno dellos     mientes tiene al so:
abraçan los escudos     delant los coraçones                    3615
abaxan las lanças     abueltas con los pendones
enclinavan las caras     sobre los arzones
batien los cavallos     con los espolones
tembrar querie la tierra     dond eran movedores.
Cada uno dellos     mientes tiene al so;                        3620
todos tres por tres     ya juntados son,
cuedan se que essora cadran muertos     los que estan aderredor.
Pero Vermuez     el que antes rebto
con Ferran Gonçalez     de cara se junto,
firiensse en los escudos     sin todo pavor;                    3625
Ferran Gonçalez a Pero Vermuez     el escudol passo,
prisol en vazio,     en carne nol tomo,
bien en dos logares     el astil le quebro.
Firme estido Pero Vermuez,     por esso nos encamo;
un colpe reçibiera     mas otro firio,                          3630
quebranto la b[l]oca del escudo,     apart gela echo,
passo gelo todo     que nada nol valio,
metiol la lança por los pechos     que nada nol valio;
tres dobles de loriga tiene Fernando,     aquestol presto,
las dos le desmanchan     e la terçera finco;                  3635
el belmez con la camisa     e con la guarnizon
de dentro en la carne     una mano gelo metio,
por la boca afuera     la sangrel salio,
quebraron le las çinchas,     ninguna nol ovo pro,
por la copla del cavallo     en tierra lo echo.                3640
Assi lo tenien las yentes     que mal ferido es de muert.
El dexo la lança     e al espada mano metio;
quando lo vio Ferran Gonçalez     conuvo a Tizon,
antes que el colpe esperasse     dixo '¡Vençudo so!'
Atorgaron gelo los fieles,     Pero Vermuez le dexo.           3645

151 Martin Antolinez e Diego Gonçalez     firieron se de las lanças,
tales fueron los colpes     que les quebraron amas.
Martin Antolinez     mano metio al espada,
relumbra tod el campo     tanto es linpia e clara;

---

**3613** The three duels take place simultaneously.

252

and the Infantes of Carrión attacked the Battler's men.
Each one of them had his mind set firmly on his adversary.
They clasped their shield before their hearts                                    3615
and lowered their lances with their pennants.
They leaned low over the saddle - bows
and dug into their horses with their spurs.
The ground trembled as they rode forward.
Each one of them had his mind set firmly on his adversary.        3620
Now they had joined in combat, three against three,
and those who watched thought that at any moment the fighters
                              would fall dead.
Pedro Bermúdez, who had issued the first challenge,
fought Fernando González face to face;
fearlessly they smote each other's shield.                                          3625
Fernando González pierced Pedro Bermúdez's shield,
but his lance cut through empty space and did not strike flesh.
Indeed the shaft split in two places.
Pedro Bermúdez held firm and did not lose his balance.
He had received one blow, but now he struck another,                    3630
shattering and breaking through the boss of the shield,
which was split from side to side and gave Fernando no protection.
Pedro Bermúdez plunged his lance into Fernando's breast, for his
                              shield did not protect him;
Fernando wore three layers of armour, and this saved him,
for two were torn open but the third remained unbroken.               3635
His quilted tunic with his shirt and his armour
was driven a hand's length into his flesh,
and from his mouth there flowed blood.
His saddle · girths were broken, none remained intact,
and over the horse's back he was thrown to the ground.                 3640
Those watching thought that he had been mortally wounded.
Pedro Bermúdez threw down the lance and took his sword in his hand;
when Fernando González saw it, he recognized Tizón.
Rather than wait for the blow, he said: "I am beaten."
The judges agreed, and Pedro Bermúdez left him.                          3645


Martín Antolínez and Diego González fought with their lances,
and so fierce were the blows, that both weapons broke.
Martín Antolínez took his sword in his hand;
it was so clean and bright that it lit up the whole field of combat.

diol un colpe,    de traviessol tomava,                                          3650
el casco de somo    apart gelo echava,
las moncluras del yelmo    todas gelas cortava,
alla levo el almofar,    fata la cofia legava,
la cofia y el almofar    todo gelo levava,
raxol los pelos de la cabeça,    bien a la carne legava;    3655
lo uno cayo en el campo    e lo al suso fincava.
Quando este colpe a ferido    Colada la preçiada
vio Diego Gonçalez    que no escaparie con el alma;
bolvio la rienda al cavallo    por tornasse de cara.
Essora Martin Antolinez    reçibiol con el espada,    3660
un colpel dio de lano,    con lo agudo nol tomava;
*Dia Gonçalez espada tiene en mano    mas no la ensayava;*
esora el ifante    tan grandes vozes dava:
'¡Valme, Dios glorioso, señor,    e curiam deste espada!'    3665
El cavallo asorrienda    e mesurandol del espada
sacol del mojon;    Martin Antolinez en el campo fincava.
Essora dixo el rey:    'Venid vos a mi compaña;
por quanto avedes fecho    vençida avedes esta batalla.'
Otorgan gelo los fieles    que dize verdadera palabra.    3670

152 Los dos han arrancado;    direvos de Muño Gustioz,
con Assur Gonçalez    commo se adobo:
firiensse(n) en los escudos    unos tan grandes colpes;
Assur Gonçalez    furçudo e de valor
firio en el escudo    a don Muño Gustioz,    3675
tras el escudo    falsso ge la guarnizon,
en vazio fue la lança    ca en carne nol tomo.
Este colpe fecho    otro dio Muño Gustioz,
(tras el escudo    falsso ge la guarnizon)
por medio de la bloca    (d)el escudol quebranto,    3680
nol pudo guarir,    falsso ge la guarnizon,
apart le priso,    que non cab el coraçon;
metiol por la carne adentro    la lança con el pendon,
de la otra part    una braça gela echo,
con el dio una tuerta,    de la siella lo encamo,    3685
al tirar de la lança    en tierra lo echo;
vermejo salio el astil    e la lança y el pendon.
Todos se cuedan    que ferido es de muert.
La lança recombro    e sobr'el se paro;

3662-63 The copyist wrote *ensayaba* on a separate line.
3667 Diego González thus admits defeat.

254

He struck a blow which caught his opponent at an angle,            3650
shattering the upper part of his helm
and slicing through its leather straps.
The sword reached Diego's cowl and even his cap,
and cut them both away;
it tore the hair from his head and bit into his flesh.            3655
Part of the helmet fell to the ground, the rest remained in place.
When precious Colada had struck this blow,
Diego González saw that he would not escape alive.
He drew his horse round to face his opponent.
Then Martín Antolínez met him with his sword;            3660
he struck him with the flat of it and not with the sharp edge.
Diego González held his sword in his hand but he did not use it.
At this point, the Infante cried out loudly:
"Save me, glorious Lord God, and protect me from this sword!"   3665
He reined in his horse and, guiding it away from the sword,
he rode beyond the boundary.  Martín Antolínez remained in the field.
Then the King said: "Come and join my company.
By the way you have fought you have won this combat."
The judges confirmed that he spoke the truth.            3670

Two of them had already won.  I shall tell you about Muño Gustioz
and how he made out with Asur González.
As they dealt heavy blows at each other's shield,
Asur González, a man both tough and strong,
smote Don Muño Gustioz's shield so violently            3675
that behind his shield he pierced his armour.
The lance passed through empty space and did not reach his flesh.
After this, Muño Gustioz dealt another blow
and behind the shield he pierced his opponent's armour.
He shattered the boss of the shield.            3680
Asur González could not protect himself and his armour was pierced.
The blow went to one side, not near the heart,
but the lance and the pennant plunged into his body
and an arm's length of it came out the other side.
Muño Gustioz pulled sharply at it, and wrenched his opponent from
                                                  the saddle
and as he tugged at the lance he threw Asur González to the ground.
Shaft, lance and pennant all came out bright red.
They all thought Asur mortally wounded.
Muño Gustioz pulled out the lance and stood over him.

dixo Gonçalo Assurez: '¡Nol firgades, por Dios! 3690
¡Vençudo es el campo quando esto se acabo!'
Dixieron los fieles: 'Esto oimos nos.'
Mando librar el canpo el buen rey don Alfonsso,
las armas que i rastaron el selas tomo.
Por ondrados se parten los del buen Campeador, 3695
vençieron esta lid ¡grado al Criador!
Grandes son los pesares por tierras de Carrion.
El rey a los de mio Çid de noche los enbio
que no les diessen salto nin oviessen pavor.
A guisa de menbrados andan dias e noches, 3700
felos en Valençia con mio Çid el Campeador;
por malos los dexaron a los ifantes de Carrion,
conplido han el debdo que les mando so señor;
alegre ffue d'aquesto mio Çid el Campeador.
Grant es la biltança de ifantes de Carrion: 3705
qui buena dueña escarneçe e la dexa despues
¡atal le contesca o si quier peor!
Dexemos nos de pleitos de ifantes de Carrion;
de lo que an preso mucho an mal sabor.
Fablemos nos d'aqueste que en buen ora naçio: 3710
grandes son los gozos en Valençia la mayor
por que tan ondrados fueron los del Campeador.
Prisos a la barba Ruy Diaz so señor:
'¡Grado al rey del çielo, mis fijas vengadas son!
¡Agora las ayan quitas heredades de Carrion! 3715
Sin verguença las casare o a qui pese o a qui non.'
Andidieron en pleitos los de Navarra e de Aragon,
ovieron su ajunta con Alfonsso el de Leon;
fizieron sus casamientos con don Elvira e con doña Sol.
Los primeros fueron grandes mas aquestos son mijores; 3720
a mayor ondra las casa que lo que primero fue:

---

**3691** Gonzalo Ansúrez admits defeat on behalf of his son. Just as Martín Antolínez held back from killing Diego González (l.3661), so here Muño Gustioz refrains from taking the life of Asur. The poet shows that the purpose of the Cid's vassals has been to dishonour the Infantes and not to exact a bloody revenge. The fate of the Infantes is singularly appropriate: they had intended that the Cid should live in lasting dishonour, and that fate is now to be theirs; whilst the illustrious marriages that they claimed to deserve (ll.3296-98) are offered to Elvira and Sol, whom the Infantes must now serve as their social superiors (ll.3446-51). For a discussion of the poet's purpose here, see A.D.Deyermond, 'The Close of the *Cantar de Mio Cid*', pp.15-16.

**3694** Law codes make it clear that it was the king's prerogative to confiscate the horses and arms of those defeated in a judicial combat.

**3703** See also l.3528. The Cid's vassals have given a further excellent example of loyal service to one's lord and scrupulous fulfilment of the individual's responsibilities, so important within the framework of the feudal society.

**3706-07** The cruellest part of the punishment suffered by the Infantes is the permanent public dishonour which has been inflicted upon them; the accusation levelled against them by the Cid was that they had brought dishonour upon themselves (ll.3268-69), and this has been upheld in the judicial combat. There is no suggestion

Gonzalo Ansúrez said: "Do not strike him, for God's sake!     3690
The combat has been won now that this is done."
The judges said: "We hear what you say."
Good King Alfonso commanded the field to be cleared.
He took for himself the arms that remained.
The good Battler's men left with honour.     3695
They had won this combat, thanks be to the Creator!
Great was the sorrow in the lands of Carrión.
The King commanded My Cid's men to leave by night,
lest there should be any fear of their being attacked.
As prudent men, they travelled by day and night.     3700
Behold them now in Valencia with My Cid the Battler!
They left the Infantes of Carrión to be regarded as traitors,
and have fulfilled the obligation imposed upon them by their lord.
My Cid the Battler is filled with joy at this.
Great is the dishonour of the Infantes of Carrión.     3705
A man who commits an outrage against a fine lady and then
                  abandons her
deserves to be treated thus or worse!
Let us leave the affairs of the Infantes of Carrión.
The punishment they have received has caused them great unhappiness.
Let us talk of this man who was born in a favoured hour.     3710
Much was the rejoicing in the great city of Valencia
since the Battler's men had won such honour.
Ruy Díaz, their lord, clasped his beard:
"Thanks be to the King of Heaven that my daughters have been avenged.
Now they may indeed enjoy, without impediment, their lands in Carrión!
I shall marry them with no dishonour and with no thought for the
                  displeasure of some."
The princes of Navarre and Aragón carried out their negotiations;
they had their meeting with Alfonso of León;
they were married to Doña Elvira and Doña Sol.
The first alliances were great, but these were finer still;     3720
My Cid married his daughters more prestigiously than before.

---

that further penalties are to be imposed, apart from the fulfilment of their financial obligations (see note to
l.3715).
**3715** This line has usually been taken as an expression of the Cid's relief that he will no longer be obliged to have
dealings with the Infantes. However, the sense is more likely to be that the Cid's daughters can now enjoy
possession of the estates in Carrión which constitute their *arras* and which will indisputably remain their property
(see Pavlović and Walker, 'Money, Marriage and the Law', pp.202-03).

¡ved qual ondra creçe    al que en buen ora naçio
quando señoras son sus fijas    de Navarra e de Aragon!
Oy los reyes d'España    sos parientes son;
a todos alcança ondra    por el que en buen ora naçio.    3725
Passado es deste sieglo    el dia de çinquaesma:
¡de Christus haya perdon!
¡Assi ffagamos nos todos,    justos e peccadores!
Estas son las nuevas    de mio Çid el Campeador;
en este logar    se acaba esta razon.    3730
Quien escrivio este libro    ¡del Dios paraiso, amen!
Per Abbat le escrivio    en el mes de mayo
en era de mill e .cc xlv. años.

---

**3724** It was through García, son of Cristina and Prince Ramiro, that the Cid's blood was eventually to flow in the veins of the kings of Navarre, Castile and León, Portugal, and France. Menéndez Pidal argues that the poet's claim was true from about the year 1140. There is, however, no real evidence here to assist in the precise dating of the poem.

**3726** The poet tells us the day of his hero's death – Whit Sunday, a detail presumably included because of its religious significance – but not the year. The Cid died in 1099, most probably in July and not in May as is indicated here. He was about fifty-six, and his death seems to have resulted from a combination of illness and the effects of wounds suffered in his campaigns.

It has been suggested that this is the last line of the original poem to have been preserved. Russell, 'San Pedro de Cardeña and the Heroic History of the Cid', *Medium Aevum*, XXVII (1958), 57-59 (p.74), speculates that the suddenness with which the poem ends could result from its deliberate truncation by the copyist, who wished to

See how the reputation grew of the man born in a favoured hour,
since his daughters were now the ladies of Navarre and Aragón!
Now, the kings of Spain are of his line,
and all gain in honour through the man born in a favoured hour. 3725
He passed from this world on Whit Sunday;
may he receive Christ's forgiveness,
and so may we all, good men and sinners!
These are the deeds of My Cid the Battler;
here this poem ends. 3730
May God grant his paradise to the man who wrote this book! Amen.
Per Abbat wrote it down, in the month of May,
in the year 1207.

exclude material which was at variance with the version of the Cid's story promoted by the monks of Cardeña.
**3733** For the problem posed by the final two lines, see Introduction, I. 'En era de' refers to a system of counting dates from 38 B.C., a year of measures of social reorganization and administrative reform so great that it had been seen as the beginning of a new era. For our interpretation of the role of Per Abbat, a great deal depends on the meaning of the verb *escrevir*: there can be no doubt that its usual sense is 'to write out', 'to copy'.

The manuscript contains, after l.3733, an *explicit* of three lines of verse in a different hand, difficult to make out, but interpreted by Menéndez Pidal as:

*The poem has been read; give us wine; and if you have no money, throw down some pledges, for you will receive plenty in return.*

The presence of this detail seems to indicate that the surviving manuscript was used for an oral performance.

# INDEX OF PROPER NAMES

*(A selective index of proper names mentioned in the commentary to the text; references are to line numbers.)*

Abengalbón 1464, 1485–86
Álamos 2694
Alcocer 553, 576
Alcubilla 399
Alfonso VI (of León - Castile) 9, 14, 20, 22, 24, 209, 473, etc.
Alfonso II (of León - Castile) 3003
Alfonso VIII (of Castile) 397
al - Hachib 957
Almohads 1181
Almoravids 696, 1181, 1620 ff.
al - Muqtadir (of Saragossa) 914
al - Mu'tamid (of Seville) 1181, 1222
al - Mu'tamin (of Saragossa) 914, 957
Álvar Álvarez 443–43b
Álvar Díaz 2042
Álvar Fáñez 14, 378
Álvar Salvadórez 443–43b, 1719, 1994, 1999
Andros 1971
Asur González 2172–73, 3374
Ayllón 397
Babieca 1573
Barcelona 961–63
Beltrán (Count) 3004
Benicadell 1163
Beni - Gómez see Vani - Gómez
Berenguer Ramón II (of Barcelona) 957
*Berte aus grans piés* 1610 ff.
Búcar 2314, 2408
Burgos 1–2, 52, 65
Cabra 1345
Campeador (Battler) 31
Cardeña 209, 252–60, 3726
*Carmen Campidoctoris* 31, 1345
Carrión 1312, 1375–76, 2289, 3474
Castejón de Henares 435, 473
Castejón de las Armas 553
Castro (family) 1464
Cebolla (Puig) 1095
*Chanson de Florence de Rome* 2698, 2703
*Chanson de Roland* 7, 406
*Chronicle of Twenty Kings of*

*Castile* 1–2, 2337
Cluny 2373
Colada 1010
Corpes 2697, 2698
*cort, cortes* 2963, 2964
Cuarte (plain; battle of) 1657
Denia 1161
Diego González (Infante of Carrión) 1372, 2284–85, 2291
Diego Téllez 2814
El Ansarera 2657
Elpha 2695
El Poyo de Mio Cid 902
Elvira (daughter of the Cid) 252–60, 3399
Enrique (Henri) of Burgundy 3002
Fáriz 654
Félez Muñoz 741
Fernando (Infante of Carrión) 1372, 2337
Franks 1002
Froila Díaz 3004
Frontinus 553, 576
*Fuero de Cuenca* 2722, 2762, 3235, 3257, 3313, 3343, 3607
Galindo García 443–43b
Gallocanta 1087
Galve 654
García Ordóñez 1345, 2999, 3112
Gómez Peláyez 3457
Gonzalo Ansúrez 3008
Gormaz (castle of) 2843
Grañón 3112
*Historia Roderici* 1–2, 9, 957, 1179, 1345, 1401, 1596, 1718
Holy Trinity (Mass of) 319
Huerta (of Valencia) 1172
Íñigo Jiménez 3394
Jerónimo (Jérôme) de Périgord 1288, 1299
Jews 84
Jimena 210, 3039
Julius Caesar 704
Lara (family) 397, 1464
León 1342
*Leyenda de Cardeña* 209
*Libro de Alexandre* 2700
Longinus 352 ff.
Malanda 3070
Martín (river) 904
Martín Antolínez 65, 67, 80

Martín Muñoz 738
Medinaceli 1382
Miedes (mountains of) 399, 415
*Minaya* see Alvar Fáñez
Molina 1464
Monreal del Campo 863, 1185–86
Montes Claros 2693
Muño Gustioz 737, 741
Murviedro (Sagunto) 1095, 1185–86
Ojarra 3394
Olocau de Liria 1087
Pedro Abad (Per Abbat) 3733
Pedro Bermúdez 611, 704, 1907
*Poema de Almería* 14
Portugal 2978
Quinea (Road of) 400
Ramón (Raymond) of Burgundy 3002, 3003
Raquel and Vidas 89
Riaza 2694
Sagrajas (Battle of) 1181
Sahagún 1312
Saint Isidore 1342, 3140–41
Sallust 435
Sancho (abbot of Cardeña) 237
San Esteban de Gormaz 397, 2820, 2843
San Salvador (Oviedo) 2924
San Servando 3047
Santa María (Burgos) 52, 216, ff.
Santa María (Valencia) 1288
Santiago (Saint James) 731
Saragossa 566, 914, 1208
Seville 1–2, 109 ff., 1181, 1222
Sisebuto 237
Sol (daughter of the Cid) 252–60, 3399, 3724
Spinaz de Can 394
Tajuña (river) 545
Tamín 636
Teruel 911–12
Tévar 943, 957
Tizón 2426
Toledo 2963
Ubierna (river) 3379
Urraca (Tower of) 2812
Valencia 627, 1095, 1179, 1208, 1210, 1401, 1566, 1620 ff.
Vani - Gómez (family) 1312, 1345, 1372
Vivar 1–2, 1375–76, 3379
Yusuf ibn Tashufin 1181, 1620 ff.